Bringing Zen Home

Bringing Zen Home

*The Healing Heart
of Japanese Women's Rituals*

PAULA ARAI

University of Hawai'i Press
Honolulu

Paperback edition 2022

Printed in the United States of America

Library of Congress Cataloging-in-Publication Data
Arai, Paula Kane Robinson.
  Bringing Zen home : the healing heart of Japanese women's rituals / Paula Arai.
     p. cm.
  Includes bibliographical references and index.
  ISBN 978-0-8248-3535-4 (hardcover : alk. paper)
  1. Zen Buddhism—Japan—Rituals. 2. Buddhist women—Religious life—Japan.
  3. Healing—Religious aspects—Zen Buddhism. 4. Zen funeral rites and ceremo-
  nies. I. Title.
  BQ9270.2.A73 2012
  294.3'438—dc23
                                                                    2011017005

ISBN: 978-0-8248-9418-4 (paperback)

All photographs are by the author.

University of Hawai'i Press books are printed on acid-free
paper and meet the guidelines for permanence and
durability of the Council on Library Resources.

Designed by inari

For Kenji,
健慈

my beloved son,
whose name means
health and compassion

Contents

Foreword

I first met Paula Arai in the winter of 1988 upon the introduction of Aoyama Shundō, a former student of mine who has now become a renowned abbess of the Zen nuns' training monastery, Aichi Senmon Nisōdō. At that time, Ms. Arai was a young rising scholar doing research for her first book on Zen nuns. She has kept me apprised of her work during engaging conversations in my offices and temple, and in coffee shops. Now Dr. Arai has fulfilled her promise by producing not only a singular volume on the history and practices of Sōtō Zen nuns, but also by writing this book in which she sheds further light on the practices and concerns of women, this time illuminating women in the home. Her original scholarly work makes an important contribution to our understanding of Japanese Zen Buddhist culture, especially in how traditions both continue and change in contemporary society.

Bringing Zen Home provides a view of lay Buddhist practice in contemporary Japan with a depth of ethnographic detail that will enable the readers to feel they are visiting a Japanese lay Buddhist home. Arai breathes life into practices that have not yet received scholarly attention. Her focus on domestic (*katei*) Zen enables us to see distinct Buddhist expressions in Japanese culture. Her analysis of the healing paradigm in Zen is particularly insightful. It displays keen insight into Dōgen's teachings, and into how those teachings are lived out in ritualized activities in the home. A central ritual focuses on the home altar where ancestors are revered as enlightened. This is an important feature of Japanese Buddhist practice about which I have held particular interest from a comparative Buddhist perspective. Arai's analysis of the practice of honoring ancestors as enlightened concludes that participants experience the deceased as personal Buddhas: she has discovered how rituals help people cultivate intimate relationships with the enlightened ancestors that foster their healing. This is a novel interpretation of Buddha nature, distinct to Japanese Buddhist practice. Establishing personal Buddhas reveals profound insight into the nature of grief and human relationships. No matter how technologically efficient we become, we must come to terms with death. We will never overcome the need for grieving. The wisdom of how to grieve in a way that integrates death into life is encoded in domestic rituals. Arai's book provides a rich view of Zen Buddhist values, practices, and wisdom, especially in the home where daily activities make up the fabric of life.

Arai's research on domestic rituals is a timely and welcome development, for Japan has been rapidly and steadily changing. Wisdom cultivated over centuries is documented in this volume, which helps preserve the knowledge. Perhaps sharing these gifts of healing wisdom with the English-speaking world also will give rise to innovative practices that will transform in culturally adaptive ways.

NARA KŌMYŌ YASUAKI
Former Chancellor of Komazawa University
Former President of Komazawa University
Professor of Buddhist Studies
Head Priest of Hōsei-ji Temple
Tokyo, Japan

Acknowledgments

It is a joy to express my deep gratitude for the large circle of people involved in this book.

First, to the twelve women whose wisdom and spiritual practices fill these pages, I offer my work as tribute and thanks. Although I cannot mention them by name, each one is written on my heart. I owe infinite homage to two female leaders of the Nagoya Zen community who contributed unstintingly to my development as a scholar and a person: Aoyama Rōshi illumined my work and my life with her blazing wisdom; and Kitō Sensei, my personal bodhisattva, has been an enduring source of guidance and radiant compassion.

An ocean of thanks to Miranda Shaw for her peerless editorial skills and for her paradigm-shifting scholarship on Buddhist women. Her opus on Buddhist goddesses opens a landscape of gender discourse and devotional healing practices that has helped me view the women in my study in a broad, cross-cultural context. A mountain of gratitude to Inés Talamantez for her nonpareil mentoring and the model of her pioneering work on Mescalero Apache culture and groundbreaking theoretical work on the ethnography of indigenous peoples.

No project can come to fruition without the kindness of others. For assistance in Japan, I am indebted to the Yanai family and the Skrzypczak family, especially to Mari for her babysitting. The Sugiura family welcomed me and my son Kenji into their home in Nagoya, making it possible for me to conduct my field research for the past twelve years. Their generosity of heart supported me through many challenges, and this book could not have become a reality without their profound support. Robin Morgan and Hideko Shimizu also offered invaluable spiritual counsel and sustenance over the years.

I received indispensable institutional and financial support from Aichi Senmon Nisōdō, Nanzan University, the Fulbright Foundation, the American Council of Learned Societies, Vanderbilt University, Carleton College, the Mellon Foundation, and Louisiana State University Board of Regents.

For lending insights on Japanese Buddhism that honed my study in fruitful ways, I give nine bows of deep respect to Nara Kōmyō Yasuaki, Fujii Masao, and Victor Hori. Special thanks are due to Nara Yasuaki for graciously writing the Foreword. To Sascha duLac for her expertise in neuropsychobiology, I bow in heartfelt thanks. Jess Lionne, Paul Ramsour, Anne Dutton, Laurie Pullen, Dee Doochin, and Beth Conklin brought the scholarly eye of their respective fields to bear on the manuscript, improving the clarity of style and refinement of content. Their friendships place the academic work in a meaningful and humanitarian context that makes each step along the way an opportunity for deepening our connections. Thanks to editor Patricia Crosby for her invaluable support.

I thank my sisters—artist Lucy and weaver Wendy—for sharing the journey of our family, which provides a well of experience and insight from which I draw deeply. My father's fascination with the human condition and kindness of heart inspire and guide me, especially now that he has become one of my personal Buddhas.

This book began amid the sublime experience of giving birth to Kenji while caring for my dying mother. Living in that space between birth and death opened me to the depths of sorrow and heights of joy that inhabit the realm of healing. My mother blessed me with unconditional love, while Kenji buoyed me with his purity of spirit throughout the fourteen years it took to complete this book. I cannot thank him enough for the patience, understanding, strength, and good humor he exhibited as he learned to do laundry, sweep floors, cook, take out the trash, mow the lawn, and tend to his own needs at a tender age. The poignant image of him at Logan Airport pulling a wheeled suitcase twice his weight at the age of two is seared into my heart. Too, I'll never forget the evening when, at the age of seven, he scrambled eggs for our dinner when I was exhausted. I am honored, Kenji, that you chose to share the healing journey of this lifetime with me.

Gratitude to the willow whose grace and supple strength embrace me with enduring love. At last to abide by the shores of the deep sea.

Prologue

When I was beginning the field research for this book, I had the tremendous good fortune to listen once again to one of Sōtō Zen's greatly respected scholar-Zen masters, Suzuki Kakuzen Rōshi. He had recently been diagnosed with terminal cancer; although he was in the advanced stages of progression of the disease, he kept up a rigorous teaching schedule. Everyone who saw him during this time commented how he glowed with an incandescent wisdom. He was teaching about the Dharma with an urgency and clarity that surpassed even his brilliant publications and lectures at Komazawa University—the highly prestigious Sōtō Zen University—where he was a senior professor. I sneaked back to the formal guest quarters (*shoin*) where he was staying at the Zen nunnery in Nagoya because I sensed this would probably be the last time I would see him (and so it was). Since he had a no-nonsense approach to things, I dared to ask him as he was facing his death what he thought about healing. He responded in this way:

> Nobody at Komazawa knows anything about healing. They won't tell you this there. You must take death as the point of departure to understand healing. It is only then that you will see that you are already healed. This is the vow of Hotoke [Buddha], of Kannon [Bodhisattva of Compassion]. It is not that you pray and then receive the compassion of Kannon. It is only a matter of whether or not you become aware that you are already healed.[1]

He made me promise that I would include this in my book and make sure it gets published. I am honored to be able to fulfill this promise at last.

CHAPTER I

Mapping the Terrain

This book took root on December 18, 1996, the day my mother died. After months of listening to the whir of the oxygen machine, a vacuum of silence filled her bedroom. Even though I had known she would die soon, when I stood looking at the threshold of life and death I felt as if one wrong move would send us off into an abyss of despair. The last several months had been one long fear of wrong moves: too much morphine or not enough, too much talking or not enough, too much water or not enough.

Suddenly all the palliatives seemed harshly out of place. Hands shaking, I cleared the bedside table of the vials of morphine, antinausea salves, and pink star-shaped sponges for removing sticky mucous from the tongue. The ultimacy of the moment engulfed me. How was I to ensure my mother's passage through this perilous transition? Kitō Sensei had encouraged me to call her. The elderly Zen nun had helped my mother and me through the past nine years, applying her healing balm of compassion. It was the middle of the night in Japan, but I knew that, although she devotes long days to ministering to others, at 3:45 a.m. Kitō Sensei would be at her temple: there she nurtures the Bodhi tree seeds she brought back from India. The telephone in my hand was a lifeline. I knew intellectually about Sōtō Zen rituals that recognize the deceased as a Buddha, but it was Kitō Sensei, in her unheated worship hall ten thousand miles away, who guided me through those first terrifying, disorienting moments.

Trusting her to know what to do, I followed her instructions for the ritual of safely sending off the deceased on her journey of death.

Frantic to treat our new Buddha properly, I rushed to find the bronze plum blossom incense burner, sandalwood incense sticks, white candle, and plain carved wooden figure of Kannon, goddess of compassion, adding some white chrysanthemums I had been keeping on hand for this moment. Not more than ten minutes after my mother breathed her last, the bedside table was transformed into a mortuary altar. As I offered a stick of incense in her honor, I saw my mother's face take on the peace that I have seen so often on images of Buddhas. Our relationship was transforming before my very eyes.

When I placed the incense in the burner, I became one with all who had done so before. In the moment that had threatened to be the loneliest in my life, I instead experienced a profound connection with all grievers, past and future. I was not alone. I was united with everyone who had lost a loved one. Kitō Sensei had guided us through this critical transition with a wisdom that transcended barriers of space, time, life, and death. At that moment, the healing power of ritual became a visceral reality.

I began my relationships with the twelve women whose experiences form the basis of this book by sharing this event in my life. In doing so, I opened my heart, creating a safe place for them to share their similarly intimate experiences. It is only in the context of close relationships of trust and mutual respect that healing can be qualitatively studied and understood.[1] Therefore, to begin such a study requires an invitation to share in the suffering and vulnerability of others. Feigning an objective observer's distance, especially in the Japanese relationally driven cultural context, would yield little about the highly personal and often painful dimensions of the subjects' lives. By exposing my shortcomings and difficulties, I received not only valuable and helpful advice, but also a bounty of details essential to understanding the women's views, experiences, and feelings. As we cultivated intimate relationships, we broke through Japanese socially scripted façades of tidiness and self-control and delved into the excruciating, infuriating, and terrifying realms where healing takes place.

Researching Buddhist Women's Healing Rituals

This book explores the lives of mature and devoted Japanese Buddhist women and reveals how ritualized activities are a critical tool in a Sōtō

Zen mode of living. Studying their ritual lives also reveals a domestic aspect of Zen that is ripe with wisdom for responding to a host of everyday challenges, difficulties, and fears. Their paradigm of healing is rooted in the Zen Buddhist teachings of Dōgen; that paradigm also includes a wide range of practices that emerge from esoteric, Pure Land Buddhist, and from homemade sources. Strikingly, rituals not formally recognized—or even practiced—as healing rituals are a catalyst for powerful healing experiences among these women. We will see how Dōgen's teachings are applied in their ritual lives, where ritualized activities actualize healing.

I was surprised that rituals not formally recognized as healing rituals figured so prominently in their repertoire. This led me to a theory about healing rituals in a Buddhist context. In a worldview where the interrelatedness of all things is the primary point of reference, healing means to be in harmony with this impermanent web of relationships that constitutes the dynamic universe. It is difficult, however, to comprehend—much less experience—something so expansive. Interrelatedness cannot be experienced deliberately. Rituals, however, can be a conduit to an intuitive experience of interrelatedness, based on the body, precisely because rituals can induce modes of being that transcend linear and rational logic and facilitate contact with the ineffable. Rituals can affect a person holistically by entering below the radar of cerebral cognition and bypassing dualistic perception. They permeate the body-mind. Language and cognitive processing, on the other hand, often fall short of or even obstruct the way to experiencing the grandeur of one's ultimate context. Therefore, rituals that do not explicitly purport to be healing rituals can indirectly facilitate a key dimension of a Buddhist healing activity—a nondualistic experience of reality.

In order to gain access and insight into the realm of domestic Zen, I employed qualitative research methods rooted in ethical considerations. Practices I developed during field research in Japan resonate with principles found in feminist ethnography that encourage "ethnographic experimentation" and are "ethically responsible."[2] I first had to establish a balance of power between each of my twelve consociates and myself.[3] It was imperative that I take the lead in establishing a deep relationship because at the beginning I had the structural power: I was the researcher with the Harvard Ph.D. in Buddhism. I was keenly aware, however, that my consociates had the real power to let me in or keep me at a distance. Without their cooperation, my understanding of domestic Zen would be superficial.

It was critical to establish relationships with women who live domestic Zen because Zen Buddhism embodies a paradox, in that its public image is at odds with the experience of most of its practitioners. Although a shift is in progress, textually oriented scholars of Zen, as well as many leading Zen monks, have largely represented Zen as an iconoclastic, antiritualistic tradition.[4] Yet ritual is at the center of the ordinary Japanese experience of Zen. Funerals and rites of supplication for health and prosperity are what draw families and individuals—especially women—to engage with Zen. My ethnographic research suggests that these rituals fill a need by offering frameworks for transformation and healing. Qualitative investigation and analysis contribute to our understanding of how rituals are used in establishing Zen Buddhist communities, transmitting the teachings, and responding to various dimensions of lay life. My research reveals that Zen Buddhist rituals offer ways to address the emotional and psychological needs of people as they respond to the inevitable challenges of human existence—love, loss, birth and death, and the longing to belong.

A focus on rituals brings to the fore the complex dynamics and concerns that shape what it means to be a Zen Buddhist woman in modern Japan and reveals how Zen ritualized activities help with healing. This dimension of Zen has not been pursued before due to the dominance of the philosophical, textual, and historical lenses through which scholars have examined the tradition. Moreover, the iconoclastic ideals and antiritual rhetoric generated from within the Zen Buddhist tradition itself have deflected scholars from exploring the roles of its healing rituals and practices. This work addresses a lacuna in Zen studies by employing a Buddhist-based ritual analysis to elucidate the techniques, meanings, and outcomes of ritualized activities.[5]

Buddhist laywomen, often supported by nuns, respond to life's challenges: birth, illness, death, and emotional turmoil. It is within the milieu of this network of female relationships that one can observe how rituals and healing activities are practiced and transmitted. This book captures the otherwise unrecognized contributions of these women to Japanese culture and society. For most of them, the only public record of their existence is their birth certificate and, for some, their marriage certificate.

As it is with life, so it is with field research: serendipity is often more important than a well-designed plan and method. Having written my first book on Zen nuns, I began with a solid relationship with the abbess of the Aichi Zen nunnery (Aichi Senmon *nisōdō*) in Nagoya. The abbess, Aoyama Shundō Rōshi, regularly conducts Zen activities for laywomen. In June 1998, she introduced my project and me at one of these events, and graciously requested that people extend their cooperation to me. By doing so, she indicated her support of the theme and of the project. I wanted the women to approach me on their own rather than establishing my own criteria and choosing people who I thought would fit. It was clear from the beginning that the women who offered to help were exemplars: women who were serious about their religiosity, involved with Zen practice in some way, and willing to serve as long-term consociates.[6] The relationships began with a budding trust encouraged by the abbess' endorsement of me as a sympathetic scholar.

The twelve women who generously volunteered to allow me to scrutinize their lives are from a distinctive generation in Japanese history. Nine of the twelve women are World War II survivors, and three were born shortly after the war.[7] Major transformations in Japanese society occurred during this period, including Japan's rise to international stature. Women of this generation are the center of their homes. They are the ritual experts, the counselors for the family, and the healers.[8] As they care for others, they attend to themselves with awareness that it is all part of one web of concern.

A range of profiles is reflected in the women who offered to be consociates in the project. Their ages at the beginning of the field study in 1998 were mid-forty to mid-seventy.[9] The women come from a range of family situations: A few had been adopted, although their birth parents were alive. One woman had an intact three-generational family, but her father died in a car crash when she was a child. Others lost their mothers or siblings when they were young. The prototypical nuclear family of mom, dad, and two children is not represented among these families. Umemura-san says quite openly, "I come from a complicated family. I am one of five siblings, and we each have a different mother. My birth mother did not raise me. I have had a half-hearted life. My body is easily sick, and I have a quiet personality."[10]

Eight of the twelve are either married or widowed. All eight have raised children, theirs by birth or adoption. Three of those eight have spent the majority of their adulthood as mothers and housewives, and five have worked at a business while caring for their homes and families. Four of the twelve have never been married, given birth, or raised a child. Each of those four has financial independence through careers. Their housing, reflecting their economic resources, ranges from a one-room efficiency apartment in the center of a city to a traditional home on the edge of a river with a prominent gate, an outbuilding, large vegetable garden, and a finely manicured traditional Japanese garden.

Each of the women has a home altar (*butsudan*) in her home. All but one actively participates in public Buddhist rituals, mostly in affiliation with Aoyama Rōshi and Kitō Sensei, both of whom are Zen nuns in the

Nagoya community. Another significant point in common among my consociates is they all have educated themselves about Buddhist teachings by listening to lectures and Dharma talks, reading books, and taking academic classes. Therefore, their understanding of Buddhism is notably more developed than that of the average Japanese. All are exemplars of living Buddhist teachings, each stressing certain dimensions and manifesting a range of qualities valued in Buddhist teachings.

I was aware when I asked my consociates to remember things important to their healing activities that memory does not preserve "facts." Rather, memory excels at creating meaning.[11] I seek to understand the women's healing paradigm and ritual lives, not explain "the truth" about them.[12] My aim is to make sense of the rich ethnographic material and to communicate something meaningful to readers. I am especially concerned to synthesize the material into culturally and religiously contextualized frames. Hence, I developed theories and hermeneutical categories about the healing dimensions of their ritual lives to illuminate their contributions that until now have gone unnoticed by scholars or even those closest to them.

I listened for hundreds of hours to these twelve mature Japanese women speak about their lives, and found they used Buddhist rituals for diverse purposes. Some rituals help deal with intractable family dysfunction, whereas others keep loneliness at bay. Finally, some Zen practices help practitioners cope with a terminal illness. By documenting and analyzing these healing experiences and ritual practices, this work reveals a central aspect of the Zen tradition.

When I asked the women if exposing their painful and sad experiences was difficult for them, many said it was actually helpful, because few had listened to them before. This confirms the findings of clinicians that "Disclosure of traumatic or painful experiences had a more powerful benefit on health and healing than talking or writing about superficial events."[13] Throughout the research and writing of this book, I have been committed to respecting what they shared.

To see these women in a fuller context, I entered into conversation with the concerns, theories, and questions of several disciplines, the rich historical, textual, and philosophical traditions of Buddhist scholarship, and current ethnographic thinking about reflexivity and qualitative reasoning. My work bridges issues in ritual studies and healing; healing and the cultural, linguistic, and sociological aspects of Japan studies; religious studies and Buddhist studies; and women's studies and Buddhist ritual healing. It demonstrates what Zen has to offer with the study of healing, ritual, women, and methodology. It shows how a focus on ritual can amplify and expand Zen studies and how scholarship on Zen can more fully inform the discourse on ritual studies.

The focus on women informs gender studies cross culturally. Moreover, this study illustrates how a tradition famous for strictly disciplined monasticism and nondualistic philosophy can simultaneously offer lay people meaningful symbolic and ritual resources for negotiating contemporary problems. As a result, this study expands the purview of what it means to be a Zen Buddhist woman in contemporary Japan.[14]

The only studies on women's experience in Zen ritual are from my own previous research into a few rituals in Zen monastic life. Hence, ethnographically driven methods were required for me to access the type and depth of material I sought. It was of fundamental importance in my ethnography to engage in enactive learning, or participant-observation, of each ritual the women engaged in, including several major public rituals, sundry modest temple rituals, and numerous private rituals. I joined with the women in performing their rituals, except those rituals that had been performed at earlier times in their lives, or when circumstances made it impossible or inappropriate for me to participate. For these few rituals, I often was able to participate in a similar ritual on my own.

My research methods are attuned to the intersubjective dynamic between researcher and consociates, and, therefore, operate in the second-person.[15] I use the second person to refer to the space and dynamics between people. It is the "we" of relational interaction. The second-person approach is especially fitting for qualitative research that aims to understand people's healing experiences. A second-person orientation focuses on the relationship of the people involved in the research. All people are treated as wholes, not divided into "objective observer" and "subjective informant." Like optometry, which depends on the patient's subjective judgment of which is clearer—"one . . . or (click) two"—to get reliable results, the only way to learn about the women's inner experiences and thoughts about their ritual lives and healing experiences is through their expressions.[16] Yet, unlike optometry, which essentially works with one-word responses, reliable results on the topic of healing requires hours, even years of interaction to cultivate not only the expressions of emotions and aspirations, but also the context in which they are experienced.[17]

There is no fixed word for "I" in the Japanese language. The nuanced complexities of navigating selves as fundamentally relational beings is evident in the fact that there are fifteen ways to say "I" in contemporary

Japanese, each one designating an aspect of the self depending on what one wants present to another person. You can indicate gender, stress social status, negotiate levels of formality, note age, or convey a combination of any of these.[18] Delineations of subjectivity and objectivity are not helpful in this sociolinguistic context, which makes a second-person mode of research especially helpful.

My decisions about how to render my consociates' words into English and how to frame and interpret them means that the reader does not have direct access to a first-person perspective. The material is shaped by my assessments of how to translate across not only linguistic, but also cultural traditions. It reflects my imagination and anticipation about who potential readers might be and what I think they want to know. The results, then, are neither first-person accounts nor third-person "objective" description and analysis. Rather, what results is an intersubjective discussion based on a triangulated relationship of consociates, scholars, and readers.

A second-person mode of research is supported by findings in mirror-neurons.[19] Although more research is developing in this field of cognitive-affective neuroscience, current research indicates that when people see each other act, the neural activity of one person activates similar neural fields in the other person's brain. These findings underscore that embodied engagement of rituals is a reliable method for learning and gaining understanding of the dynamics of ritualized behavior.[20] Reliability is established through the empathic experience of being with the women for long periods spanning a dozen years.

I agree with Diane Bell's ethnographic approach that the researcher bring an awareness of herself "as an instrument of observation."[21] Reflexivity is necessary in obtaining reliable field materials and doing ethically responsible research.[22] Ethically, "one must bring oneself to that dialogue, values and all—for that is what one is asking of one's respondent."[23]

What I bring to my research includes several years of living and studying in Japan, as well as the formative experience of having been raised by a Japanese woman in North America. The post–World War II Detroit context in which she, a native of Yokohama, Japan, raised my sisters and me presented specific concerns. She carried the responsibility of a civilization on her shoulders. Not only was she foreign to her American family, she needed to be vindicated in the eyes of her new neighbors. Ten years after a Shinto marriage to an Anglo-American man, she moved away from all things familiar. She was determined to teach her children how to be polite and behave well in this new environment. Although hardly anyone in

Detroit at the time knew the difference, in her mind "polite" translated into inculcating Meiji-era (1868–1912) values that were already waning in Japan. Such an upbringing, though not without its confusions and frustrations, proved invaluable in navigating the subtleties and nuances of conversation with elderly Japanese women. One of my consociates even gave me direct affirmation. On two separate occasions, Yamamoto-san said, "I feel like I am speaking to a Japanese person who understands the feelings, too."[24] I have no doubt that I would not be writing this book were it not for the specific elements of my historical and cultural circumstance.

I conducted interviews, engaged in embodied learning, translated across distinct linguistic and cultural foundations, and drew on the available textual materials such as ritual manuals, scriptures, prayers, and pilgrimage songs. Textual sources sometimes provided the content of the rituals, whereas qualitative field materials helped to explain what the rituals mean to people who experience them. Theoretical materials on ritual and healing were drawn from both Japanese and Western literature. I deliberately did not turn to these secondary sources, however, until after I had completed the primary field research, because I did not want to apply frameworks of analysis that developed in a different context before I knew the paradigms and concerns of my consociates. After understanding the internal dynamics of the original materials, I am better able to assess which theories will illuminate the material and which might highlight important differences with the current literature. This approach echoes Jean Piaget's concepts on cognition: accommodation and assimilation.[25]

I did not need to worry, however, about designing a way to maintain a power balance and deepen trust through continuing to show my vulnerabilities to the women who volunteered to show me theirs, a concern of qualitative field researchers that derives from commitment to gain reliable information.[26] They came to know me more personally than I could have crafted by research design, through methods I certainly did not think to include in my Fulbright grant proposal. After being hospitalized with pneumonia, I successively went through tonsillitis, acute conjunctivitis, and dizziness accompanied by tinnitus that laid me flat on my back for nearly two weeks—all while solo parenting a two-year-old. Thanks to these conditions during the one-year intensive field research phase, my research developed in ways that were ultimately more interesting than they might otherwise have been.[27]

During our interactions, these women showed me how they try to maintain health through careful attention to the intimate relationship of body-mind and heart. They told me of the close link between physical and spiritual health. More than anything else, though, they shared the treatments, rituals, and practices they perform in the home.[28] This was the real treasure.

Without my asking, each woman independently helped me realize that their knowledge about the healing powers in rituals lies more in their bodies and habits than in their self-conscious, effable thoughts. Awareness that the knowledge I sought was centered in their bodily actions evolved into a notable dimension of the methodology. I realized that I had to learn "how" they do things, not just ask "what" they do and "why." So in addition to each woman investing no fewer than a dozen hours of formal recorded interview time (some even exceeded twenty hours), total interaction time with most women far exceeded one hundred hours per person. The activities with which we occupied the time include those as natural as tending a garden and eating organic vegetables, going to museum exhibitions, or taking walks to view autumn foliage and spring flowers. This time spent being a participant-observer in their religious and self-defined healing activities gave me the most insight into their practices. In allowing our meetings to take on a broad format, they collectively found ways to express their personalities and to communicate holistic information about their healing experiences. In fact, direct verbal questions and answers did not yield the most important information. Rather, human relationships are at the center of this project, for it is in wrestling with being human that healing is sought. Thus, their narratives are the core of the field materials. These stories, whether painful, inspiring, sobering, or humorous, illuminate their paradigm of healing.

I had to learn how these women viewed and experienced themselves. Considerations of how research methodology relates to distinctive cultural formations of self are central to my aim.[29] I have already noted that there are fifteen ways to say "I" in Japanese, depending on the relationship of those interacting. The context for this vocabulary revolves around the Japanese relational construction of self-identity.[30] In Japanese culture, public face (*tatemae*) and private face (*honne*) are clearly delineated, especially among the generation of women I was interviewing.[31] In this cultural context, people are adept at sincerely expressing their public face, making it difficult to discern how much their public and private faces might differ. Moreover, it would be considered improper for you to express your private face to someone with whom you have only a public relationship. Although I tried to make clear to the women that they were consocinates in this study, at first they perceived our relationship as one of interviewer and interviewee, which falls into the "public" category.

Exposing my personal vulnerabilities was the key to creating a safe place for them to reveal their private face, giving me access to subtle, complex, and sometimes fraught details of their situations. I consider this self-reflexive method a way to make the critical reasoning process transparent. It is messy, but life is not always tidy. Even though I know I cannot convey the full reality of these women's lives and experiences—and all I do convey is filtered through the multiple lenses of my training, background, linguistic and cultural differences, and different concepts of knowledge—my aim is to capture a reliable portion of the fabric of reality.[32] In a real way, then, the messier the material, the more confident I am as a scholar that I am getting closer to the "truth."[33]

The criteria for qualitative research—rigor, breadth, and depth—are met through a variety of methods and sources.[34] The interviews and interaction with my consociates form the primary empirical material for the project. These are amplified by my embodied engagement with their ritual activities, private writings and artwork, and reference to relevant historical, thematic, and theoretical writings. I also have generated new theories and hermeneutical categories to explicate my findings.

Theorizing Healing in Religio-Cultural Context

The root of the word "heal" is "to make whole." I use the word "healing" as a heuristic device to convey what these women understand and have experienced about making their lives whole. As a heuristic tool, healing brings into focus what they value, think of themselves, aim for, and do.[35] To understand their views, it is important to examine the root assumptions that constitute the mature Japanese Zen Buddhist women's worldview. After all, "What makes ideas 'real' are the system of knowledge, the formations of culture, and the relations of power in which these concepts are located."[36] I have devised a "worldview compass" to help orient us to their way of understanding and experiencing the world (see chart below). "North" designates the fundamental framework or primary reference point. Some examples of primary reference points are gods, goddesses, emptiness, reason, and harmony. "East" points to the concept of self. Concepts of self are quite varied, including notions of a distinct body and mind, eternal soul or souls, no soul, and the capacity for rebirth, resurrection, or burning in an eternal or provisional hell realm.

Worldview Compass

"Primary Reference Point"

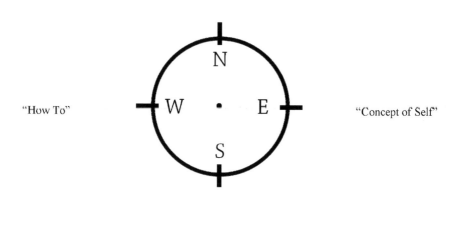

"How To"   "Concept of Self"

"Aim"

"South" designates the fundamental aims in life. Salvation from original sin, liberation from cycles of suffering, awakening from delusion, social harmony, and harmony with nature are examples of aims found within a handful of religious traditions (Christian, Hindu, Buddhist, Confucian, and Taoist, respectively). "West" directs attention to how to go about reaching those aims.[37]

North, the primary reference point, orients a person, society, or tradition. It is similar to how sailors use the North Star: it helps people know where they are and can help guide them to where they are going. Every culture, religion, society, period, and individual is oriented to the world in some fashion. Most are not conscious of what underlies their sense of being. Often it is easier to see this orientation in comparison to another orientation. For example, if you grow up seeing yourself as an interrelated event in an ever-changing cosmos, you might not be able to articulate that until you meet someone who is oriented to an omnipotent and transcendent god. Other primary reference points people navigate by include scientific exploration, fiscal strength, political power, humanity, and ecological sustainability.

For these women, the Buddhist framework of emptiness is the primary reference point. Emptiness puts focus on the interrelatedness of all events and things in the universe. Events and things are empty of independent existence. For example, flowers are dependent on nutrients in the earth and rain from the sky. The rain comes from the water that has been cycling the planet for millions and millions of years. Tracing the nutrients in the soil back as far as possible, you would end up at the "Big Bang." When the Buddhist point of reference is set to emptiness, the universe is a vast flux of events and elements in an interdependent causality of relationships. This point of reference expects change and encourages you to see yourself as a part of something big. The women in this study filter this basic Buddhist orientation through a Japanese context that stresses concrete details of daily life in the here and now. Recognizing how even little things contribute to your life is a driving force in human relations, resulting in a culture of obvious and subtle expressions of gratitude. In the vast web of events, even difficulties are seen as somehow contributing to a more meaningful life.

East on the compass represents the concept of self. The relational concept of self that characterizes these women is continuous with the Buddhist framework of interrelatedness. The self is ever, always, and only understood in the context of relationships. As in other Confucian-influenced cultures, a person's family name in Japan precedes a person's given name because the family is the primary identity. Within a family, one is mostly known and called by the appellation of who one is in relation to other family members: grandmother, father, older sister, younger brother. In general society, a person explains who they are in terms of their largest organizing unit. For example, "Toyota's (car company) Koyama Toshiko." Notice, there is no "I." The first person singular is neither grammatically nor socially required. In Japanese, an identity apart from relationships is difficult to establish.

Moreover, the self is understood as an integrated body-mind-heart unit. It is part of a Buddhist cosmology that Dōgen brilliantly articulated. He made a paradigm shift when he translated a phrase rendered in the Chinese version of the *Nirvana Sutra* from "All sentient beings have Buddha nature" to "All existents are Buddha nature."[38] Dōgen made a subtle grammatical move by interpreting the Chinese verb "to have" as part of a noun, "existents." Moreover, by removing an explicit verb the whole phrase becomes an activity. The implications of this grammatical shift continue to reverberate. Some could interpret this move as the logical conclusion of a nondualistic philosophy. Others might note its resonance with the seamless worldview of indigenous Japan. Whatever the case, this is one of Dōgen's most important teachings, and it is particularly pertinent to the activities of his female followers. Women are Buddha nature, just as men are, and, for that matter, just as rocks and rags are.

South is the direction on the worldview compass that indicates aim. Aim is what measures meaning and significance. It is what makes living and working hard worthwhile. A person can be driven by many aims. Here, we are highlighting healing. In the largest sense, healing in a Buddhist context is "a metaphor for growth, with the Buddha named as Supreme Physician and the Buddhist teachings termed the King of Medicines."[39] Some discussion of my consociates' healing paradigm follows below, but more of the specifics will unfold over the course of the book as I explain the theories I developed to make sense of my field research and discoveries.

My understanding of healing as an aim began with learning their vocabulary and its significance. Until I began doing field research, I had thought about the project in academic English. My initial conversations with consociates revealed that my original concepts did not resonate with them. The ideas did not translate well into conversational Japanese. In order to understand how *they* experience the world, I had to allow them to define the terms.

The vocabulary they used to discuss healing revealed in part their understanding of it. It is notable that the word they all used to refer to "healing" was a different grammatical form of the word I had initially tried out. My use of the equivalent of the gerund form of "heal" (*iyashi*—"Have you ever experienced a healing?") elicited only blank stares. On the other hand, using what I call the "gratitude tense" (*iyasaremashita*) yielded enthusiastic nods of understanding.[40] I was struck that they could comprehend being "a humble and grateful recipient of healing" but not someone who "experienced a healing." The difference between these two ways of talking about healing is fundamental and has far-reaching implications. There is no English equivalent to the verb tense I have labeled the gratitude tense. It is my term for the verb conjugation that eloquently expresses gratitude for having been humbly given the gift of being caused by the universe to be healed. It is technically a passive tense, but it is not used in a dualistic sense that something happens to one by virtue of an outside force. They use it to express the nondualistic worldview of interrelatedness. It is not that they have nothing to do with what happens—it is more that there are countless factors in play. It is a way of articulating that no person can act by herself, because there are no isolated entities. All is interrelated. *Iyashi*, or the gerund form of the verb "to heal," implies that healing is a discrete phenomenon. It stands alone and apart. *Iyasaremashita,* however, sets healing in a context-specific relationship. For these women the relationship is with the universe. Although they understand the universe to be a vast network of interrelated phenomena, in their daily lives most of these women do not think of the universe in terms of its grand expanse. Rather, they experience the universe in more direct and intimate ways: in the dew at dawn, ducklings swimming in their mother's wake, and laundry drying in the sun. It is something that one receives, humbly and gratefully. The source from which healing comes is not explicitly stated in the term itself, but in its deepest meaning that the source of healing is the universe, and is not their "small" self. As their stories of *iyasareteiru* experience unfolded, it became clear that the Buddhist nuns and laity who are the focus of this study saw healing as a way of life. It is a paradigm that includes a specific orientation to the events of life, primarily gratitude.

Using the gratitude tense fosters healing because it fosters awareness of the interrelatedness of all things. It helps these women see that illness is not the enemy. It helps them relate to difficulty in a positive way that does not generate more suffering. It helps them cultivate or maintain the perspective that they are not alone. For these women, then, all of life, including the way life is viewed and experienced, is an activity of healing.

Health in a Japanese context is not just about individual biomedical assessments. It also takes into account the quality of your relationships with the living and even the deceased.[41] For these women, healing has physical, social, and emotional aspects. If one of these aspects is out of balance, all become strained. The women realize the power they have to affect a situation depends on how they interpret it. A narrow and negative approach usually results in a worsening of social relationships, caustic emotional states, and even adverse physiological conditions.[42] An expansive and positive approach can lead to more harmonious relations, relaxed emotions, and a stronger constitution.

By understanding healing in the context of relationships with people who are integrated mind-body beings, these women see physical manifestations as expressions of hopes, fears, challenges, and commitments. They do not see sickness as a failing, however, especially not the failing of an individual. Unpleasant physical conditions primarily indicate that something is out of balance, whether relationships between people or the environment. In this context, somatization is an acknowledged mode of expressing distress or dissatisfaction. That this is a more general Japanese cultural understanding is evident in the common expression, "Their exhaustion came out" (*tsukaregadeta*) on hearing that someone who has been working with intense commitment becomes sick. I added the pronoun "their" to render the phrase into grammatical English, but in Japanese, no pronoun is required. The Japanese language allows for implicit understanding of a subject. This seems to come out of an awareness and value placed on recognizing that people and things do not act alone. When sick, it is acceptable to rest. Otherwise, in Japanese society you are expected to perform. Danforth observes how "somatization is particularly common in societies where mental illness is heavily stigmatized, where it is improper to discuss personal or family difficulties with outsiders, and where no form of psychotherapy is available."[43] This describes Japanese society in general.

With few social or medical resources for dealing with problems of the heart-mind (kokoro), these women show us how they weave healing into their daily lives. For these women, the heart-mind can decide how to respond to events.[44] They know they can make social, physical, and emotional matters worse and suffer more, or they can respond with a large and stable emotional frame that makes human relations and attitudes toward physical conditions better. In other words, they can choose to heal. Assessing how much is in continuity with past practices is beyond the scope of this study, but it is safe to presume that these women draw on a foundation of a long line of women who have tried to be responsible and strong in the face of complicated human interactions, physical challenges, and heart-wrenching situations. In sum, for them healing is not about finding a cure nor is it about direct cause-and-effect relationship. Rather, it is a worldview or way of living and facing challenges of the nonbifurcated body-mind in the context of intricate human relations and natural forces.

On my worldview compass, West indicates how to accomplish the aim, given the particular primary reference point and the operative concept of self. Ten types of activities animate the "how to" dimension of my consociates' worldview. They are experiencing interrelatedness, embodying a nondualistic self (body-mind as one), engaging in rituals, nurturing self, enjoying life, creating beauty, cultivating gratitude, accepting reality as it is, expanding perspective, and embodying compassion.[45]

The teachings of Dōgen undergird the assumptions at work in the women's activities. In a departure from most formulations of the relationship between practice and enlightenment, Dōgen taught, "practice is enlightenment" (shushō ittō). In other words, you are enlightened when you practice. For Dōgen, enlightenment is an activity (verb), and not a state (noun). When you meditate while sitting (zazen), you just sit. You do not sit in order to be enlightened. Understanding "practice is enlightenment" is the key to understanding ritualized activities as acts of healing. In a Sōtō worldview, healing, too, is a verb, not a state. Healing is an activity, a way of living. Therefore, engaging in ritualized activities *is* actualization of healing. In broader terms, one could even say ritualized healing activities or practices are Buddha activities, a way to actualize Buddha-nature. Worded another way, they are compassionate activities. When you act compassionately, it is affirmation that you are healed. Moreover, one who sees you whole—sees that you are Buddha-nature—is a healer.

Theorizing Ritual in Religio-Cultural Context

Ritual as a heuristic device focuses on meaningful body-mind activity.[46] Ritual is a field that opens a window on embodied religiosity in motion. Rituals are rich arenas for exploring, as Bloch articulates, the "non-linear organization of everyday cognition."[47] Engaging in rituals can be an effective way to move people and accomplish complicated things, such as healing in the face of a terminal diagnosis. Rituals enlist images, metaphors, symbols, specific bodily motions and gestures, and smells and sounds;[48] enact philosophical ideals;[49] and employ implements that are encoded with meaning and power.[50] For these women, ritual is not a process: it is a manifestation or actualization of aims.

To understand the ritual lives of these Japanese women, it is important to understand ritual in Japanese religiosity. Ritual is a key prism through which to view Japanese religiosity, because the category "religion" is foreign and relatively new to Japanese culture. Along with "experience (in general)" (*keiken*) and "(personal) physical experience" (*taiken*), the word "religion" (*shūkyō*) entered Japan during the Meiji Period (1868–1912). Ritual is an agile and dynamic heuristic device that enables us to see the nonbifurcated body-mind as it navigates the Japanese Buddhist worldview. The view afforded by ritual is less cluttered and distorted than the view afforded by trying to see directly through the lens of religion.

Nevertheless, ritualized activity viewed through the category of religion can be illuminating. The literature in ritual studies that has burgeoned over the past dozen years offers tremendous insights into the critical role ritual serves in religious traditions. Specifically in the highly ritualized Japanese culture, ritual studies are key to understanding how religion functions. When asked, contemporary Japanese people typically comment that they are not religious, yet they can be observed performing numerous religious rituals. Participating in rituals throughout your life and behaving in the appropriate ritualized manner is part of what constitutes Japanese identity. Indeed, the ritualized body of the Zen arts, such as the tea ceremony and calligraphy, has had a profound and pervasive impact on Japanese culture. Ritualizing your body in certain ways, such as using your body in the different types of bowing, is part of what makes a person a respectable person. This study will explicitly address this central aspect of Japanese culture, highlighting the healing contributions of particular religious rituals.

The impulse to ritualize daily behavior derives in part from Confucian influence.[51] The Japanese cultural habit of equating proper action with moral force resonates with the Confucian-based paradigm that focuses on the importance of ritual propriety. Herein, daily actions are understood to occur in a context of ultimate importance: human society. Zen practice, especially in Japan, applied the Confucian influence to methods of face washing, towel folding, and all-manner of daily activities. Respect is embedded in each gesture, so the performer embodies respect when performing the act. Although in the Zen monastery exacting standards are the norm, women are often the ones to set the ritual and aesthetic standards of a home.

In part due to Confucian influence, ritual practices have a long and rich history in Zen. Stressing the functional dimension of Zen ritual practices,[52] Hasebe Kōichi goes so far as to assert, "there can be no Chan [Zen] without ritual."[53] According to Kuromaru Kanji, "the true expression of the precepts could be realized only through the rituals of Zen monastic life."[54] Rinzai Zen scholar and monastic G. Victor Sogen Hori asserts, "The concrete practices that form the path to that spiritual insight consist of ritually performed acts."[55] Practice equals ritualized activity designed to manifest Buddha nature. Such a positive view of ritual in Zen is not uncontested, however. Lin-chi (d. 866 CE), according to Bernard Faure, "denounced rites for their empty formalism."[56] With Zen moving into yet another cultural context, D. T. Suzuki framed Zen to his North American Anglo audience as a tradition that "eschews . . . all ritual."[57] Although having divergent views, another prominent Buddhist scholar of the time, Hu Shih, also saw Zen as antiritualistic.[58]

Specifically in the context of Japan, the works of Zen scholars Faure, William Bodiford, and Ishikawa Rikizan have made significant inroads into this multifaceted topic from hermeneutical and historical perspectives.[59] Fujii Masao has documented ritual in the broad context of Japanese religious life.[60] Two edited volumes also help fill out the picture of ritual history and activities in Zen: Bernard Faure's *Chan in Ritual Context*, and Heine and

Wright's *Zen Ritual*.[61] From an anthropological perspective, Ohnuki-Tierney has given an overview of the types of rituals sought by Japanese who are ill.[62] LaFleur's study on Buddhist memorial services for unborn fetuses explores the ethical aspects of this rite, as does Hardacre's treatment of the marketing dimension of fetal rites.[63] My project builds on their work and joins the stream of other works that are coming out in related areas.[64]

Northup aptly observes how Japanese women empower themselves by interpreting the things they do in an important way. They have ritualized their daily activities and have endowed them with meaning: "Cooking, cleaning, parenting, bathing, dressing, managing, sewing, networking, creating, teaching—the endless host of women's unglorified daily activities are being mined by women seeking a distinctive spiritual expression."[65] Moreover, Sered found for women more broadly that, "given the this-worldly orientation of women's religions, spiritual and earthly benefits tend to be intertwined."[66] Indeed, she observes, "ritual solutions for the problems of suffering in this world are the foci of most women's religions."[67]

Sleuthing was required to find out what a "ritual" is in the context of contemporary Japanese Zen Buddhist women. There is no evidence that Dōgen thought in terms of the category "ritual." Neither do the women who served as consociates for this study, because the English term "ritual" finds no easy translation into Japanese. There are general terms that include the Confucian term *li* (in Japanese pronounced "gi," as in "geese"), such as *reigi* (etiquette) and *girei* (formal ritual). *Gishiki* (ceremony) and its generic suffix, *shiki*, are added to a wide range of activities to indicate specific ceremonies, as in *seijinshiki* (coming of age), *sotsugyōshiki* (graduation), *kekkonshiki* (wedding), and *sōshiki* (funeral). There is even a term for a Buddhist service (*hōyō*). Notably, there is no abstract category with the overarching sense that accompanies the current usage of the English word "ritual." In fact, I had difficulty communicating with my consociates that I was interested in understanding their use of "ritual." Even those with advanced academic training were not clear what I meant. It is therefore unavoidable that I project a Western academic category onto the material if I am to communicate to a Western audience familiar with the Western category of ritual. In *Ritual Perspectives and Dimensions,* Catherine Bell cautions about the dynamics of this phenomenon: "While such developments may foster easier communication and shared values, they may do so by means of political subordination and substantive diminution of the diversity of human experience."[68] I make every attempt to understand my consociates in their larger cultural, historical, and personal context.

I have not found a thoroughly satisfactory way to communicate the
activities highlighted in this study in English without using the term "ritual." I am cognizant, however, that as Bell states, "Western scholarship is
very powerful. Its explanative power rests not only on tools of abstraction
that make some things into concepts and other things into data but also
on many social activities, simultaneously economic and political, that con-
struct a plausibility system of global proportions. Hence, it is quite possible that categories of ritual and nonritual will influence people who would
define their activities differently."[69] My delineation of the category "ritual"
does not accurately or fully capture how the women understand themselves and their actions, nor does it communicate the understanding I have
of the topic in colloquial (nonacademic) Japanese. In Japanese, we talked
in amorphous ways that communicated volumes. We used phrases such as
"events like this" (*kōiuyōna koto*). Even after thousands of hours over years
conversing with dozens of Japanese nuns and laywomen, no clearer termi-
nology emerged. There is no abstract framework within which delineating
certain activities as ritual made sense. In their seamless worldview, many
everyday activities are invested with a sense of importance, such as where
to take off shoes and how to place them once they are off. This confirmed
to me that the concept "ritual" does not quite explain their experience or
represent their worldview. Despite its limitations, I have chosen for the
sake of communicating with an English-speaking readership to enlist the
term "ritual," because I agree with Bell, who argues, "[t]he form and scope
of interpretation differ, and that should not be lightly dismissed, but it
cannot be amiss to see in all of these instances practices that illuminate
our shared humanity."[70] The study of ritual will continue to complicate
matters as increased cross-cultural and interdisciplinary investigations
proceed. For now, it raises interesting questions that bring into focus some
important points and exploratory speculation.

My first speculation is that back in the thirteenth century Dōgen might
have thought of *sahō* in a manner similar to what I think of as "ritualized
activities." My translation of *sahō* is "method of actualizing." I take my translation and interpretation cues from Dōgen's teachings, especially *shushō ittō*,
"practice and enlightenment are one,"[71] and the articulations of it found in
his "Genjō Kōan" fascicle of the *Shōbōgenzō*.[72] The root assumptions are (1)
there is no dichotomy between subject and object, (2) there is a holistic understanding of body-mind, and (3) there is only the present moment. Contemporary Zen monastic women demonstrate with their actions that they
agree with Dōgen's concern to manifest certain qualities, including clean

floors, a nourished body-mind, and footwear kept in respectful order.[73] To manifest these specific qualities requires exacting care, as anyone who has tried to eat properly from a lacquered set of *oryōki* bowls in a Japanese Zen meditation hall can relate. To extend this line of analysis to the rituals under consideration in this study, a fruitful question might be, What are the rituals actualizing?[74]

Japanese lay and monastic women employ Dōgen's practices and teachings to guide, empower, and heal themselves.[75] The ethnographic field materials reveal that many Sōtō Zen women are steeped in Dōgen's distinctive teaching on Buddha nature. The avenues these women created to work toward their goals within an imperfect institutional structure reveal the influence of Dōgen's teachings. Dōgen's teaching that we *are* all Buddha nature is not directly invoked during the rituals women perform, but the rituals bear out that teaching. Moreover, the rituals are in no way dependent on male permission, authority, or recognition. The rituals begin with assuming everyone is Buddha nature and proceed from there. In this way, they empower women to actualize their Buddha nature and heal them from delusions that trigger despair and loneliness.

For many women, ritualizing has become the "primary mode of claiming power to invent, control, and interpret the symbolic resources of their traditions and cultures."[76] Characteristics of ritual Northup found in women's ritual practices in the West resonate with those I found in Japan. They include spontaneity and informality, ecumenicity, and nonreliance on texts.[77] Martinez found women in Japan who were concerned with doing rituals were "subsuming potentially dangerous power, harnessing it to the need to care for the health and well-being of their family and household ancestors."[78] The women I worked with are similar, although only two of the twelve would characterize their power as "potentially dangerous." All are determined in their use of power, and all are dedicated to wielding it in ways that help heal themselves and others.[79]

Through my field research (primarily in Nagoya), I discovered Zen rituals ranging from colorful to monochromatic, from intense silence to loud drumming accompanied by esoteric chanting. By formalizing how to eat, sleep, sit, and walk to ceremonial rituals of devotion, mourning, supplication, and gratitude, rituals are integral to the tradition. In addition, many Zen Buddhist women in Japan seem to effortlessly weave together diverse elements in their practice. Indeed, exploring the rituals practiced by Sōtō Zen laywomen today exposes a broad spectrum of activities and ceremonies, including functional, daily, annual, private, public, expensive, inexpensive, esoteric, and even homemade. Their selection illustrates the array of rituals available to Zen Buddhist women seeking affirmation and healing. They include those that are aimed at significant moments in the life cycle, women's issues, and family issues, as well as moments of transition. Highlighting different seasons of the year and phases of life, their ritual practices range from chanting to the goddess Kannon while soothing a feverish child to ensuring that sundry spirits not go hungry, from copying scriptures with prayers for family harmony to sleeping on a pillow covered with a cloth believed to be efficacious in curing cancer.

The range and significance of these practices are even more intriguing when considered in light of the fact that they are not outlined or advocated in scripture. Absent ritual texts, ethnographic investigation is essential in expanding our understanding of the contours of Zen experience in the ritual lives of Buddhist laywomen. Their religiosity reveals a mixture of serendipity, historical happenstance, familial and marital relations, and personal choice. In the following chapters, I provide a description of such previously undocumented rituals, analyze common Zen rituals that have yet to be examined in terms of their healing implications, provide new insights about contemporary Japanese culture and the ways Japanese women experience religion, and discuss what modern Japanese Zen Buddhists actually do.

Our conversations started with my asking questions like, "What sutras do you chant?" or "Do you do something at your home altar on a regular basis?" and "What do you do there?" Their answers yielded information not covered in the abstract concept of ritual: recommendations for what elixirs are good for colds, why it is important to have something beautiful on view like a flower arrangement or an object of art, and what it means to keep an adult child's elementary school drawings in a home altar.[80] In addition to close observation of their ritual life, placing their ritual experiences in the context of the vicissitudes of their lives illuminated a number of important dynamics. They would not be meaningful, fully appreciated, or perhaps even noticed without the vantage point of the lifespan. From a long-term perspective of their lives, the changes that the rituals helped to foster became visible. For example, it is now apparent how the mortuary rituals that figure centrally in Japanese Zen Buddhism are a manifestation of the wisdom that grieving is a never-ending activity. Healing from grief does not mean that grief will stop. On the contrary, healing involves expecting and preparing for the changing seasons of grief—or, in other words, living with grief in a life-affirming manner.

It is well documented that in Sōtō Zen funerals the deceased person is recognized as a Buddha.[81] My contribution is to add the experience of the living, those who recognize their deceased beloved as a personal Buddha. Chapter 3 discusses this experience at length. The home altar where the dead are recognized as Buddhas is the heart of Japanese Buddhist homes. It raises the question, What power do the funerary rituals have in helping someone be a Buddha?[82] In Sōtō Zen, becoming a Buddha is not a concern, even when a person is alive. The key word is "becoming." Dōgen teaches, "All existents are Buddha nature." Hence, there is no need to *become* something you already are. So, Sōtō Zen Buddhists do not have to do philosophical gymnastics at the point of death to recognize someone as a Buddha, as would be the case in other streams of Buddhism.[83] Buddhist rituals often have been cast as secondary to meditation practice, even superfluous on the path to enlightenment. The death rituals examined in this ethnographic study reveal that the rituals that help people dissolve attachments and experience interrelatedness are key ingredients to the cessation of suffering.[84]

Understanding the dead as personal Buddhas adds to the categories for interpreting Buddha-hood. Viewing Buddha-hood through the hermeneutical category of the personal Buddha enables us to see how memorial rituals facilitate dissolving delusion of self and other as separate entities. It helps loosen the grip of fear the prospect of death can have. It also helps a person accept the present reality more fully. In turn, memorial rituals can help generate gratitude and generosity, qualities requisite for an enlightened being.

A long-term vantage point also brings into focus the tremendous flexibility and creativity women bring to their ritual practices. Although all of the women have home altars, the rituals they perform and the meaning and significance it has for them varies widely. In addition to home rituals, some always do certain rituals at a temple, and one almost never does. Some go to one temple for one ritual and another temple for another ritual. Some only go to one temple. What is meaningful and helpful for one woman is not so with another, or it is not meaningful in the same way. Different people bring different concerns, yet it is because of the group gathering that all find it a meaningful ritual. Moreover, what works in one phase of life does not necessarily work in another. As a person ages, she seeks new rituals to help with the changing concerns, needs, and situations. The diversity of ritual practices counted even just among these twelve women is striking. Another dimension of these women that comes to the fore when studying their ritual practices is the seamless way they cross sectarian boundaries, especially when viewed from a larger historical and cultural context, which I will only briefly outline here.

Circumstances in the early 1600s resulted in the expulsion of Christianity from Japan. In an effort to enforce this regulation, the government required all families to register at a neighborhood Buddhist temple. Hence, many families—the unit of decision making on such matters—became formal followers of the sect of Buddhism of their neighborhood temple. To have such large-scale declaration of affiliation to a particular Buddhist sect, however, was an unprecedented event in Japanese Buddhist history. Nonetheless, since then, many families have stayed with that sect, primarily because the memorial rituals for ancestors keeps them connected to the temple of affiliation at the death of a family member. It is difficult to relocate ancestors. Therefore, despite having lived in the city all their lives, many family members return each summer to their ancestor's temple in the countryside for Obon, the nationally recognized memorial ritual.

As a result of the Tokugawa Period (1603–1867) sociohistorical circumstances that required families to have a Buddhist temple affiliation, most Japanese are familiar with Buddhist rituals. However, it is not uncommon for someone to explore other traditions and teachings, because Buddhist teachings are inherently open to multiple approaches to learning and practicing love and compassion. It is not surprising, then, to hear that Kawasaki-san was Christian for a while. She concluded that Buddhist and Christian love are the same. She does the appropriate rituals when she is supposed to with no sense of dissonance. The underlying assumption in experiencing no dissonance likely derives from the lack of an indigenous concept of absolute truth. This seems to carry over into the common practice of mixing Buddhist sect practices, too. Listen as Kawasaki-san tells of her exploration.

> I like Dostoevsky and I thought Christianity was so great. I was interested in Western literature. I needed to know Christianity to understand. Until I was about twenty or twenty-two, I went to church. My family thought I was odd. I was really taken by Christianity. I was baptized. Then I learned I was a Buddhist family. I think the teachings may have some differences, but I think Christ and Buddha's "love" is the same.

> When I got married [to a Sōtō Zen Buddhist family], I thought I should be with my husband's ancestors. Since I thought Christ and Buddha were the same love, I thought I should just perform the rituals at the home altar. It took me a while to adjust. I'd pray at the family Buddhist altar and then go to the kitchen and chant "Ave Maria." I was not confused about being

Christian and doing this. I just did what you do at the times you're supposed to do them. This is the Japanese way. I felt no dissonance.[85]

One of the main features of domestic Zen is the lack of concern for knowing what practices go with which tradition or sect. We will therefore look at all manner of rituals.

Only a few of the consociates actually came from historically Zen families. Despite the common social practice of not making individual decisions about temple affiliation, all of the consociates deliberately sought out Zen practices and teachings for personal reasons. Each cited different reasons for having done so, but all found what they were looking for in Zen—at least, in part. Most of the women did not hesitate to do any ritual practice that they thought might suit and help them. These are mature women, known for not letting external structures impede their progress or limit their aims. Perhaps it is no coincidence that all the laywomen who sought out Zen nuns to be their spiritual guides would have such an attitude, given that Zen nuns have proven that institutional structures and regulations, as well as established practices, can be changed, especially if they are not in accord with their understanding of the Buddhist teachings.[86] In this context, then, it is a matter of no consequence that most of the consociates draw on the teachings and practices of a range of sectarian traditions. The most common weaving of practices and traditions was with the Sōtō Zen sect and the Jōdoshinshū True Pure Land sect. Two of the women also integrated the practices of the Sōtō Zen sect, an exoteric tradition, and the Kegon sect, an esoteric tradition. Such cross-sectarian practice is an indicator of the flexibility the women exercise in pursuing their spiritual needs. Also brought to light from a perspective of their lifespan are rituals not found in any formal religious tradition; this is an indication of their creativity in finding resources to meet their needs.

As one faces increasing challenges in life, there is a tendency to engage in more rituals. It seems to come out of awareness that we are not alone and cannot do things alone. The rituals are a way to enlist support from those who know. Noguchi-san is aware of this: "Life is so hard. You can't live just on your own power. Gratitude increases with age, because I see how I have been able to live so far due to all that has happened to enable me. *Ikasareteiru*" (she uses the verb "to live" in the gratitude tense).[87] Over a life, gratitude increases, too.

Many women turn explicitly to Zen because it validates everyday activities, including cooking and cleaning. Family concerns can be approached in the mode of practice. It is part of Japanese religiosity in general to be concrete about spirituality. Indeed, such ritualization of daily activities may help the limbic system. "The neocortex rapidly masters didactic information, but the limbic brain takes mountains of repetition."[88] The repetitive dimension of cooking, washing dishes, cleaning floors, doing laundry, and tending to trash and recycling is ripe territory for the limbic system, feeding, nourishing, and entraining it in specific ways. The emotional dimensions of ritual also prime the limbic system.

The rituals explored in this book cannot be done "wrong" because they are events women weave into their lives. To note what does not work is to miss the point. It is not about perfect performance. It is about healing in the midst of a mess.[89] Rituals of healing embedded in daily life are especially impervious to failure, because healing is about an orientation in life, and is not about a narrow cause-and-effect process. That is why what constitutes healing rituals for my consociates are not readily obvious to those looking for phenomena called "healing rituals" in some specific cause-and-effect relationship.

It is not that explicit healing rituals have no place. Formal healing rituals are often large and public. They are a place where people of similar orientation can gather together in community, often itself an important dimension to healing. These rituals tend to be infrequent, and usually are held annually. They are designed to offer minimal individual attention, often in a formulaic way, such as when each person does the same thing by turns.

Rituals performed in the home during daily life—though not labeled by the practitioners, or even by the tradition, as healing rituals—are primed and framed by the public healing rituals. The role of these more personal rituals is that they are honed to fit each person. They are actually often the result of a creative deviation from a more common ritual. These tailor-fit rituals can reach deep, because all the idiosyncrasies that constitute a person are accounted for and, hence, are personal affirmations of that person's interconnectedness. The recent emphasis on positive emotions in mental health resonates with my approach at exploring the qualities and dynamics helpful for these women.[90]

Through the hermeneutical lens of ritual, several things become clear. First, ritual in a Sōtō Zen context is an actualization of Buddha nature. Rituals performed in this mode help heal, especially by expanding perspective at the same time attention is directed through the whole body-mind on the present moment, a place where illness and wellness do not exist. Such distinctions require comparison to a past or future, which do not exist in the present moment. Chapter 2 explicates my theory about the components and dynamics that constitute the way of healing as experienced by the Buddhist women studied. Through assessing this healing paradigm, it becomes clear that experiencing interrelatedness is the key that unlocks the dynamics for all other elements to be helpful in healing. Once this occurs, all the factors mutually amplify each other, resulting in heightened experiences of healing.

My concept of personal Buddhas is advanced in Chapter 3. It explores the role of mortuary and ancestral rituals in helping people integrate loss into their lives. This book takes an intimate look at grieving. It extends beyond the immediate period of the rites and looks at how mourners weave loss into the fabric of their daily lives. Exploring memorial and ancestral rituals from this perspective leads us to recognize both the centrality of the dead in Japanese Buddhist religiosity and the ways these ancestral rites can serve as healing rituals.

A ritual lens enables us to see a dimension of Zen that I call "domestic Zen," a concept developed in Chapter 4. It is a messy Zen that responds to the needs and demands of people facing a wide range of challenges, including difficulty in giving birth, problems with child-rearing, complex family dynamics, and death by natural and unnatural causes. They range from lighting incense at your home altar, to cutting carrots, to chanting, to ingesting Sanskrit syllables written on rice paper (*washi*). In addition to these rituals, I analyze several others in terms of how they contribute to the ten-fold healing paradigm.

I further my interpretation of the aesthetics of healing in Chapter 5. That chapter investigates the phenomenon that beauty factors into all the women's healing activities. Whether they are composing a poem or arranging flowers, or just enjoying a walk to see the plum blossoms in late winter, the power of beauty to help heal was emphasized by all the women. With expanded perception, inherent beauty can be revealed in that which appears ugly, for everything is a resource for beauty. Likewise, healing is found in the pain, not by destroying the pain. The women see themselves in relationship with (*tsukiau*) their pain and injury. Disease, pain, loss, and spiritual and family problems are the "abrasives" that a person can use to polish her heart.

The rituals documented and analyzed in the book respond to a range of needs, hopes, and fears, and span a gamut of methods, complexity, and simplicity. Even as I write about the ritual lives of my consociates, I am mindful of Bloch's concern that there is tension and problems that attend "rendering into a text something which is not a text."[91] Keeping this tension in mind, I frame their activities in a broad context in order to interpret the roles, functions, and dynamics of the rituals. This helps elucidate how they are woven into their lives over time, demonstrating that both large, public, explicitly recognized healing rituals, and personal, informal ritualized behaviors in the home are necessary for healing. From this perspective, it is also apparent that scholarship on healing rituals requires the ethical imperative to devote extensive time in a relationship of mutual respect and trust.

CHAPTER 2

The Way of Healing

Yudō 癒道

I know I am healed when I am kind.

<small>UMEMURA, JAPANESE BUDDHIST WOMAN[1]</small>

The healing way of my Japanese Buddhist consociates involves discipline, ritualized practices, and expanding perspectives. Expanding perspectives facilitates a different experience of life for these women and transforms their relationships with events, circumstances, and people, including themselves. As I searched for the source of their practices and understanding of healing it became clear that their healing path is grounded in a Buddhist worldview. With this development, the medical analogy of the root Buddhist teachings on the Four Noble Truths took on new significance. This medical analogy appears in early texts (fifth century BCE), with no precedents identified in other literature, suggesting a distinctly Buddhist creative development in framing its religious orientation.[1] Although others have written about healing in a Buddhist context, it was viewing Buddhism through the lens of women's ritual lives and practices that enabled me to see the medical analogy and to understand Buddhist teachings and practices as a path of healing.[2]

Indeed, from this perspective it becomes apparent that healing is at the center of Buddhist teachings. The medical analogy of the Four Noble Truths likens the first Noble Truth (suffering) to a diagnosis. It is an observation of a condition, not a fated state. The second Noble Truth (ignorance) is the cause of this condition. Ignorance of the impermanent and interrelated nature of ultimate reality is the lens through which deluded beings view things, propelling them to greed and hatred. From the Buddhist perspective, humans are prone to ignorance because they experience life largely through the six senses of hearing, seeing, touching, smelling, tasting, and thinking. The input through these sources reinforces a distinct but false sense of being an independent self. For example, when I stub my toe, your toe does not hurt. Mine does. So it seems like I am separate from you. A sense-based perspective of things leads to suffering because it frames perception to focus on experience as a matter of interacting with independent objects that, in turn, can be desired or rejected. Although, conventionally, distinctions can be made between this and that, ultimately everything is not separate. But when we make decisions based on the view that there are separate things, we suffer because our actions are not synchronized with the way things ultimately are: impermanent and interconnected.

The Buddhist assumption is that people are born with a longing for good things to be permanent, and that they seek fulfillment of their desires and elimination of their aversions. According to Buddhist teachings, this longing is the primary condition from which people must be healed. Therefore, healing involves the transformation of habitually deluded ways of looking at the world through the lenses of attachment and aversion. The prognosis, though, could not be better. Suffering is neither a terminal nor a permanent condition. The third Noble Truth heralds that the cessation of suffering is possible. My consociates attest to the tenaciousness of ignorance, however. This leads to the fourth Noble Truth that outlines guidelines for treatment, which is to live according to the Eightfold Path of awakened views, intention, speech, action, livelihood, effort, mindfulness, and concentration.[3] Dissolving the ego through the Eightfold Path requires surgical precision to extricate the delusions that insidiously shape perception and fuel suffering. These women approach life as a healing activity that transforms their lives. It is a way of life that emerges from a Buddhist worldview and its values and practices. Their concept of healing, in keeping with the larger frame of the tradition, is oriented to diminishing and ultimately overcoming suffering.

The particulars of these women's healing activities and experiences emerged during lengthy in-depth sessions during which they recounted stories of how they responded to the challenges and losses in their lives. To move from learning a myriad of details about specific people and complex events to understanding their significance required that I view my original ethnographic data in its greater historical, cultural, religious, and linguistic contexts. It is only from this larger vantage point that many of the dynamics of their healing activities reveal a shared orientation and consistent qualities, values, and aims.

I created the phrase "way of healing" (*yudō*) to name the theory of healing that I have developed from this ethnographic data, because it invokes the ancient East Asian paradigm of the "Way" (*tao*). Tao is broadly construed as an ethical and aesthetic guide to transforming the body-mind to be in accord with the activity of the universe. The Way often involves actively refining the nonbifurcated body-mind by means of discipline and respect. The metaphor of the Way traces deep into Chinese history, having experienced efflorescence in textual articulation around the fifth century BCE. In the Japanese historical and cultural context, the concept was adapted into Zen-based arts that were formulated during the Muromachi Period (1336–1573). This Zen Buddhist religiocultural development is known as Gozan Bunka, or the Culture of the Five Mountains. It gave rise to the aesthetic paths of *shodō* (the Way of calligraphy), *sadō* (the Way of tea), *kadō* (the Way of flower arranging), *kadō* (the Way of poetry), and *gadō* (the Way of painting).

These Zen arts can be practiced as a spiritual discipline that furthers one along the Way, perhaps even to enlightenment. The healing paradigm focuses on the activity of the body-mind in the present moment. In other words, the Way is the activity of living fully in the present moment, which is the goal. Flexibility of the highest order is a primary skill of the Way. When you receive a terminal diagnosis, are informed that your sister was murdered by her husband, realize you will never give birth to your own child—these are the times when being flexible enough to flow along with the ephemeral stream of activity is most helpful. This healing paradigm insists on a fierce awareness of your delusions, desires, and aversions. These are the dimensions of the paradigm of the Way that I want to resonate in my theory of healing. The specific formulation I have given to this path is novel, but it is most meaningful when viewed as continuous with the extensive historical, cultural, linguistic, and religious stream running through East Asian civilization.

The Way of healing of my Buddhist women consociates is most fundamentally a path of retraining themselves to act in harmony with the way that things are: impermanent and interrelated. Healing, here, is not a result of action. It is, rather, a way of acting, seeing, thinking, and "holding your heart." It is an art to seek out ways to heal and not suffer. More specifically, it is an art of choosing to be grateful in the face of fear-driven and torment-ridden possibilities. This way of living and interpreting the world, self, events, and others requires practice and discipline. It is more an orientation to living than a clearly delineated and consciously followed course. There are guidelines but there are no absolutes. It is mostly in hindsight that one can see that there have been consistent values, attitudes, and activities that, when taken as a whole, constitute a way. Healing is activity that involves a myriad of factors, though there are ten salient principles that emerged from the lives of these Buddhist women.

The Ten Principles in the Way of Healing

The ten principles that constitute my theory of their "Way of Healing" are

1. experiencing interrelatedness,
2. living body-mind,
3. engaging in rituals,
4. nurturing the self,
5. enjoying life,
6. creating beauty,
7. cultivating gratitude,
8. accepting reality as it is,
9. expanding perspective, and
10. embodying compassion.

Each principle is distinct. Although there is overlap, there is no redundancy. Each adds a dimension to the healing paradigm. Often one element augments another—for instance, interrelatedness increases a person's feelings of thankfulness and heightens her sense of beauty. This in turn commonly sharpens her sense of fun. Performing rituals sometimes manifests in a deepening of the body-mind connection and results in a person taking better care of herself. Indeed, any factor can initiate an increase in any of the other factors. The more this happens, the more quickly and thoroughly a person heals.

My consociates' healing way demonstrates the complexity of their lived tradition. My ethnographic data indicate the power that rituals can have in fostering an experience of interrelatedness. Focusing on the power that rituals have in generating an experience of interrelatedness illuminates the core of the Buddhist mode of healing. When fully engaged, healing occurs in each act of compassion and every expression of gratitude. My consociates confirm that rituals help to facilitate healing because rituals are an experience of the nonbifurcated body-mind. The rituals they employ show them how to be healers, especially to be healers of their delusions that falsely divide and unnecessarily discourage. The difficulty lies in the task of realizing profound interrelatedness in the midst of illness, conflict, misunderstanding, and loneliness. Through assessing my consociates' healing activities, it becomes clear that experiencing interrelatedness—not merely being cognizant of it— is the key. Once this occurs, all factors amplify each other, resulting in heightened experiences of healing.

Experiencing Interrelatedness

Buddhism is an experiential tradition. It teaches that you must test a behavior or activity for yourself to see if it helps stop suffering. Nothing is taken on faith. Therefore, Buddhism has a rather pragmatic undercurrent running through it. Likewise, healing is a pragmatic experience. What works for one may not work for another. However, all the women found experiencing interrelatedness helpful in healing.

Implicit in the meaning of healing that functions among the women is the antithesis of healing: a desperate sense of loneliness where excruciating anguish is accompanied by paralytic fear and an insatiable desire for things that cannot be. Suffering arises out of a mistaken sense that a person is separate, alone, and unsupported. Healing, conversely, arises out of a sense of peace that does not shatter in the face of horrific events and delusional activities. Healing occurs when you have a bodily heart-felt awareness that you are integral to an all-encompassing network in which compassionate support is both given and received. In other words, healing derives from experiencing yourself as interrelated to everything in the universe. "Experiencing interrelatedness" is the first principle in my theory of the healing paradigm.

Conceptually, interrelatedness is the flip side of emptiness. Interrelatedness stresses the connections and mutual causality of phenomenal reality. Emptiness highlights the view that everything is empty of intrinsically individual substance. For example, the human body is made up of the same elements, such as carbon, that make up the stars. It is difficult to find something that we are not related to in some way. It is in this cosmic sense that everything is interrelated and empty of independent existence. Gyokko Sensei explains it this way: "Things are related through boundlessness. Past, future, and present are connected by a net of emptiness."[4] Tanaka-san puts stress on her concept of time, which she pauses to reflect on consciously whenever she is facing a frustrating situation that requires an approach, not just a single response. She reminds herself, "All time is empty."[5] Seeing things in this way helps her put things in perspective, enabling her to maintain sight of what is most important. Part of Kawasaki-san's healing activity is to view herself as part of a span of 5 billion years into the past and future. When she sees herself in this way, she can be healed. She adds, "Just being aware of this is healing. If you think this way, death is not a big deal. I don't feel fear. You received your form from others and then it goes to others. You don't disappear. This is the flow of life."[6] Gyokko Sensei phrased her sense of interrelatedness with a pithy but compelling image: "People are the cells of the universe."[7] Implicit in this view is the understanding that she belongs and that she is an integral part of something great. She declares, "I think the Buddha Dharma is the universe, nature. It's endless relations. There are no limits. When water moves from a high place, it goes down. It's really well-done activity. Nothing is more refined than nature. This is the Dharma."[8] The universe is not just a vast expanse. It is a meaningful and ethical dynamic of events, where you reap what you sow. Umemura-san said, "Being embraced is to be healed."[9] In both a literal and metaphorical way, when a person is embraced, she feels interrelated, not alone, cared for. Experiencing this emptiness-interrelatedness is the core of my consociates' healing activity.

In order to experience the universe this way, any focus on desire, hatred, and fear must be dissolved. The attachments that derive out of these foci obscure the interrelationships, invariably resulting in suffering. Their healing paradigm is based on activities that loosen the grip these attachments have by fostering an experience of interrelatedness. The following aspects of their healing paradigm explain how these women foster such an experience.

Living Body-Mind

The women in this study view the mind and body as one, a fundamental assumption of their worldview. It is so "normal" to them it did not seem to warrant mention. Yet, this view of the body-mind as one is a significant component of their healing paradigm because it explains how they can turn to chanting and prayer in the face of terminal illness and believe those activities will help them heal. By not bifurcating the resources available to a person, they find avenues of healing that no allopathic doctor would prescribe: holding a rock that has the word "OK" painted on it as they are transported into surgery, or adding a few drops of "sacralized" water into a cup of morning tea to ward off a cold.

This holistic view is shared by general Japanese culture, and is even found in the spiritual education (*seishinkyōiku*) programs held by companies, as noted by anthropologist David Plath: "The programs tap that most widely taken of all Japanese stances toward liberation: that it can be more readily achieved *in* one's everyday roles—by learning to perform them 'wholly'— than by seeking an other-worldly release *from* them."[10] The root of this worldview is current concrete activity, and that is where value is placed.

This is a pragmatic approach. The mind cannot cut carrots and put them in the pot all by itself, no matter the level of concentration. The body must move, and the body can only move in the present. If this is true for an act as straightforward as getting carrots into the soup, how much more so is it true for healing and helping, which can only occur in the present?

Dōgen's (1200–1253) imprint is evident in the concept of self that these women maintain. Aoyama Rōshi teaches that Dōgen took the common phrase, mind-body, and switched it to body-mind.[11] The implication of this innocuous change is significant. Dōgen taught that in order for you to actualize your true nature (Buddha nature), it is most effective to discipline the body. The assumption is that the mind will move in tandem, just as water takes the shape of whatever surrounds it. Since the mind can be so capricious, Dōgen focused on training the body. The assumption is that if the body moves and acts in accordance with respect and nonwaste, and treats everything as part of an interrelated whole, then the mind also will naturally experience compassion. Likewise, once you learn to wipe a table efficiently, effectively, and respectfully, that is the way you will always wipe the table, without thinking, "I should treat this table and rag better." You can think all kinds of wonderful thoughts, but if your body does not act accordingly, then your true nature is not manifested. Dōgen's approach makes it difficult to be hypocritical. Although the women did not describe their goal in idealistic terms such as the actualization of their Buddha nature, they strive to do most tasks in a day with embodied conscientiousness and care.

Most of my consociates received Dōgen's Sōtō Zen teachings through the interpretation of Aoyama Rōshi. Although she is a master of a Zen characterized by clean lines and minimalist aesthetics, this is not what she stresses. Seated meditation is also not her focus. Rather, she teaches a Zen of daily living. Indeed, for my consociates, Zen living is hard work. They mix daily demands with faith in miraculous cures.

Aoyama Rōshi further outlined the relationship between body and mind in the following way: There are three dimensions. (1) The first is Buddhist law (*Buppō*), which refers to the universal and natural laws of the universe. Buddhist law is the context for the other two dimensions: (2) Buddhist teachings (*Bukkyō*) are the ideals of the tradition, which appeal to the heart-mind, and (3) the Buddhist Way (*Butsudō*) consists of the actual practices that vary in locality and era. This involves the discipline and training of the body. According to Aoyama Rōshi's teachings, the Buddhist Way is needed to shape the fluid heart-mind.[12] The Way is made up of the formal disciplines (*kata*) of daily tasks like eating, cleaning, and bathing. For example, since lacquer has certain properties, it is important to make sure it is very dry after washing it, so the discipline for drying a lacquer dish is to wipe it with two different cloths so moisture does not remain on the surface. These disciplines are not arbitrary, but are based on what is needed to care for each object. This approach can be described as entering through form (*katakarahairu*).

From this nondualistic perspective, even sickness is a Buddha. In order to heal, we must also relate to sickness as such. In other words, what is here now is what we must live with. We cannot live later, and we cannot force life to be a certain way. This healing way is based in a holistic worldview where sickness is part of the world. The women stressed that they must relate with sickness as an active part of their lives. The word *tsukiau* is used when referring to interacting with people in the context of a friendship. The word connotes a friendly familiarity between the people who get together and do things on a frequent basis such that formalities are replaced by casual comfort. Therefore, to use the word *tsukiau* with your sickness assumes that an active relationship exists between you and the sickness. How you interact is the concern, not whether you interact. You can be kind to your sickness and rest when your body feels tired or refrain from foods that aggravate the sickness, or not. One consociate, Gyokko Sensei, said that to relate well involves adjusting her activity level to suit her condition. For example, before her legs began to hurt, she could do eight out of ten things. Now she only does six out of ten.[13] In a similar vein, Honda-san said that her key to a good relationship is to not strain herself unreasonably.[14] You can also choose to be uncaring about a condition and strain the body with overwork or partake in behaviors that are detrimental, such as eating salty foods despite hypertension or ingesting large amounts of sugar despite diabetes. If you are kind to the sickness, then conditions often go along smoothly. If you are unkind to the sickness, conditions often get worse.

In contrast, a dualistic worldview sets up an adversarial dynamic between health and sickness where sickness is something to be attacked. It is an object apart from yourself. From this perspective, sickness can be construed as an enemy. It must be eradicated in order for you to heal. On the contrary, from a nondualistic view, you can experience sickness as something with which you are in relationship, not something you want to defeat, destroy, or conquer. *How* you relate to the sickness makes all the difference.

To relate well with a sickness, however, does not imply that the sickness will go away. Indeed, you also can relate well with a terminal diagnosis. The question is, Will the relationship be open to inevitable changes or will hostility and bitterness reign? A good way to relate well would involve acceptance without resentment and peace in the face of demise. Although only one of my consociates has had to face a terminal diagnosis, several have had to learn how to live with chronic ailments. All of them hold that having a peaceful relationship with your condition is the ideal.

Umemura-san lives with the thought that body-mind means health in the context of daily life. "I had a 38° C [100.4° F] fever in my late twenties and medicine would not cure the fever. After that experience, I realized that the body and mind work together. I became much more mindful about caring for my heart, especially to not let stress build up."[15] She explains what she did to care for her body-mind:

> I thought that I must do something. Friends were dying of cancer. I had given birth to my second child. I was sick a lot as a child. A doctor told me that I was a person inclined to be sick because I was weak. I started doing yoga. I was under a teacher who treated yoga as religion, meaning it is that which forms the backbone of life. It suited me! I was so happy to get involved with this kind of yoga rather than yoga just treated as stretching the body. We started with the *Heart Sutra* and other chants for twenty minutes. To have the two hours away from childcare and housework, and have time to myself made me so happy! I was healed by it, but it was not because of just one thing—the chanting, or whatever. It was the whole experience.[16]

Healing must come from moving the nonbifurcated body-mind. It cannot be done with just the mind or just the body. The ideal is to be retrained so that your "instincts" are in harmony with the way things are. The aim is to manifest your full nature. Oftentimes, ritualizing activities helps the women accomplish this manifestation in their daily lives.

Engaging in Rituals

Rituals can help people deal with a broad spectrum of pain, including emotional pain, serious illness, family discord, and loss. Rituals have this capacity because they are a way of cultivating the heart needed to relate well with illness in a healing mode. The third principle in the way of healing is "engaging in rituals." A key to being healed is to experience interrelatedness, even interrelatedness to illness. This is not easy. These women have found that various rituals facilitate the changes in perspective needed to experience the fact that they are already embraced by the universe—aches, pains, tumors, and all. Rituals are effective in cultivating such awareness, because they involve the body. The mind alone can comprehend interrelatedness, but this knowledge does not bring about healing. A visceral experience of interrelatedness is required for the healing to occur. These women have found that some rituals are especially effective in facilitating such an experience. An important point, though, is that the women are not necessarily cognizant of this dimension of ritualized activity. They experience the results, but they do not perform the rituals *in order to* experience interrelatedness. They perform the rituals in order to remember deceased loved ones or mark the changes of the seasons. That is the power of rituals. They accomplish some things they do not intentionally seek but that nonetheless are beneficial. Some results that are helpful are elusive when sought directly. By its infinitely expansive nature, experiencing interrelatedness is a target that dissolves in the mere effort to aim at it. Rituals affect the body even if the mind is not conscious of what is going on, and that is the key to rituals' healing power.

Rituals shape, stretch, define, and redefine the identity of those who perform them. As you engage in a ritual, your consciousness changes. The power of ritual, however, is not an ability to communicate conscious knowledge, but to frame experience in such a way that it may be apprehended meaningfully. Ritual can have the impact of lived experience because it is performed by the body. In this way, people can learn about what is important through experiencing "fresh" what those before have experienced. Real life is very messy and organic, whereas discourse about life tends to be tidy and linear. Ritual is found somewhere in between. Performing a ritual with a long tradition can make a person feel connected.

Rituals can unite while words divide, because language is inherently dualistic. All of my consociates agreed with this statement. One woman in particular struggled to realize that cerebral understanding alone often does not help a person feel whole and connected to the universe. From an analysis of the numerous examples they provided, I realized that since rituals are multivalent, you can perform a ritual to honor a loved one on the third anniversary of her death and not only successfully show respect, but also, thereby, experience being embraced by the universe. You can feel that you are not alone, and this is what heals. Tom Driver, scholar of ritual studies, offers his insights into ritual: "Ritual . . . refuses to recognize clear lines of demarcation between the psychological, the socio-political and the material worlds."[17] He continues, "Ritual acts as if everything is alive and personal."[18] Ritual tries to make sense out of the raw materials of lived experience. Two additional ritual studies scholars, James Boyd and Ron Williams, amplify the significance of ritual in lived experience. They articulate why rituals are important and why they are complex: "Rituals aim at harmonizing disparate elements of culture and expression; they affect both our minds and hearts, rationalizing our activities and empowering us to act. And these rituals bring together diverse realms of experience—ethical, aesthetic, technical, religious—mirroring our activities and expressing our inner emotional life in voices ranging from descriptive to evaluative, worshipful, and performative, they are necessarily complex and multivalent."[19] In other words, rituals help a person feel connectedness through bodily action that integrates dissonant aspects of experience.

Healing is messy. Engaging in rituals to heal can be especially helpful, because rituals thrive in complex and emotionally charged conditions. Competing aims, conflicting conditions, and hope for otherwise improbable results—like wanting to live long enough to watch a child grow up even as the systems in your body start shutting down—evoke intense emotions that words alone cannot convey. Rituals can heal, even in such situations, because they do not operate in chronological time. Rituals provide a space to tolerate the otherwise intolerable when they are designed and performed accordingly. A number of the Buddhist rituals the women engage in have helped them live with otherwise untenable conditions, because they experience themselves in an incomprehensibly vast space—large enough to contain the source of angst along with a peace that transcends particular conditions. Rituals are adept at working with and guiding emotions. When emotionally upset, your attention often becomes more narrowly focused, limiting the options that seem possible. The proper ritual can help calm a person and expand his perspective, opening up options of response. Deep emotions become embedded in the body, so moving the body can help shift and guide those emotions. Although meditation can help you gain a vast sense of self, time, and place, it often takes a long time before you experience that sense. Rituals, however, can help in times when you cannot even sit quietly, and they can be immediately effective. Sōtō Zen rituals that the women have found to help in healing facilitate remaining in the present. Without comparison to past events or desires for the future, healing can take place in the present moment. In an expansive experience of the present, the ego self dissolves along with a consciousness of suffering.

Rituals work through the senses to cultivate wisdom in the bones. Unlike discourses on wisdom, which focus on understanding the empty nature of ultimate reality—and hence are sometimes too abstract and cold to comfort someone who is experiencing excruciating pain—rituals can help you experience with your whole body-mind that you are subtly and profoundly interconnected and, therefore, supported by countless relationships. Zen scholar-monk Victor Hori notes, "Ritual formalism and mystical insight reside together. Japanese expect this."[20] The typical Buddhist ritual performed at home and at temple altars engages all the senses. Lighting a candle provides a glow for the eyes and heat for the body. Lighting a stick of incense provides an aroma for the nose. Ringing a bell provides sound for the ear. Chanting reverberates in the body. Food offerings made will be eaten and stir the tongue and fill the body. These typical ritual acts affirm the gift of life in concrete ways experienced by the body. It is in this way that rituals make symbols real. In the chaos that can ensue after a death or other tragic event, rituals can help affirm order.

Since rituals can be performed in harmony with the rhythms of grief and recovery after trauma, the rhythm of the seasons are learned through rituals that punctuate the calendar: ringing in the New Year with 108 gongs of the temple bell (*Joya no Kane*), throwing beans on February 2 to ward off misfortune and welcome fortune (*mamemaki*), celebrating the equinox (Ohigan), and welcoming home ancestors in the summer (Obon). The body learns these rituals from childhood, making the connections between a person's self and community, and the natural environment.[21] Encoding children's bodies with the natural passing of the seasons prepares them to accept the various seasons of human life, as well. After growth comes maturation and death, decay, then renewal. The mothers among my consociates faithfully participated in these rituals with their families, but it was only with reflective thinking and stepping outside these experiences that the wisdom in their bodies about these rituals could be seen. Once observed, they could articulate the function and deeper value of the rituals. These women are sensitive to the beauty distinctive to each season. Indeed, this very awareness of their natural surroundings is part of the healing activity of rituals.

In addition to specific formal rituals, ritualizing daily activities is part of the healing paradigm of these women, especially if an experience of interrelatedness is remembered in the body. Many renew this experience each morning at their home altars. Chores like cleaning, cooking, and doing laundry become ritualized as they are imbued with meaning. Ritualizing activities both cultivates and expresses bodily knowledge. By bodily knowledge, I mean things that the body knows how to do without "thinking." For example, the way a teacup is formally held is a learned ritual that these women have done so often that it is done without thinking. Such bodily knowledge cultivated through ritualizing domestic activities accomplishes much, including care for self and others in the household. To ritualize a routinized activity can foster a sense of comfort and belonging. Many such ritualized actions are subtle, but they pervade your daily life. These are the little but concrete details that weave together your identity. They are rarely done consciously and are not noticed except in their absence.

Some of the most effective rituals the women engaged in were "homemade." They were effective because they were tailored to the aesthetics, fears, and hopes of the person who created them. They often drew on traditions that were creatively modified to suit personal situations. Humans seem to have a proclivity to ritualize activities that are important. They help people embody ideals. In Sōtō Zen, ritual actualizes Buddha activity.

The focus of this study is on the rituals or ritualized activities that help the women heal. Neuroscience research has begun to explore the effect rituals have on the brain, and evidence suggests that rituals work with the limbic system.[22] Rituals that have a rhythmic quality produce positive limbic discharges. The effect is increased social cohesion. For example, there is a qualitative difference between chanting with a group at a temple and chanting by yourself at home. Chanting with others helps you feel more connected to others, because you are mindful to breathe and coordinate with others to stay on the same beat. Perhaps such activity synchronizes people in other ways as well. What happens to heart rates? Various hormone levels? However, even not knowing the details of neurological and biological activity that occur when engaged in rituals, the fact that people across history and cultures have developed ritual activities suggests a powerful correlation between human aims and the capacity of rituals to facilitate preferred developments. Ritual behavior is one of the few modes that enable a person to engage holistically with the complexity and challenges of human experience, because rituals can juxtapose contradictory and "unreasonable" elements in one organically related sphere of embodied motion. In ritual, you can communicate with the dead, receive direct messages from various Buddhas, heal in the face of a terminal diagnosis, and feel embraced even when living alone with chronic pain.

Rituals excel at bringing the mind and body together in full attention on the present moment. This capacity is one reason why rituals are a primary resource in the quest for healing and resiliency, a staple quality in those who find happiness in adverse conditions and who succeed against difficult odds. Operating from an integrated body-mind focused on the present opens possibilities to galvanize forceful amounts of clarity and strength. Doing so enables you to discover options and possibilities that remain faint and blurred when you are pulled in many directions at once. Ritualizing an activity raises its importance and, by extension, affirms the significance of the person who performs it. Ritualizing helps quell tortuous doubts about whether what you are doing is "good enough." Ritualizing gives no space for the erosive effects of self-doubt and lack of confidence, because ritualizing inherently embeds meaning and connections beyond your self. Of course, you can be nervous about performing a ritual well, but the nervousness implies a respect for what is happening and thereby reinforces the importance of the act. For all these reasons, engaging in daily rituals is one of the ways the Japanese Buddhist women maintain their strength and sanity. Rituals help them nurture themselves, which in turn enhances their ability to serve the needs of others.

Nurturing the Self

Those who perform rituals, even with intent to benefit others, benefit from the mindful actions. Exactly what neurophysiological changes occur when a person engages in meaningful actions is not yet fully understood, but neuroscientist Dr. Sascha duLac suggests there is likely a shift in the "autonomic system from 'prepare-for-action' to 'integrate-and-regulate' (i.e., from sympathetic to parasympathetic)."[23] When the system does not need to expend energy preparing for a possible challenge or dangerous event, more energy is available for other things, such as immune system functions. In this way, rituals that help calm and focus a person, especially during a difficult or traumatic time, can be a helpful part of self-care.

Understanding who the self is and recognizing the needs of the self—nurturing the self—is the fourth principle in my theory on their healing paradigm. In their Buddhist context, these women see themselves as an integral part of the universe, interconnected to all things. This large-scale perspective is key to adjusting their perspective as events arise in their lives. Nurturing the self at this level begins with understanding that you are not alone and that what you do with your life matters. Rituals that focus on healing for yourself as well as rituals that focus on helping others are part of their healing activity that involves recognizing who the self is in the context of your relationship with others.[24]

Fundamentally, from their most expansive perspective, the self is the universe. Everything is a matter of perspective. When you hurt others, you hurt yourself. When you help others, you help yourself. This is not only the Buddhist view of how people affect each other, but is part of the Japanese relational concept of self. This concept helps shape the women's healing activity. Recognizing that you are not alone and that you both intimately and subtly depend on other people—while others intimately and subtly depend on you—helps you feel the interrelatedness of things and makes you aware that you are needed. These experiences are an integral key to the efficacy of their healing paradigm.

On a more immediately experiential level, nurturing the self involves several concrete and direct dimensions. Getting proper nutrition is basic. All of the women are conscious and careful about their food. Adequate sleep is also basic. Managing stress, a significant concern, results in a wide range of creative activities. One woman makes a deliberate effort to relax and not hold on to things. "If you let stress build up, it will be bad for your blood flow. When blood does not flow, many things go wrong with the body. Relaxing is so important. My key to not building stress is to not expect anything. Since you are the only one who can decide, I decide to relax, not build stress, and not be attached to things."[25] She nurtures herself with conscious relaxing and disciplining her mind to not wander off into unhelpful streams of thought. Noguchi-san, realizing that she must lead her own life and not limit herself to other's expectations, has taken significant strides in accepting events and situations in her life that have not gone as she initially preferred.

> I now realize that you can apply a lot of effort and accomplish certain things, but there are also things that rely on things outside of you, and you cannot control them. So, things that happen are not always what you want. About fifteen to sixteen years ago [at which time she was sixty-four], I realized that I had to live my life consciously. I feel like I have enough. This has happened gradually. I think this is part of preparing for death. It will help me not be afraid. I don't want to die with attachments. I have no attachments to material things now.[26]

Again, we see how not having attachments is part of how to take care of yourself. Although she lives a very active life, awareness of the inevitability of death and how she wants to die is also part of her effort to live consciously. This maturity is the result of having been thoughtful about how to nurture herself through the vicissitudes of life and not build up bitterness about what did not go the way she had hoped. She is aware of what she can do, and she attends to that with deliberate care.

Taniguchi-san also nurtures herself by an aim to live consciously. She even says she is grateful for some health problems, because as she ages they motivate her to think more carefully about what she should and should not do. Having to think about her health helps her have a sense of needing to stay sharp-minded. She says she would rather have some health problems than be perfectly healthy. A key to helping her maintain a positive orientation is to say "thank you" at night for the day she lived, and in the morning say "thank you" for the day she has to live.[27]

All of them take walks, especially where they can view flowers. Several of the women also write poetry to nurture themselves. Although these dimensions will be developed more in Chapter 5, here I offer a sample of the way in which the beauty of nature helps one woman heal. Nagai-san reminisces how nature had the power to ameliorate even physically challenging times: "Even though civilization has developed so much, I think that the past was better. When I watched the clouds change shape, that was better nutrition for my heart than now. Now you can't see the stars much. The actual life was hard. We ate only sweet potatoes and such."[28]

Nurturing the self is a critical component of their paradigm on two different levels. First, it is essential on a mundane level, because no matter what happens, you still need to eat, bathe, and take out the trash. Second, skills that nurture the self affirm your self-worth in the face of uncontrollable circumstances. After she brushes her teeth, she not only has clean teeth, but also a sense of personal competence. This is self-affirming. Rarely is brushing your teeth or performing other basic tasks of daily life an intense experience of nurturing the self, but they can be when healing is acutely needed. Sometimes getting through a difficult situation is a matter of living with pain and loneliness, and having things to do that make a positive difference can make the time seem less intensely painful. If a person does not have skills for nurturing the self, then the pain can become intractable. From my consociates' perspective, taking care of basic needs like shelter and food is a source of satisfaction. Indeed, the skills of caring for their surroundings fare them well when they need to live with tragedy. Those who have experienced debilitating suffering know the liberating healing power of ritualized acts of self-care. These acts often become a lifeline to the parts of a person that continue no matter what else has changed, no matter how painful or unwanted the changes.

Another aspect of nurturing the self that is critical for their healing paradigm is the sense of responsibility for your own life. Gyokko Sensei lives by the motto, "If you make something someone else's fault, you cannot be healed from the wound."[29] These women see that they are responsible for their own lives. They do not blame others for their problems. Rather than focusing on what others have done, they focus on what they can do to address a situation. They are aware that they cannot control other people or the circumstances. All they can do is choose how they will act. They try not to place conditions on their happiness. They consciously try not to take the attitude that they will be happy if _____ (fill in the blank) happens. To maintain this perspective requires discipline—to not lose sight of the support they receive from the universe as well as to not lose sight of the power they have to shape experience by how they interpret and respond to events.

An odd twist on caring for the self is an illness recognized in Japan called "women's illness" (*fujin-byō*). It is an illness only diagnosed in women, hence the name. Many symptoms fall into this category, such as stomachaches, joint pain, and frequent headaches. Women's illness seems to stem from the value placed on accepting responsibility for what happens, so complaining is deeply discouraged. Other family members, especially husbands and in-laws, can do things to help or hurt the situation, but the woman must not complain. If she is physically able to work, it is morally unacceptable for her to take a break, so some women manifest their discontent by becoming physically ill, which is morally acceptable. When a person is sick, others naturally help that person. Perhaps that is why when someone is sick the Japanese say, "Her exhaustion came out." It is an acknowledgement of how hard she has been working and an affirmation that she needs to rest. When a person is sick, normal expectations are relaxed. Although not pursued as a direct course of action, a few of the women have reflected on their situations and acknowledged becoming physically ill was effective in resolving untenable human relations.

One of the women works very hard on not becoming angry. She has deliberately disciplined herself. As the Dalai Lama, one of her favorite Buddhist teachers, explains, "If one's mind is disciplined and tamed or at peace, then it will lead to joy and happiness, whereas if one's mind is undisciplined and not at peace, then it will lead to unhappiness and suffering."[30] Patience and disciplining the mind are part of how many of the women nurture themselves. Failing that, the women say they cannot see the larger picture nor can they help themselves, or anyone else. In addition to being essential for expanding perspective, having nurtured themselves to cultivate a patient and disciplined mind helps them experience joy.

Enjoying Life

Enjoying life is easy when things are going well, but there are many times when there are ample things one could complain about. That recognition is an important aspect of their healing paradigm. So, what is needed is to gain a perspective that opens up an avenue to enjoy life, tumors and all, which is the fifth principle of my way of healing theory. It is a skill that the women say has become increasingly important, or, at least, they have recognized its value as they have matured. Finding the humor in a situation is part of the activity of transformation where a different set of symbols is found that enables them to accommodate the painful reality of loss, injury, or trauma. They said it is primarily in finding joy in the subtle things in daily life that is most important. Gyokko Sensei, a woman in her late sixties at the time of this interview, laughed while explaining that "suffering comes knocking even if you ignore it, so you must make a deliberate intention to invite in fun things."[31] Most of these women are very good at enjoying life. Whether it is collecting shells along the seashore, sipping tea while gazing at a waterfall framed in autumn's crimson foliage, having a tea ceremony while viewing flowering plum trees, or walking under the nighttime cherry blossoms (*yozakura*) along a river, each woman finds ways to have fun.

When thinking of eventual death, the beauty of nature inspires Umemura-san to enjoy life more consciously: "I am not afraid to die, but I dislike that I will stop being able to enjoy the beauty of nature—the beauty of the sky, the mountain scenery—when I die. Therefore, if I see the beauty of greenery or a flower, I gather my strength and determine to apply effort."[32] Umemura-san consciously redoubled her efforts to enjoy life after a conversation with her son. "My [adult] son told me that I had not [previously] taught him that life was fun just after I told him, 'Life is fun!'"[33]

A surprising number of the women have also mentioned Norman Cousins' experience of healing by laughing at funny movies.[34] It is clear they welcomed outside affirmation of their views. Scientist Richard Davidson further affirms their optimistic approach to healing. "There is initial experimental evidence that certain types of positive emotion in general may actually improve the immune system."[35] Such information, however, is not the inspiration for their awareness that laughing and enjoyment of life help healing. It comes out of their life experience, which is based on a Buddhist orientation to the world. Noguchi-san explains, "To really laugh and enjoy life requires not being attached to certain results and relaxing. Having no worries."[36] In turn, to not have worries requires acceptance of what has been, is, and will be. (Accepting reality as it is the eighth principle of healing.) The positive impact on the immune system of laughing underscores the healing benefits of enjoying life.

What they mean by enjoying life is not about seeking out methods of being entertained. It is about realizing a supple and flexible body-mind. If you have this, then you can enjoy life without setting conditions on what is needed to experience joy. It is the feeling that you are happy to be alive. Without a general sense of well-being, it would be easy to descend into a negative cycle of interpreting things in ways that prolong suffering and increase a sense of loneliness. Therefore, being able to adjust your perspective to see and enjoy the beauty in what is in the present moment here and now is an essential aspect of healing activity.

Creating Beauty

Beauty and creativity are factors of healing that arose without my solicitation in all the women's conversations. Whether or not the form of the beauty is from the traditional Japanese aesthetic, engaging with some form of beauty is clearly a critical component of their healing paradigm. There are many dimensions to this issue, and Chapter 5 is devoted to a thorough explication and analysis of them. Here I will take up three aspects of beauty that are part of their healing paradigm. One aspect is observing beauty: paintings, flowers, furniture, clothing, and so on. A second aspect is explicitly creating beauty: writing a poem, painting a picture, arranging flowers, making music, and so on. The third aspect is beauty in action. For most of the women, beauty is expressed not just in objects, but also in action. How the body moves, holds a teacup, or bows are all acts that can be done with beauty (or not). Even house cleaning and arranging food can be performed as acts of beauty.

These three aspects of beauty are part of the healing activity in the following ways. Viewing a beautiful painting or flower can remind you of things beyond any immediate pain. It can help expand your perspective and remind one how interrelated things are. Creating something beautiful can facilitate a visceral experience of joy. In so doing, it can also be a way that one nurtures the self and helps manage stress. One can make something to give to someone, both cultivating and expressing gratitude. This embodiment of compassion can buoy a person in times of despair. Expressing beauty in action is done with an integrated body-mind, an embodiment of compassion, and an expression of joy in living. Beauty in action is central to engaging in rituals. One of the modes for learning about beauty is through the body-mind engaging in the rituals of the seasons and interaction with nature. Kawasaki-san explained that awareness of the subtle changes in the seasons is the foundation of beauty in Japan.[37]

Being aware of beauty is fundamental to healing. Living itself comes from multiple elements working together to support life. If this fundamental condition is not recognized, then you cannot see clearly. When you see clearly, gratitude is an energizing response, because it corresponds to the activities taking place in the present. Seeing beauty is based on a penetrating awareness of the fundamental nature of how things work. Umemura-san says that for her, "To think in terms of 'life is a gift' (*ikasarete-iru*) is important to healing. You do not live on your own. You eat, and the food supports you. To recognize this is vital."[38] Whether it is a conscious or intuitive awareness does not seem to matter. Seeing beauty is to be aware of and embrace how life is supported. It is an acceptance that involves seeing the beauty in events as they occur. From seeing beauty, gratitude is less than a breath away.

Cultivating Gratitude

When one sees or creates beauty, my consociates observed, it is not a strain to see what enormous support one receives from the universe. The fact that we are alive is proof that the universe embraces us. This awareness can sometimes make us feel connected and cared for, particularly when we feel lonely. The type of gratitude these women find especially healing is not construed as *me* being grateful for *things*, because that sets up a dualism, which is incongruous with an interrelated worldview. If we are aware that we are already—without having to do anything special—an integral part of the world that is in a vast mutually influential web of give and take, gratitude is a natural response.

With gratitude, the body relaxes and the mind is eased. Even allopathic medical specialists are doing research that confirms that an optimistic view of the world is beneficial to the body's health. In *Love and Survival: The Scientific Basis for the Healing Power of Intimacy*, Dr. Dean

Ornish, founder of the Center for Integrative Medicine at the University of California at San Francisco, concludes, "the reason altruism may be healing for both the giver and the recipient is that giving to others with an open heart helps heal the isolation that appears to separate us from each other."[39] Stress causes the immune system to weaken and puts a strain on other systems of the body. But a general sense of well-being can allow the immune system to work its natural healing function. Hence, gratitude is a critical element in the healing activity.

Gyokko Sensei says it is particularly important "to say 'thank you' in the midst of a crisis, because there is something better than what you can see at that moment."[40] Gyokko Sensei's practice to express gratitude as part of healing resonates with psychological research of people who keep a gratitude journal. Although she is not seeking external confirmation, it is interesting to see the common qualities cross-culturally and the evidence of increased health potential. Psychological research confirms that those who recorded the things for which they were grateful on a daily basis reported significantly increased feelings of happiness. They also engaged in better health behaviors compared to those who did not keep a list of things for which they were grateful.[41]

The healing potential of gratitude comes from a combination of learning by experience, being taught by respected people, and reflective living. For Yamamoto-san, despite having been raised in a temple, it was not until her adult life that she experienced the power of a ritualized expression of gratitude and respect. "Until less than a year ago, I have felt awkward about doing a bow with palms together (*gasshō*) to a person, because it is a ritualized expression of worship. I do it at an altar. I have an elderly uncle who is ninety-two and a high-ranking priest. He gave me a *gasshō*, and I was deeply moved that such an advanced person would do this ritualized expression of worship to me! It made me feel different, because *gasshō* is what you do for a Buddha."[42]

Yamamoto-san felt what it was like to be treated with such deep respect and she felt the gratitude through her whole body. She now bows with palms together to people with a motivation to have them feel what she felt. She told me this story after I had visited her home several times. I had noticed how when she bowed to send me off in the taxi, she stayed bowed until the taxi rounded the corner a long block from her home. It made me feel truly welcomed, and that she was genuinely grateful for our heart-revealing conversation.

It is not surprising that Yamamoto-san often noticed things to be grateful for in daily life. "When I feel happy are the times I think I am healed. It mostly happens in the little things, like when hanging out the futons in the sun. When I feel grateful is when I feel happy, like when I am grateful to be in a warm place eating a good meal. The root of healing is gratitude."[43] Gratitude practices that Gyokko Sensei finds effective are not burdensome. "What's most important is to continue [doing the practices], not when you chant the *Heart Sutra*. Do it when you can. Things change. It's the quiet, sitting time that Buddha teaches, the cracks between all the things to do—cooking, childcare, work, and so on. At those times, say what you are grateful for. You can just say 'Thank you for today.' To be grateful is the important thing. You need the quiet time to sit for things to happen."[44] Gratitude can be cultivated by just sitting at a home altar and being quiet. It is something she finds a way to do each day, helping her to maintain a sense of connection to that which supports her, and keeping her perspective trained on the positive. As she often says, suffering will come without being invited, so this perspective is important.

For Noguchi-san, feeling gratitude emerges out of an awareness that she is not living just on her own power.[45] She knows in her bones that it is the constellation of elements and events that work together in a manner that enables her to breathe, walk, travel to other countries, and have a safe home. Noguchi-san also knows that expressing gratitude includes helping others, and she spends many hours carefully reading books aloud into a tape recorder so that people who are visually impaired can "read."

When grateful, these women do not have to work at seeing the good things in a situation—those things just appear. Also, when in a grateful state of being, they do not need to work at not complaining. Gratitude is, in a sense, a shortcut on the path of healing. Yet, gratitude's full power to heal occurs in conjunction with the other aspects of their healing paradigm.

Accepting Reality as It Is

Part of cultivating gratitude involves developing an accepting heart: healing requires accepting reality as it is. That means putting no conditions on healing and rejecting nothing. Accepting everything that occurs in your life, however, is extraordinarily difficult. Several of the women said that if you actually accepted everything, you would be a recognized Buddha.

Rejecting your actual situation and condition, however, consumes vital energy. Wishing things were different from what they are causes suffering. If we fight within ourselves, we cannot relax. If we are not relaxed, then there is stress, which weakens our immune system. Jon Kabat-Zinn, founder and director of the Stress Reduction Clinic at the University of Massachusetts Medical Center, corroborates this point: "If you can come to accept how you are in any moment, it frees up huge amounts of energy that can go to healing."[46]

Gyokko Sensei knows this to be so, but has come to this understanding through her Buddhist practice.

> Once I realized that the point is to be here, there is no reason to rush or be anxious. Ride the flow of nature. If you don't do this, you suffer a great deal. With this, I saw how I didn't have to suffer. It's very difficult! The reasoning is not hard to understand, but to do it is *difficult!*[47]
>
> To accept everything is the final and highest form (*sugata*) of humanity. You complete life when you can do this. The image that guides me is an image of a woman simply bowing, hands together in prayerful gesture. She receives all without judging and without anguish. This is the image of Kannon [goddess of compassion]. Kannon's heart accepts everything.[48]

Notice how Gyokko Sensei explains her highest ideal to accept all things through an image of how to move the body. The gesture of the bow with palms together seems to help her embody, or at least focus on, the act of acceptance. It is a gesture that does not allow grasping or hurting. It is not, however, a passive gesture. It is a gesture of actively choosing not to impede the flow of reality. Gyokko Sensei's goal in life is to accept everything with peace, joy, and gratitude, as if she were bowing.

A way to gain a heart that accepts reality is to treat each thing with respect (*mono o daiji ni suru*). To be aware of the value of things requires an open and accepting heart. A person's heart, in turn, becomes more accepting the more she sees the importance of things. To appreciate the value of something requires paying careful attention to it.

Healing as awareness requires acceptance of impermanence. Expanding your sense of time is a way to help the heart become more accepting. There is a larger framework in which the significance of something can often be more easily understood. For example, if you are in a closet you can stand or sit, but there is little room for anything else. However, if you are in a gymnasium, you can sit, stand, dance, or even do handsprings and a back flip. The same happens with the heart: the bigger it is, the more options there are. Gyokko Sensei explained how she thinks of accepting things in her heart. She says that if a flame burns straight up, it will burn out quickly. However, if it has a chance to dance, it will last a long time.

To not exhaust our hearts, we need to loosen them and allow things in. Accepting is a matter of growing the heart bigger so everything can fit.

In Japanese, the verb *yurusu* is commonly translated as "forgive." It has the valence of permitting and allowing. It involves making room in your heart and mind to allow things to be, even things you do not agree with and do not like. Gyokko Sensei holds that "in order to accept all, you need to be open-minded, magnanimous, and forgive, and make room for things."[49] Inevitably, negative events and adverse conditions arise. Negativity builds up walls and separates that which is interrelated, so there is an inherent strain. Maintaining a rejection also drains energy away that could be used in other ways. If the negativity is left too long, it will calcify and be harder to clear away. So, "the task is to make things that are a '−' into a '+.'"[50] To turn things into a "+" requires growing to make room. Gyokko Sensei further explains.

> You need to throw out the past to make room to accept the present. It's really about how much you are in touch with the power of boundlessness (*mugen*). If you are sincere and unobstructive, not calculating gain and loss (*sunao*) and let things flow like a stream, then forgiveness and allowing room for things occurs. Water that is hardened will not move. Depending on the matter at hand, you can forgive or make room for something by responding with silence, but it is important not to turn anger in on yourself. As you forgive and make room for, your heart melts.[51]

Then it is easier to expand, and the more you accept into your heart, the more your heart expands. Expanding helps facilitate accepting even things that are not immediately appealing or preferred, because it diminishes the impact of the event.

Acceptance means to "ride the waves" of good and bad.[52] Acceptance does not mean that you agree with everything or that everything is compassionate. Some conditions are more difficult than others. Each situation opens up innumerable potential responses. Gyokko Sensei encourages the response of making your heart = "0" (zero). She said, "If I am zero, then all can happen and enter. Zero equals boundless power. With zero, you can forgive and make room for things. Then there will be nothing that you can get snagged on or reject."[53] Gyokko Sensei is quick to stress that "to forgive and make room for others, you need to forgive and make room for yourself. Then you can become generous with your heart."[54] "It is a matter of how you hold your heart. Everyone has Buddha heart-mind. With chanting sutras, making offerings, and such practices, I have learned to see my shortcomings. I did not see them before. The practices help me become zero, which enables me to see and accept. When I become zero, then I can be taught. It is hard to become zero, though. It is easier for me to become zero when I am chanting."[55] The ritualized activity of chanting helps her achieve the mode in which she wants to be, to have an accepting heart that allows all things in, yet does not destabilize her.

Another woman, Honda-san, turns to nature to open her heart. She says that it is the place where she feels most accepted.[56] "At my sister's I am not at complete peace, because I am thinking of *ki o tsukau*. (There is no English equivalent due to different assumptions of self and human relations. In broad terms, it means using vital energy to try to be sensitive to others.) Nature is the place I feel most at peace. I rode a bus and went to the sea. An egret came and played in front of me. I thanked it. I spent two hours there, embraced by nature. Here I am a human, so small in the universe."[57]

Honda-san begins with explaining her feeling of being at her sister's, because being among family with whom you have a close relationship is a place that you would think you might be most able to relax and feel accepted. Yet, she still feels like she must maintain awareness of how her actions affect her sister. It is only in nature where she feels she does not have to worry if she's good enough. She has ritualized sitting by the ocean. Here she can accept all manner of things into her heart and maintain peace. When you are grateful, things will flow in different ways. Better things come to those who accept, and especially those who are grateful.

Kitō Sensei teaches people to "have a Fudō heart."[58] Fudō is a Buddhist guardian who protects the Dharma. He is the embodiment of stability. His most common representation is of a red body, muscular frame, piercing eyes, solid stance, surrounded by dancing flames. His intense expression makes it clear that he is strong enough to handle any obstacle to compassion. His visage should not be mistaken for intolerance, because Fudō accepts all. Kitō Sensei seems to speak from experience when she says, "an accepting heart is fearless."[59] To accept with fearlessness requires expanding your perspective far beyond the details of your personal perspective.

Expanding Perspective

Expanding their perspective seems to be the key to the women's healing activities. Although the details vary, they all indicated that in order to enjoy life, cultivate gratitude, and accept reality as it is, expanding their perspective was critical. A narrow perspective diminishes their ability to see things in a positive light, because the limited view takes events or situations out of their fuller context, distorting them. If decisions and actions are based on this distorted view, then complication ensues as actions become less and less appropriate to the situation. Conversely, an expansive perspective gives you more information to make more-informed decisions. Seeing things in their largest context diminishes distortion, allowing us to see more clearly.

To expand perspective, Aoyama Rōshi encourages reflecting on the length of human culture in relation to the assumed age of the earth.[60] To make it easier to comprehend the relative amounts of time, she transposed 4 billion years into one year. On this scale, the earliest humans did not appear until about 4:00 PM on December 31. Another way she suggests to keep things in perspective is to remember that gravity works on plants, rocks, women, and men, making no preferences.

Expanding your perspective requires learning from whatever happens and seeing what goodness, wisdom, or strength can be gained, especially from physical or psychological suffering. Choosing a positive view, however, is not always easy or clear. One of the first things we commonly do when trying to understand a situation is to look for something familiar to orient ourselves. But setting up a comparison with something else previously experienced or imagined often leads to a negative view, because looking for a point of reference outside the current situation can result in making it more difficult to see what is right in front of you. Positive views, on the other hand, tend to be found when looking at the greater context of the present moment. The logic these women use is that since everything is interrelated, there must be something positive going on—otherwise, there would be no life.

High levels of clarity and honesty are necessary for transforming the heart, because sometimes the apparent choices all look undesirable, such as deciding between spinal surgery that could cause further nerve damage or continuing to live with chronic back pain. Recovery requires transforming experience with new symbols. When trauma, loss, and injury happen, these experiences are rendered in some fashion. The activity is to transform negatively valued metaphors into positively adaptive ones. It involves transforming the experience of suffering. This activity includes cultural, social, psychological, and physiological domains. Rituals can facilitate transforming the experience into a different set of symbols, because rituals have power to positively drive transformational activity. They facilitate the transformation by making metaphors visceral.

An expansive perspective also makes it easier to decrease cognitive dissonance that arises, especially in the fast pace of change these women have experienced during their lives. The larger the context, the fewer the contradictions, because contradictions often appear as a result of the distorting effects of a narrow lens. Moreover, not dividing things into subject/object dichotomies makes it easier to turn conflicts into complementary approaches. It also enables you to see how you are interrelated with others, opening up more avenues of compassionate response, especially responses to difficult situations.

Gyokko Sensei has learned how to not see in dichotomous terms, but she admits that it has taken her into her sixties to do it. "There are good things and bad things. Both are OK. There is no such thing as all good things. This is natural. Be natural. I can now say this, having reached this age. The foundation is to be patient. It is about how to respond."[61] If you take the events as resources for growing, then your perspective is expanded. Patience is a key ingredient in seeing from a larger perspective. The ritualized activities that help calm are useful in many ways, including that they help people find the patience to see more broadly, and, hence, make better decisions about how to respond.

One of the ritualized behaviors that helps Umemura-san in this regard is this: "I think to 'cut off and change' is healing. You need to keep repeating it. I learned this from breathing in yoga."[62] When you are attached to something, you cannot see broadly, because your view is obstructed by that to which you are clinging. You need to cut off the attachments that tether you. They limit your ability to respond to situations. So, letting go is the first step to changing. Umemura-san has found that consciously breathing deeply expands the space in which she sees herself moving.

Noguchi-san adds that recognizing what part she has to play in how things occur helps her keep her heart and mind open to ways of interpreting that cultivate her capacity to respond to situations with a greater sense of possibility and generosity. "Taking responsibility for how things turn out is a critical aspect of healing. It does not mean that you have control over what happens or how others behave. It refers to the capacity to interpret the meaning and significance of events. This is tremendous power that has real impact on how you feel and what you do afterwards."[63] Expanding your perspective involves what frame of reference a person uses to interpret events. The bigger the frame, the more likely the interpretation will help one heal.

What follows is an example of a ritual that healed a person through obliquely crafted mirror-image metaphors on the primary Buddhist concepts:

emptiness and interrelatedness. Such expansive metaphors cannot be made directly, because the very effort to clearly delineate them will result in their failure to evoke their limitlessness. The ritual that sustained Honda-san through the worst of her incapacitating hip pain caused by nerve damage is scripture copying (*shakyō*).[64] As is often the case with many of the rituals that these women found so helpful to healing, this ritual is not formally recognized as an explicit healing ritual by the tradition. The ritual, as she performs it, consists of going to the Zen nunnery in Nagoya on the third Saturday of the month and using brush and ink to copy the *Heart Sutra*. It is a short scripture written in classical Chinese.[65] It is famous for its line, "Form is emptiness. Emptiness is form." At the end of the day, there is a place to write your prayers that you hope will be answered. Indeed, it is not uncommon for people to go to the ritual only when they have problems just so they can have more efficacious prayers.[66]

Honda-san carefully brushed the strokes of each character of the *Heart Sutra* after arriving by taxi, a luxury that put a strain on her limited income. To even get into a taxi was a major accomplishment. She had been dragging her body with her arms through her small apartment to get herself ready to go, trying to minimize the pain that accompanies each movement of her left leg. She described the pain she had to live with in those days as even worse than if a dentist accidentally touched a nerve in a nonanaesthetized part of your mouth, because the source of her pain did not move away. It stayed in place, generating pain with each breath. She said that at times tears would quietly and uncontrollably leak out of the corners of her eyes as the pain coursed through her. And yet she almost never failed to go to the ritualized copying of the sutra. After she recounted how the scripture copying ritual sustained her and healed her, I asked her what I thought was a reasonable follow-up question: "At the end, if you do not mind sharing, what are the types of things you offered up in prayer?" She matter-of-factly responded that she never prayed for anything. I was shocked. "Didn't you pray for the pain in your hip to go away?" Now *she* looked surprised and confused as she sputtered, "No, I never even thought about it. It never occurred to me." Thinking that I should be a respecting ethnographer and not add any more queries that might indicate a criticism of her practice of the ritual and try to analyze what her worldview might be on my own and knowing that Japanese is such a delicate, indirect, and subtle linguistic instrument, I blurted out, "*Nande?!* Why not?!" She was visibly uncomfortable about being pressed for a reason. She had just poured out her heart to me about how much pain she had been in—not an easy task for someone who is the epitome of politeness and a master of thoughtful caring for others—and had gone on to share the beauty and joy she received from just going to the scripture copying ritual. It seemed difficult for her to understand what more she could possibly explain to me. At that point I gained control of my perplexity and incredulity, and slipped in, "That's what I would have done" (referring to praying for pain to go away) and moved the conversation to another topic. It took years for me to see how the scripture copying ritual helped her with her pain if she was not even praying for her hip to stop hurting.

The key to understanding why she never prayed for her own pain to be removed lies in her confusion with why I thought she would have. I could not even imagine such thorough and steady acceptance of debilitating chronic pain, although I respect those who do. Honda-san does not resist her life circumstances. She does not even privately wish that things were different. She also does not passively watch life go by without her. Honda-san has disciplined herself to perceive her situation as no one's fault. In fact, she claims that nothing is bad about her life. She realizes that she has power to shape her life, and she chooses to define herself and her needs by her own standards. She does not buy into the societal expectations of her. She did not marry, has no children, and lives a very simple life. She has found contentment. She is a living example of Ornish's point, "The more inwardly defined you are, the less you need and the more power you retain."[67] She never felt sorry for herself. Putting inked brush to paper while the incense wafts through the air of the worship hall (*hondō*) with a wooden carving of Kannon-sama, the goddess of compassion, gazing down on all who come, one viscerally experiences being in the impermanent stream of the numberless flowing together along the Way. With each stroke of black ink on white rice paper, she traces the gray path of "Form is emptiness. Emptiness is form." 「色即是空。空即是色。」 Countless people have followed this path before her, and countless more will do so in the future. In this continuous flow, each present moment is complete. In each moment, there may be pain but there is no suffering. In each moment you belong, just as you are, in this vast and beautiful expanse. There is no need to pray for anything.

To accommodate such a view requires focusing on the larger picture. Catherine Bell explains, "the fundamental efficacy of ritual activity lies in its ability to have people embody assumptions about their place in a larger order of things."[68] The fundamental assumption is that they think they are not living independent lives based on only their own power and effort. All of the women used the verb "to give life to" (*ikasu*) in the gratitude-tense (*ikasareteiru*). It is technically the causative-continuative tense *sareteiru*, but what is implied is they see they are alive because the myriad interconnections in the universe work together to generate and support life. Some say this is due to *Buppō*, the Buddha Dharma of the interrelated nature of reality. Others explain it as the work of the Buddha. Yet others explain it in more scientific and ecological terms, including Taniguchi-san who gave the following explanation: "Life (*inochi*) is like water which becomes fog. Fog becomes river, and so on. Nothing is lost. You cannot choose for things to be different from what they are, but you can choose how they are perceived and interpreted."[69] Whatever the metaphor used to explain, this perspective of their lives seems to naturally give rise to a profound sense of gratitude for all things. Ever adjusting their perspective with the vicissitudes of life enables them to accept their lives into their hearts, to feel grateful for and create beauty out of what is. To do this is to embody compassion. Embodying compassion is the ultimate healing.

Embodying Compassion

In one of Suzuki Kakuzen Rōshi's last Dharma Talks at the Zen Nunnery in Nagoya, he spoke about the meaning of compassion.[70] He wrote on the chalkboard the pictogram (*kanji*) for compassion (*jihi*). The word is a combination of the characters for loving affection (*utsukushimi*) and sadness (*kanashimi*). Sadness is part of compassion, because to be compassionate requires that you understand but not be limited by suffering. He explained that when you realize everyone is a Buddha, you will act compassionately. This necessitates an accepting heart that is peaceful and acts out of a bodily awareness of our interrelatedness. Even the deceptively simple act of listening is an embodiment of compassion.[71] Many of the women stressed how the healing power of active listening is profound. It is a basic form of compassion. Several women explicitly stressed this is why Kannon-sama, the embodiment of compassion, is called the "One who hears the cries of the world" (*Kanjizai bosatsu*).[72] They explained that what happens when you are listened to is you experience not being alone. You know you are heard because everything is interrelated. Compassion arises out of an awareness of the interdependent causal nature of reality. Compassion is to act in ways that diminish suffering. The rituals of Kannon facilitate this.

Research psychologist Paul Ekman has an instructive perspective on compassion. His detailed study of emotions and facial muscles helped give rise to the following insight. His perspective on compassion is instructive.

Neither empathy nor compassion is an emotion; they refer to our reactions to another person's emotions. In *cognitive* empathy we recognize what another is feeling. In *emotional* empathy we actually *feel* what that person is feeling, and in *compassionate* empathy we want to help the other person deal with his situation and his emotions. We must have cognitive empathy in order to achieve either of the other forms of empathy, but we need not have emotional empathy in order to have compassionate empathy. (emphasis in original)[73]

The Dalai Lama holds that human nature is fundamentally compassionate.[74] Once interrelatedness is experienced, compassion is generated. This is the law of the Dharma, according to Buddhist teachings. Acting with compassion is healing, because it manifests our fundamental nature.

Embodying compassion is the most powerful healing power. Honda-san thinks, "The existence that has the most healing power is a human. Healing power comes from the heart."[75] Those who embody compassion move people in powerful ways. Indeed, meeting the right person can in and of itself be healing. Ogawa-san recalls a pivotal person she met: "When I think back, I would say that meeting the nun Katō Sensei was a healing meeting. I might not have continued being so serious in Sōtō Zen if it had not been for her."[76] Katō Sensei healed Ogawa-san by her presence, for Katō Sensei fully embodied compassion.

Kitō Sensei had that effect on me, too, in Bodh Gaya, India, in the fall of 1987. We met when she had returned to the Japanese Temple where she had been the resident monastic for four years when the temple was being established. I was there assisting on a Buddhist studies program with U.S. college students. My life course has been deeply shaped and indebted to that meeting, first giving rise to my book on Zen nuns, and now this one. She is also a healing presence to a number of the other women who participated in this study.

Honda-san knows that taking care of her own body-mind is essential to helping others. "When I help someone I have to have a stable, calm, heart. If I don't, it won't be positive for anyone. It becomes a battle within myself. The body and heart just gets exhausted."[77] It takes strength to be kind. Yamamoto-san explains, "One who can smile is strong. I think you can only be kind-hearted if you are strong. 'How do you get strong?' You do not complain or say anything bad about anyone, ever. I write in my journal, but if someone were to find it, it would be terrible, so I don't write everything [laughter]."[78] It is easy to be mean. It takes discipline and patience to be kind.

Kitō Sensei also teaches that prayer opens the heart of compassion.[79] To pray knowing that you are heard is healing. It is striking to hear Ornish, the first medical doctor to scientifically prove the reversal of heart disease by changing lifestyle, echo the importance of being heard.

> When you share your darkest secrets and mistakes with another person who listens without judgment, it is like shining a light in the darkness. A powerful social bond of intimacy is forged with the listener. When someone else can have compassion, forgiveness, and acceptance of those dark parts of ourselves that seem so unlovable, it makes it easier for us to accept those parts within us. When we can do this, we are less likely to project our darkness onto others and hate them. If we don't acknowledge our anger, for example, we are more prone to violence.[80]
>
> As important as these [diet, exercise, drugs, and surgery] are, I have found that perhaps the most powerful intervention . . . is the healing power of love and intimacy, and the emotional and spiritual transformation that often result from these.[81]

Hearing an allopathic doctor articulate the benefits of listening to healing is cross-cultural affirmation. Ornish adds, "Just as chronic stress can suppress your immune function, altruism, love, and compassion may enhance it."[82] He also stresses, "The essence of compassion—which is the essence of healing—is to realize that we are not so different from each other in the experience of being human."[83] Kitō Sensei's thinking seems to be in conversation with Ornish as she reasons from her Zen Buddhist nun experience that if we are heard then we have confirmation that we are connected. It is proof that someone cares. It is not so much the act of speaking and pouring out your problems as it is being heard that does the healing.[84] Kitō Sensei, however, has never even heard of Ornish or his scientific studies. Taniguchi-san stressed what "Embodying Compassion" meant to her. She explained that in order to be a good listener we need to have a receptive heart.[85] In turn, in order to have a receptive heart, we need to be open to various perspectives.[86] To be a good listener is to be a healer. To be listened to is to be healed.

Compassion figures in these women's healing activity both as a source of healing and as an expression of healing. To receive compassion and to be compassionate are both part of their healing paradigm. By their definition of healing, one who is healed is one who is compassionate. Compassion is the alpha and the omega of healing activity. In other words, to be healed one must be a healer. This is the pinnacle of my theory of their way of healing. When they are aware of their interrelatedness, compassion pours in and flows out. Compassion does not come from an intellectual understanding of interrelatedness. It comes from experiencing themselves as integral to the whole. When they experience their wholeness, the natural response is gratitude. Gratitude opens the heart wide so that light can shine brightly onto their interrelatedness, illuminating what compassionate activity is appropriate for the moment. From a grateful heart flows a flexibility of response that is based on an honest perspective of the big picture—that is, a view of how each event, person, or thing is ultimately part of the whole that embraces each of us. The view is not necessarily cerebrally perceived nor is the response based on an active cognition of the dynamics of the situation. That is one of the main characteristics of the power of compassion. It is a response to the world that comes from the heart of impermanence and interrelatedness.

Umemura-san has reflected a lot on how she would know if she were healed. Her answer is simple and revealing. "I know I am healed when I am kind."[87]

Living Dynamics of Healing Activity

Researching the rituals that facilitate the physical and spiritual healing of contemporary Japanese women led to an understanding of their wealth of wisdom, strength, humor, beauty, and compassion. These virtuous qualities were mostly cultivated through painful, difficult, and challenging work on their experiences. Through understanding their efforts to find relief from suffering, it became evident that the healing power of Buddhist rituals lies in the rituals' capacity to provide people with a conduit for experiencing interrelatedness, which is the lynchpin of my consociates' healing activity. Healing is a worldview or a way of living and facing all kinds of challenges of the nonbifurcated body-mind. Therefore, for these women, all of life can be lived as healing activity.

The ultimate Buddhist healing is to move from suffering to the cessation of suffering. These women do many things to help foster that healing. They also recognize that there are many factors that are beyond their control. It is a healing that happens on a daily basis in the midst of cleaning house, checking fevers, working, making lunch boxes, and chanting sutras at the home altar while everyone is filing off to work or school. They are mature women who have learned through various life experiences the truth of the basic Buddhist teaching that everything is impermanent. This gives them hope that things sometimes might be bad, but they will not stay that way. They strive to ride the waves that inevitably come, navigating through their threatening tumult with as much kindness as they can summon.

Since the women know their healing lies in responding to things as they change and not hanging on to things that cannot be, they expose themselves to an increased awareness of vulnerability at the same time that they experience a heightened sense of support from the universe. It is in finding balance among these ever-changing dynamics that they are able to respond to situations with gratitude and compassion.

The ten principles that outline the contours of their way of healing are illuminated in the ethnographic materials.[88] The chapters that follow offer numerous examples for the reader to see the ten dynamics in motion. I will highlight the prominent elements that organically come to the surface among the ten principles rather than offer a systematic analysis that covers each aspect point by point. With the ten aspects in mind, however, you can see how they intertwine and mutually enhance each other.

Hoping to see the plum blossoms still in bloom, Kitō Sensei took me on an excursion to a field of plum trees she used to take small children to when she was a teacher early in her life as a nun. We alighted the train with others also happy they had made it in time to see some blossoms still on the trees. It was disconcerting, though, to see how the fields of plum trees on the rolling landscape were dwarfed by high-tension electrical towers that loomed ominously above. These wires made the spirit of the plum blossom all the more poignant, for it is a flower famous for blooming in adverse conditions. After we enjoyed the numerous varieties of plum blossoms, we sat on a bench. She pulled out a traveler's tea set, complete with a small thermos for hot water, and made us tea with the petite bamboo whisk that just fit the diminutive tea bowl. We reminisced about how she had this set with her in India in the autumn of 1987 where we first met and she made us tea then, too.

Much has happened since that meeting that set my life on a trajectory of studying and working with Zen women. The time was ripe to ask her my question: "Kitō Sensei, what does healing mean to you?" Kitō Sensei answered my question with a query. "Isn't healing that you breathe, your heart pounds? [Silence.] You are already healed. [Silence.] You can't do this with just your own power. Isn't it that Hotoke [the Buddha] gave you breath that you are healed? [looking around at the orchard of plum trees] You are in Great Nature. It is not that you see it, but that your heart pounds even when you sleep. You are healed. Let it all be as it is: birth-death."[89] Then she wrote me this poem on the back of the card I was taking notes on.

梅は寒苦をえて
清香を発す。

Plum blossoms overcome the suffering cold
Giving off pure fragrance.

Rain, snow, and sleet are all necessary ingredients for the beautiful fragrance the plum blossoms freely give to all who approach. Their fragrance is especially healing to those who have to travel a significant distance to come to a place where nature is relatively intact. The very fact that we are able to sit and drink tea together is evidence of our healing. In a resonant vein, Aoyama Rōshi teaches, "We are here now as we are because we have received the generous gift of the universe's activity."[90]

In this way of healing, it is important to remember the Japanese word uses the "gratitude-tense" conjugation of "to heal": *iyasareteiru*. Tanaka-san stresses that to use another conjugation "sounds a bit selfish, like the concern is just with the self getting better."[91] Using the same "gratitude-tense" conjugation, Gyokko Sensei describes how she thinks about living. "I think I am *ikasareteiru*, not *ikiteiru*. I am being given the gift of being caused to live, not just living."[92] The effect of using the "gratitude-tense" is that it takes the stress off the individual and keeps the activity in the context of a complex web of interrelated events. I asked Honda-san about her views on this topic.

As you age, your energy gradually declines. So as my energy declines and when my leg began to hurt, I realized that it was a big mistake to think that humans are living (*ikiteiru*) on their own. I thought that it was that we are receiving life (*inochi*) from somewhere. When you are sad and suffering, you do not just die on your own. Although there are people who do take their own lives, I can't do that no matter how much I suffer. I began to feel gratitude. I guess it began when my leg began to hurt. For me it was my leg, for others it is cancer or something or they feel pain in their heart. If I had been always healthy, I probably would not feel this happiness. I cannot judge if I have become a better person because of this, but I think I can say that I have made some progress in being grateful.[93]

Ikasareteiru and *iyasareteiru* come out of the same orientation and root assumptions. They go hand in hand for these women. This conjugation places each person as an integral element of a vast interrelated universe. It is imbued with gratitude, an appreciation of all that goes into living and healing. In a sense, to live with gratitude is to be healed. All ten principles need to be active in the present moment. It is not a linear cause-and-effect paradigm. It is Dōgen's concept of "being time." In "being time" there is only the present moment where matter and time move as one. Things do not move *in* time. Rather, when things move, time moves, and vice versa. It is the difference between believing that flowers bloom *in* spring where time and matter are separate, and seeing that flowers *are* spring (*haru wa hana*).

A primary strategy they employ when faced with a rough spot is to hone the art of steering their perspective. For example, from one angle, a diagnosis of cancer is devastating and debilitating, but from another angle, it can be a catalyst for heightening your gratitude for life and open unexplored avenues of trust. Seeing the universe as intimately interrelated is the key to their ability to see things from a positive view. If everything is seen in this light, then everything becomes something for which to be grateful. A line from the Zen text *Hekiganroku* makes the point succinctly: "Medicine and sickness cure each other, and the entire earth is medicine."[94] This positive perspective is the source of their stable centeredness. If blame for a problem is placed, then the wound will fester. Healing is possible, however, if one accepts the flow of events. This requires seeing events from a vast perspective. One might say that the compass required to navigate the way of healing must be calibrated to infinite emptiness, because viewing the universe as the point of reference yields the most healing results.

CHAPTER 3

Personal Buddhas
Living with Loss and Grief

You must take death as the point of departure to understand healing.[1]

SUZUKI KAKUZEN RŌSHI, SŌTŌ ZEN MASTER[2]

Yamaguchi-san was raised on preparing to die. Not in a dark way, but in a realistic way. "My dad [a Buddhist priest] said we are designed to die. These words stick with me."[3] Death is not feared because it is understood in resonance with Kishi Iban Zenji's poetic illustration given at a funeral: "The moon sets but does not leave the sky."[4] Remembering teachings of Uchiyama Rōshi, Aoyama Rōshi spoke about death during a Dharma Talk at her nunnery. "Water does not disappear, it just moves around. We want to scoop it up. So, when it is returned to the stream, it is sad. Viewing death from this perspective recognizes the affection and sadness, as well as the transformations of nature."[5] These metaphors associated with death help guide the women as they engage in rituals to help them establish their balance after the loss of a critical relationship.

The death of a loved one is a staggering event that leads to psychic, emotional, and physiological adjustments. Your body and brain must grow accustomed to regulating in this new context. Since rituals require bodily activity, they help a person find her new balance and a new mode of relating to a loved one who has passed on. Funerary and memorial rites specifically help people integrate loss into their lives, because grieving rituals enable people to face the excruciating pain of loneliness that threatens to paralyze them as they transform their lives after the death of a loved one.[6] Specifically, Japanese Buddhist mortuary rituals help a person live with death by helping her experience being interrelated to everything.[7] The rhythms and contours of grieving rituals are examined within the context of Japanese Buddhist women's worldviews and conceptions of self, suffering, and healing. The findings are based on in-depth field data that consociates revealed about their relationships with the deceased. Through their willingness to expose their vulnerabilities and loneliness, I began to see that the intimate relationships they carry on with deceased loved ones is not only the context for but perhaps also the source of the healing power of the rituals in which they engage.

The Healing Power of Funerary Rites

The dominance of funerary, memorial, and ancestral rites in the ritual landscape of contemporary Buddhism in Japan is so pronounced that scholars and lay people commonly refer to the phenomenon as "Funeral Buddhism."[8] Most people even report their primary engagement with Buddhism is when someone passes away. In addition, the biggest summer holiday, Obon, is a Buddhist rite to honor ancestors.[9] Although scholars have researched the topic of Japanese ancestor worship, the question of whether funerary, memorial, and ancestral rites offer healing for those living in modern Japan has not been thoroughly explored.[10] Throughout this study, the positive roles mortuary and ancestral rites play in contemporary Japan become evident, especially in the lives of mature Buddhist women.

In a Japanese Buddhist context, mortuary rituals help one learn about death, making the prospect of dying less frightening. These rituals are not done with the aim to bring "closure" for the living. This concept does not fit the Buddhist worldview where everything is interrelated. Everything transforms, articulated as reincarnation. "Closure" is more suitable for an individualistic concept of self that also sees death as more of an ending, not a transition. A Western psychiatrist explains his approach to helping people who are grieving: "Mourners must emancipate themselves from the lost person."[11] In a Buddhist context, this is not a logical aim. "Emancipation" in Buddhist teachings comes from awakening to interrelatedness, not accepting separation. Ontologically, the deceased cannot be lost. Rather, the deceased has undergone a radical change.

Ritualizing activity is not unique to Japanese culture or religiosity, but the details of how and what activities are ritualized are what give Japanese religiosity its distinctive aesthetic. Zen practice in Japan is a rich arena in which the propensity for ritualizing activities—from holding teacups to removing shoes—occurs where lines of delineating sacred from profane are, at best, blurred. Ritualized activity in a Sōtō Zen context is not a process of becoming: it is an event of (ideally) actualizing Buddha nature—mindful all is interrelated, impermanent, and ultimately empty (of substance and individuation)—in the present moment. By the same token, healing is not a process of curing or getting "better." It is a mode of experiencing events in the present moment from the perspective of Buddha nature where compassion neutralizes suffering, though pain may be chronic and death may ensue. My research reveals how women empower themselves and others as they experience their interrelatedness with all things. Ritualized activity takes such prominence in Japanese Zen due to its embodied (not dichotomizing body and mind) and holistic orientation where even the boundaries of life and death are not divisive, especially in the moments of sitting and talking to deceased loved ones who on death become recognized Buddhas in a person's home altar.

There are many memorial and ancestral rites, large and small, local and national. Home rituals and the public Jizō Nagashi ritual are the primary focus of my analysis here. Researching home rituals offers an understanding of the dynamics of identity cultivation and transformation in the face of loss. It also provides a rare view of how the dead can function in the women's healing paradigm. In the privacy of the home, ancestral rituals are often performed at the family home altar on a daily, monthly, and annual basis. A Buddhist altar is a place where birth and death meet, where the living and dead interact. As such, it is a "nest" for healing. Outside the home, visiting the gravesite (o-haka-mairi) is also done on monthly and annual intervals. The annual, day-long Jizō Nagashi is a poignant rite not widely performed. Depending upon the relationship of the participant in the ritual to the deceased, it can be experienced as a memorial rite, ancestral rite, or both. It is distinctive for it includes participants riding in a large boat on a lake.

Examining a large public memorial ritual gives insight into the role of the greater community and environment in their healing way. These rituals provide the basis for illuminating how, on death, a person becomes a personal Buddha to the loved ones still living.[12] Exploring memorial and ancestral rituals from this perspective sheds new light on the power these rites have in the healing paradigm, leading us to recognize both the centrality of the dead in Japanese Buddhist religiosity and how these ancestral rites can serve as healing rituals.

The concept of healing as I use it here is based on the Buddhist worldview where everything is understood to be interrelated and impermanent.

Combining this context with the Sōtō Zen Buddhist development to accord the deceased with the status of Hotoke-sama (Honorable Buddha), distinctive rituals have emerged and become the fabric of many modern Japanese Buddhist healing experiences. Recognizing someone has attained enlightenment upon death has had significant ramifications for the development of Japanese Buddhist rituals. Among other possibilities, this elevated status is critical to the grieving and healing paradigm of the survivors. The rituals are designed to make the deceased loved one remain a part of the living people's lives, yet not in the same way as they were in life. The exalted status of death makes them more powerful and their newfound wisdom enables them to help their loved ones.

The origins of the rhythm of Buddhist mortuary rituals extend through Chinese terrain to India. Several traditions and embellishments have been added and subtracted over the millennia.[13] My focus is on observing how the punctuation of the rituals usher a person through the emotions and adjustments many experience with the loss of a loved one. The intensity of rituals at the time of death corresponds to the intensity of the experience: Loved ones stay with the deceased person throughout the first night, ensuring incense is continuously kept lit. Some will chant or sing Buddhist hymns (*go-eika*). The funeral is a public high mark. Then, in the home, every seventh day after death for seven weeks special sutras are chanted. A nun or monk is sometimes called in to do the chanting.

During these forty-nine days after death, the person is thought to be nearby. The living often are in a liminal state, unable to plan ahead or do things they usually do. On the forty-ninth day, the spirit (*tamashi*) is thought to move beyond. This often corresponds to the time the living can begin to increase their interactions with the outside world. Several of the women noted how going grocery shopping went from a haze of half-hearted decisions back to a familiar task. Composing a grocery list, as simple as it seems, involves planning and recognizing that you are going to continue living. The concreteness of not needing to calculate a portion for the person who has passed is oftentimes painfully sobering.

The one hundredth day after the passing is another marker. At this time, many can fully return to work and other responsibilities. Today many must resume work sooner, but it is still about this time that many report being able to function fully.

Monthly rituals also punctuate the time after death. For example, if someone died on the seventeenth of the month, the seventeenth becomes the monthly death anniversary (*meinichi*) for that person. Certain death dates are particularly auspicious, and some even aim to die on those days.[14] On the monthly anniversary, many engage in extra rituals, such as visiting the grave, washing the gravestone, and making offerings.[15]

Japanese have been socialized to not expect someone to be completely reintegrated into society until a whole year passes. For example, New Year's cards—an important ritual for recognizing ties with friends and colleagues and acknowledging obligations and affections—are not expected from a family with a deceased member in the first year. Others refrain from sending cards to that family as well. This "absent" ritual is a subtle yet quietly deferential way to express respect for the deceased. The usual exchange of celebration in greeting the new year would be awkwardly forced, given the great loss that attends a death.

The first year after a death is always momentous. It includes the "firsts" that have been lived through that year: the first meals without the person, the first time sleeping at home after the person died, the first New Year's day, the first Obon, the first birthday the deceased did not have, and the first death anniversary (*isshūki*). Hence, the first death anniversary is second in importance only to the funeral. The third anniversary ritual (*sankaiki*) is actually performed two years after the death. The organic logic of calling it the "third" anniversary makes sense, because it is the third major ritual marking the death, including the funeral, and the pace of the second year after a death moves notably faster than the first year.[16]

Honda-san gives us an intimate view of her experiences when her parents passed away.

> I got a job [at a university] because the professor had a grant from the ministry of finance. I did the accounts. I used a computer—you know, with the cards with holes. The calculator I used was very noisy. I enjoyed it. I stopped working because my mother passed away of a heart attack when I was twenty-five. It was the summer, July 16 [1969]. It was when the U.S. Apollo [11] was being broadcast on NHK at 9 p.m. She said that she was going to take a bath before then.
>
> I had gone to the dentist that day, so I didn't eat with everyone. I had gone into the kitchen to fix something to eat, which is beside the bath. I thought I heard a cat, because there are lots of cats around [outside] our house. But then I thought it was a little different. I peeked into the bath, and my mother's neck was like this [slumped over gesture]. It was a heart attack.
>
> That was the day that my younger brother had just returned from Waseda [University]. My older brother lived in the house. My father had already passed away. So with the strength of men, they [my brothers] were

able to lift her out of the bath. I quickly called an ambulance. When it arrived, the medics said that it was probably bad. Then I called a doctor. When
I explained the situation, he told me it was probably bad. She was still breathing, but her eyes were rolled up. She was not conscious.

She thought she had a stiff shoulder and put Salon Pas [medicated pads]
on herself all the time. Since we were all basically healthy, we didn't go to
the doctor much. My mother was very old-fashioned and ferociously patient.
I am regretting it, because I saw it all. I wish I had said, "Why don't you go
see a doctor?" When I think now, I really regret it. This lingers in my heart.
She died so suddenly! That is probably why I turned to religion. I realized
later that she had been fifty-three, I was twenty-five—and I had only half
my life left! When I looked back at my own life of twenty-five years and
what I had done, I thought, I have only a little more time!

Also, I thought, humans can die so easily. She just died. My relative who
is a doctor said the heart feels tight for a bit, but it is not a long pain. So my
mother probably did not suffer much. I was relieved when I heard that. When
I think about it, maybe that was a big influence on my life [she says as if she
has not seen it this way before]. Being single and religious, since I saw that
form [of my mother dead in the bath], when I look back at my life now that I
am being interviewed—maybe this was a big influence in my life. I am now
fifty-five, but when I was fifty-three I thought, "Now I have made it to my
mother's age." All my siblings felt the same way. Our father passed away
when he was fifty-four. When he was forty-nine, he fell ill from an aneurism,
then my mother cared for him. It was very hard. His night and day got upside-down—he was up at night and asleep in the day. My mother never got to
sleep. Three years after my father passed away, my mother passed away.

It went to her heart. My father was a big man, 170-some centimeters
[more than 5 feet 6 inches] tall. It [taking care of him] required a lot of
strength. He would get rough, and it was hard on my mother, so I offered to
take a turn for my mother at night. Since I was slated to become a bride, my
mother didn't want me to get injured, so she told me it was OK. I did offer
once to let her sleep well even just for one night, but she said she couldn't. I
can't [refuse help like] that, but an "old-fashioned person" could. I would
have accepted the help. She protected her daughter. She wouldn't let her
daughter be injured. She took it all into her own body. From a child's perspective, our mother was phenomenal. It is less religion than it is my mother.

I later learned from relatives my mother did a lot of scripture copying. I
had not known. She went to worship at Nittai-ji [a Sōtō Zen temple in Na-
goya]. She didn't tell the children.

My mother passed without being sick. At fifty-three she was not like an old person. It was like a flower fell. So it was a stronger impression. My father had been sick for so long.[17]

After Honda-san recounted the circumstances around her mother's and father's deaths, I asked her about what the funeral for her mother was like. She became much more emotional. Her thoughts wove together a tapestry that gives us insight into a significant shift that set her life off in a different trajectory than she had previously imagined.

I asked neighbors and relatives how to do a funeral. There was no time to be sad during the funeral. I was more concerned not to do anything wrong, to do a proper job. That night I cried, but during the funeral there was no time to be sad. Afterwards, I saw the image of my mother coming home and saying, "I'm home (*tadaima*)." After that, I felt impermanence. It was summer, July 16. I felt the impermanence intensely. Life and death I felt intensely. Is it OK to die so easily? I felt empty, futile.

My older sister was pregnant with her second child, and my mother was happy for her. We felt like this child might be the reincarnation of our mother.

Yes, the next day was my grandfather's one hundredth day [since passing away]. He passed away on April 10. This was my mother's father. After my father passed away, he [my grandfather] was the one who we turned to for direction on major issues. My mother had washed her hair, because she was going to wear a kimono to go to the service the next day. At the time, I thought, he has taken her with him.

Another odd thing is that my mother had just gone to visit all her cousins and relatives, some she hadn't seen in more than ten years. It must have just been coincidence. My younger brother had just returned from university on that day, too. So to say it was all just coincidence sounds odd, but it was.

If you let me brag about my mother, she was a deeply compassionate person. Although it is rude to my father—he put us all through college—but the influence of my mother is profound.

When you have health, you get selfish. When you don't have health, you think, if you have health, there is nothing to complain about. Humans relax on top of their health. I felt there was no person I could rely on, because you never know when they will go. I felt so empty after the funeral.[18]

Moving from a keen sense of impermanence to integrating her mother's death into her life took time. Honda-san did all the traditional rituals for the first seven days after death, the forty-ninth day, the one hundredth day, the monthly anniversaries, and the special annual services.

Knowing what you "should" do when someone dies is deeply comforting.[19] Since Kawasaki-san has been around when a number of people passed away, she knew what to do when her mother-in-law breathed her last. Her neighbors knew what to do, too. "When someone dies, a priest from the Sōtō temple rushes over."[20] When her mother-in-law, Obāchan, passed away at age seventy-four, they went through the liminal phase as the death washed over the family. It was the summer, and they were fortunate that the whole family was present.

> After she passed away, we lit incense, filled a bowl full of rice, gave her water, and placed a string of prayer beads on her. We chanted as a family, "Namu Amida Butsu, Namu Amida Butsu." [Kawasaki-san was crying a bit with the memory.] We called the funeral home. They came soon and made a funerary altar (saidan) here. The altar has a picture of Obāchan in the highest place. Also placed on the altar was the mortuary tablet [with the deceased's new Buddhist name engraved on it that the priest provided]. On both sides, a lot of flowers, and one level down we put fruit. We put black cloth over the chests in the front room, so you couldn't see them. In the entrance to our home we put a sign that read mochū [in mourning, indicating that they were deeply engaged]. In the place of the Shinto altar (kamidana) we placed a white sheet of paper so the impurity of death doesn't go to it. We closed the home altar. For the first forty-nine days, the pollution is around. But the home altar was only closed for the three days of the funeral. She was in the casket under the funerary altar for the three days. The funeral home worker put dry ice in the casket, so it was OK. Her facial expression was very soft and relaxed. She died in the arms of her son. A Sōtō monk came to chant for the funeral. Neighbors and friends came and brought incense. She was properly laid at home for three days, because there are sometimes people who wake up. If during those three days the candle or incense goes out, the new Buddha may lose the way. So we do not let it go out, as taught to us by the priest. In the middle of the night, family members took turns and just rested lightly by the altar.

During those three days, I was unfocused. It still didn't seem real. Everyone was in a fog. Neighbors helped out cooking and the funeral home worker took care of the altar. Family didn't have much to do. The next-door neighbor invited us over to eat since our house is small. People didn't have places to park their cars, so neighbors moved their own and asked us to please have people use those spaces. The next-door neighbor said to put the flowers in front of their own home if the space was needed. We were just in a fog. Neighbors did everything.

At the crematorium, there were about twenty people. My child wrote a letter and put it in the coffin. He had turned eight on the day she died. We put lots of flowers in and things that she used daily, like her sandals and handbag. We chanted the *Heart Sutra* and many Nembutsu. For the forty-nine days, we offered breakfast, lunch, and dinner. On the seventh day [every seven days for seven weeks] there was the Buddha court, so we had a priest chant sutras. And on the forty-ninth day, her spirit left the home. Then we put the ashes in the family grave. We did feel that she was here during the forty-nine days. There was a warmth. When we went to the grave to chant and make offerings (*omairi*), she felt really close.

There is a warmth when the funeral is held at home. And there is a sense of leaving when [the person is] taken to the grave. When it is at the hall, it is a separate world. None of the mess of the home is present. It is the world of the funeral. And it is easy to fit into it. When it is done at home, it does not seem as much like a funeral ceremony, because there is this and that and all kinds of things of the home to attend to. We could not concentrate. Our air conditioner was not enough to keep people cool and guests had no place to stay.

[What follows refers to a funeral for her father-in-law held subsequently.] At the hall it is like you are a scene in a movie and you are the main cast. The room was so large. The altar was in the middle and was spectacular, but it seemed like it was made, like a movie screen. People spoke with a microphone. It was not a funeral where neighbors are coming in and asking what they can do. There was not that kind of intimacy. The funeral home served tea and announced when things were going to happen. They did it properly. It was done well, but . . . it was like everyone had done their duty. People, even at the crematorium, were not as deeply sad. The siblings were telling funny stories about what he had done in the past. They laughed and said they were bad to be having so much fun at a funeral.[21]

Funerary rituals help direct the emotional responses and feelings that are stirred in the face of death of a loved one. The shift from funerals held at home to, increasingly, those held at funeral homes, is a strong testimony physical space matters.[22] The traditional ritual was designed at home, and it seems to have a profound effect on the funeral experience and what emotions are inclined to arise in that space.

At the first night of death ritual (*o-tsuya*), you have a funerary altar, and light
a candle and incense. Before, no matter what time someone passed away, you
would have the death ritual that night. Now, things are more commercial-
ized, so he [father-in-law] died too late in the evening to call the priest. So,
we were up for two nights. We took turns and slept though. He passed away
in the hospital, and we had the services in the funeral home.

Japanese Buddhism has the ritual of seven days, seven days (*nanoka nanoka*). Every seven days you have a priest come for seven rounds. For the
priest to come for the death ritual, chanting the morning of the funeral, the
funeral, and the first of the seven days rites (*shonanoka*) it was ¥1,000,000
[$10,000]. To pay for the funeral home services, it was ¥2,500,000 [$25,000].
[The cost of the grave site is separate.] Japanese priests make a lot of money.

When I saw the funerary altar, I thought, oh, this has changed. It used
to be very simple. Ever since the [Shōwa] emperor's funeral [in 1989], they
have started copying that style. Everyone saw it on television. It was a Buddhist funeral, but it was a Shinto design.[23]

A primary change in the aesthetics of the funeral is the choice of flowers. Buddhist rituals use many colors and varieties, but now white chrysanthemums have become the norm. Since people have come to associate white
chrysanthemums with funerals, they now symbolize funerals and death.[24]

Tanaka-san recounts how "During a funeral, there is no time to be
sad. You are too busy. There are so many rituals. There is at first the death
ritual, and when that is finished then through to the seventh day, then
after that you can be sad. Until then, there is no time to be sad."[25] The
cumulative effect of having numerous rituals, however, often results in
people being too busy to experience much sadness while in the midst of
them. Once through them, though, you are, in a sense, primed to feel sadness in a manner that fosters acceptance and integration, so death is not an
end but a transformation. The bone-gathering ritual is a poignant example
of how this occurs.

After the cremation, those closest to the deceased perform a somber
ritual of placing the remaining bones into the urn. Picking up bones requires
a steady cooperation and mindful coordination of fine motor skills. Two
people, each using a pair of chopsticks, pick up a bone together and put it in
the urn.[26] Pressure of grasping, angle of holding, and speed of motion must
be carefully calibrated, because respectfully and successfully placing the
"Buddha" in the urn is paramount. All gathered must cooperate in various
pairings to collect the bones to place into the urn. This act can help repair

rifts and smooth over collateral damage caused in the wake of a loved one dying. The people participating demonstrate the capacity to work together in the ritual when achieving the keen level of coordination required to succeed in the delicate task. It helps them experience their relationships as extending beyond the ties that had bound them together through their mutual relations to the deceased.

Noguchi-san offered her reflections on what bones reveal about a person: "There are people who have nothing left. Like people who had cancer and had weak bones have nothing left. I feel this person really suffered, and I feel pain. Others have beautiful bones left. It seems lifestyle and disease makes the remains notably different. I have been given the opportunity to see numerous people's bones. People who die of the heart, they have beautiful bones left. Having done this so much, my attachments have dissolved. They just go away."[27]

Honda-san also freely offered her experience with her mother's bones. "Bones have spirit, because not that much leaves the person at death. So, many have a sense of intimacy with the bones. I felt the bones were my mother. We put her throat Buddha (*nodobotoke*) in a glass window so we could see it."[28] Ritualizing the handling of bones is a sobering ritual that clearly helps these women accept the reality of death. It also enables people to relate with the deceased in a rare and profoundly intimate manner. It establishes connections between the living and the loved one who is now in a deceased form. Having a specific bone named a Buddha reinforces the shift that the person in death is an improved version. The bone ritual makes death more familiar and integrates death and life in a direct and concrete way.

Settling the materials left in the wake of a deceased person can require settling matters in the heart. Honda-san reveals the way she worked with her heart after her mother's passing. Her family had "some money," so finalizing the estate was a matter of consequence. Though male privilege was not notable in life (due to her parents' childrearing approach), upon their death it appeared.

> I have envied my brother, because we were a family with some money. But to envy (*uramu*) is to cause yourself suffering. I became aware of the suffering. I am tricky. I just try to find the way that does not cause myself suffering. To doubt someone is to cause suffering to yourself. You know how you have an emotional self and a self that can see clearly? They were at odds with each other. Which would win? Eventually I realized a person's happiness comes from a stable peace of heart-mind. Since someday we all will die, I didn't

want to be in confusion and get sick. There was a battle in my heart. I wanted to stop the pain and I wanted to be calm and cheerful. If you are suffering, you must resolve it yourself. No one can do it for you. Isn't that right? It was a confusion in my own heart, so I am the only one who can take it away and clear it up. In the end, I realized that I was causing myself suffering. I wanted to have a calm heart. I came to think of it [unfair estate settlement] as not a big deal. I did not want to be obstructed by petty things. I am always thinking how to be peaceful. There are even times that I can't do this. Kitō Sensei has a beautiful face, doesn't she? That is my goal, my guide.[29]

What helped Honda-san find peace was her gratitude to her parents and acceptance that everyone will die. Once she was at peace about dying, she could find peace about the difficulties with her brother about the estate. The various rituals taking her through the death of her parents helped her accept their deaths and accept the natural inevitability of her own death. This was the key to healing her heart and resolving her parents' estate.

Aoyama Rōshi explains how "when a person moves their body and does these rituals in a heartfelt way, then the sadness is expressed and one does not sink. In this way the sadness transforms into a different strength."[30] Moreover, engaging in memorial rites helps people, especially young people, form their identity by knowing their family's past.

Having clear mortuary rituals helps many face the inevitability of their own deaths. Generally, a positive valence is put on the concept of death. Here is Nagai-san's thoughts on death. "My image of death is you are greeted by people with tons of bouquets of flowers and everyone gets along and has fun. People who are over there are all happy. So, I feel relief when I think of them. I feel that the Honorable Buddha is close through my parents. But not that they are the same Honorable Buddha. In a vague way, however, I feel my parents equal the Honorable Buddha. I feel they are alive in the other world."[31]

Indeed, many imagine "after death" as a place and time of interaction with other loved ones. It is not a lonely experience. This engenders relief in many when they think of their own demise. Nonetheless, the calmness is stunning in one of my consociates who has no children. Noguchi-san has clearly given this careful thought, and she speaks frankly about what she wants.

Since I have no children, I am more comfortable with my remains being left at the cremation place. I don't want to be a burden on anyone. They [her family] are mad at me, but I don't want a gravestone. Since I've been to several ceremonies of gathering the remains, I know they only take a few select pieces: parts of the skull, the throat Buddha, and a few others. So, there is a lot left over. Mine can just go with those. I want a funeral, because it is a nice marker for the living, but I don't want anything after that.[32]

She said this with an even, calm, clear, matter-of-fact voice. It was evident she has accepted her life conditions without resistance. She has healed from not living a life that fits the dominant pattern and social expectations. This is a notable accomplishment. In this sense, her funeral will be her crowning healing ritual, especially since she is not planning on having any of the traditional follow-up rituals that transform a deceased person into a personal Buddha.

Taniguchi-san engages in all the formal rituals, but she holds that "the real memorial ritual is to live well."[33] In keeping with her seriousness of purpose, Taniguchi-san asks herself, "Are you living in a way that it is OK to die at any time?"

Personal Buddhas as Intimate Healers

Each time Honda-san comes back to her studio apartment, I noticed she calls out, "I'm home." She is engaging in a common Japanese family greeting reserved for those coming in and out of their home. Honda-san, however, lives alone. She is addressing the photos of her parents on her homemade bureau-top Buddhist altar. They passed away more than three decades earlier, yet they are still her family. Her heart hears their response, "Your return home is welcomed (*okaerinasai*)." Honda-san has transformed a ubiquitous household greeting ritual into a healing ritual. With each greeting into the empty apartment, she knows she is not alone.

The ritualized exchange of words coming and going from home are not usually recognized or engaged in as a healing ritual. It is especially difficult to see the possibilities through the stilted English rendering, "Your return home is welcomed." It does not capture the emotional content of the phrase, for there is no English equivalent for the verb *kaeru*. *Kaeru* is reserved for returning to the place where one belongs. It elicits sentiments of warmth and acceptance. It is encoded with the affirmation: You are safe here. Indeed, if it were not for meeting in her home, I would never have known this ritual had occurred. After I was sure it was a regular practice, I asked Honda-san what it meant for her to engage in this common ritualized "exchange" and to confirm if my understanding of the practice was on target. She was quite comfortable discussing the matter, and she gave no indication there was anything out of the ordinary to vocalize her part of the exchange while knowing the other part could not be given in kind. With a sense of matter-of-factness she explained, "In my home I have my parents' pictures. I give flowers, water, and food. When I leave I ask them to take care of the house, and I say I'm leaving, and I'll be back (*ittekimasu*). I have done this since living on my own. I have not felt a sense of loneliness."[34] In contrast, Honda-san reflected on when her mother was alive and they were in different places. So, death has the effect of bringing her mother closer, because her mother can now be with her everywhere. For example, when Honda-san is walking through a crowded subway station and her legs get spasms of pain, she feels her mother's immediate support. If her mother were alive, she would feel alone if her mother were not actually beside her.

The ritualized "exchange" coming in and out of her home is simple. No one taught her how to do it. She did not assess the situation and make a conscious decision to continue this domestic ritual to heal from her parents' death. Yet, that she created this homemade healing ritual is testimony to her ritual mastery. This simple ritual enables her to experience her interrelatedness on a daily basis. It is also part of what helped her change her perspective on her life. She does not feel alone. Although she has had boyfriends, she never felt the need to be married. To go against the strong current of expectations that a "good" woman marries required clarity about the meaning of her life. She resolved the tensions by nurturing herself, enjoying life, and cultivating gratitude for what she has. Honda-san prefers a simple life and lives carefully within her means. This enables her to be generous and graceful in helping others as the need arises, whether it is cooking for an ill friend, caring for nieces and nephews, or listening as a colleague turns to her for support when struggling with doubts and frustrations. She is conscious that if she had a family of her own to tend she would not be able to be there for others as readily or as often. Being able to provide that kind of help to people gives her a deep sense of meaning. Her role in society is to be the "aunt" who can be there to serve when needed, and she is needed by many. Her personal Buddhas support her healing. In turn, they enable her to help others heal.

These personal Buddhas play a vital role in Japanese Buddhist rites, especially with regard to sources of healing. Whereas it is primarily the living who receive healing in Sōtō Zen, the ancestors are the focus of healing in Reiyukai Buddhism. Hardacre explains that in Reiyukai "healing is believed to have the soteriological function of saving the ancestors."[35] For my Zen Buddhist consociates, it is only in seeing how the rituals affect a person, usually over an extended period, that it becomes evident the ritual is indeed part of their own healing activity. Key factors in the analysis of this phenomenon include the identity constructions of the dead and the seeker of healing and how this relationship bears on their healing paradigm.

Most consociates in this study of healing rituals tend to their Buddhist altars with great care. They consider the home altar to be the anchor of their home. Its weight helps maintain stability in times of turmoil. It is a physical location for the heart-mind of the family. Whether the altar is an elaborate gilded one in a designated Buddhist altar room (butsuma) or a picture on a bureau, it can be effective in helping focus and ground healing activities.

Devoting precious space to an altar is clearly an indicator that having a designated sacred space in the home is valued. In a standard home altar, there is a central Buddha image, usually based on the family sect affiliation. If someone has passed away in the family, there is usually a mortuary tablet (o-ihai) with the posthumous Buddhist name (kaimyō) of the deceased and the date of death recorded on it. These mortuary tablets vary in height and ornamentation, from four inches in simple black to twelve inches with gold leaf and intricate carving. A picture of the deceased is usually placed at the altar in a prominent location. This helps foster the sense that the deceased person is still part of the family and community. Having ancestors "present" provides depth to the family structure and relationships.

Aoyama Rōshi has noticed in her many years of working with the bereaved that when someone passes away in a family, it makes the Buddha closer and more intimate. This occurs because the deceased is now understood to be a Buddha. People become more actively devout and feel the Buddha in their lives. This indicates the deceased is not merely referred to by the appellation "Buddha," but many people actually experience their deceased loved one as enlightened, attaining the perfection of wisdom and compassion through death.

The home altar centered on the dead person as a personal Buddha is a physical presence that cultivates relationships and healing. Indeed, the altar's very physicality facilitates facing difficult situations, because it helps people focus their attention in a place where they feel understood and supported. The support and understanding is experienced, according to most of my consociates, because the Buddha in their home altar is a family member.

The Buddha in the home altar is not thought to be omniscient, but is thought to know all that is important to any family member. The deceased becomes an enlightened personal healer for her kin. This personal Buddha knows family members' deepest level of private face (*honne*). When both were alive, it was not possible for one person to know another's private face in regard to all things. The vantage point of death, however, enables the deceased to know loved ones completely. Furthermore, becoming a Buddha means that the deceased has become a wiser and more compassionate version of who he was in life. In life, shortcomings, idiosyncrasies, and various tensions and misunderstandings make it difficult to see another clearly. In death, though, the family member can become a personal Buddha to the survivors. Personal Buddhas allow a person to *amae* (be purely dependent) with no need to calculate how much is being received versus how much is being offered (past, present, and future).[36] The relationship with your personal Buddha is liberating, for you do not need to consider that what you say, do, or think might have negative ramifications due to things being taken out of context and used against you in the future, which is always a possibility when dealing with the living. More than one woman even confessed—after more than a dozen hours of interviews— that she gets along better with her mother now that her mother is dead![37] There is no pressure to be good and hide your faults with personal Buddhas. They love you as you are. You can relax and be. Nagai-san even finds her personal Buddhas more effective than professional psychologists. "When I've spoken to psychologists, it seems like I am talking to a wall. It makes me wonder if my feelings have been understood, because they do not get upset. But they must do that as professionals."[38]

Although the oldest son of the family has the clan (*ie*) home altar in his home, often inheriting the house too, the current practice among the generally traditional women I worked with exhibited a wide variation.[39] It was surprisingly common that the women had a home altar–type space that included her own family. If an only child was a daughter who never married, she inherited the family home altar on her parents' death and maintained it, with her parents as her personal Buddhas. If an unmarried woman had siblings, she created her own home altar in her home, and her parents became her personal Buddhas. If a woman had been married and lost her husband, her husband became her personal Buddha. Among the women who lost their in-laws, there are some who had grown so close that their in-laws became their personal Buddhas. None of the women was limited by the traditional practice of the family's home altar being in the eldest male's home. This illustrates how Japanese practice is, at least currently, significantly different from the traditional Chinese mortuary rituals that reinforce Confucian family values of loyalty and filial piety.[40] The primacy of the male family line meant women were expected not only to join their husband's family, but also to not engage in rituals for their birth family. My consociates, who are otherwise notably more traditional in terms of values and practices than most contemporary Japanese women, did not indicate that including their birth family in their altar practices was unusual. Rather, it was natural for them to keep connections with their whole family. That they do their practices at the Buddhist home altar as part of their healing, not as "mere" ancestral rites of obligation, is a key to understanding their choices.

Indeed, maintaining a Buddhist home altar seems to be a virtual inoculation against the fear of death. Death is just part of the family. It is profoundly sad to lose someone, but unless there are extraordinary circumstances surrounding the death (such as suicide and murder), death is not so readily a traumatic experience for these women. Listen to Honda-san: "When my mother died I felt 'it is ok to die,' because even if you die you can still meet each other. I don't know if we can meet 'over there,' but I am not afraid of death. I feel like we can meet each other with our best aspects now that she is gone. Only the best is left. All the bad things disappeared. Death is a mysterious thing. I used to be very scared about where I would go after death."[41]

John Traphagan has also observed that the "living and dead are mutually involved in enacting and maintaining each other's well-being."[42] In fact, Ogawa-san finds deep comfort being near her altar. She explained, "I sleep in the same room with the altar. I have no interest in sleeping in another room. My parents used to sleep in there, but right after they died, I went in there. I feel they are close."[43] Sleeping in the same room with a home altar is not uncommon. Sometimes the reason is due to limited space, but, as we see with Ogawa-san, this is not her reason. It is the same with a handful of the other women, too.

Recognizing the deceased as personal Buddhas means the living and dead are not separated. The concept of personal Buddha takes the teaching of interrelatedness and stretches it across the illusory boundaries of life and death. Intimate relations people have with their personal Buddhas function to dissolve the delusion of separate entities. The transformation of the relationship between the living and the dead is concretely fostered through offerings, chanting, prayer, and conversation at the home altar. They validate the deceased as a Buddha each time they make the offerings that are reserved for Buddhas. Offerings are made by the most devout twice a day, morning and evening. The offerings typically consist of five elements as listed in the *Nirvana Sutra*: light (candles), flowers, incense, water or tea, and food (rice or fruit). In homes where rice is made for breakfast and dinner, rice offerings to Honorable Buddha are made first, then rice is served to others. Some women, however, only offer a cup of tea in the morning and reserve the full complement of offerings for special occasions. Such occasions are the annual or monthly death anniversary and Obon. In addition, people who give the five types of offerings regularly usually give more elaborate offerings on special occasions, often including favorite foods of their personal Buddha.

After the offerings are made, those who are busy and perfunctory may ring the bell, put their hands together in prayer and say "Good morning" with a bow of the head. The fuller ritual often includes ringing the bell after the incense is lit, holding prayer beads (*juzu*), and chanting some scripture. The most commonly chanted scripture is the *Heart Sutra* or *Hannya Shingyō*. *Kannon-gyō* or one of its shorter versions, such as *Jikku Kannon-gyō*, is chanted by those with more time. If there is something on the mind of the person, it is often during this time that she will talk about her concerns with her personal Buddha, beseeching their advice, assistance, or forgiveness. Expressing gratitude and making promises to improve on something is often articulated at this time as well.

Honda-san describes her home altar and typical way of interacting. Even as she is aware the rituals at her home altar help, she is also aware that there is a nonrational dimension to the activity and laughs about it. Such laughter does not dilute the potency or efficacy of the ritual.

> I have a picture that was taken of the family when we gathered for burying the ashes at the grave. Of course I have my parents' pictures. I don't use incense, because my studio apartment is too small and I am scared. My father liked sushi, so I get him some [as an offering]. I don't chant. I do put my hands together and say simple prayers. I ask them if they are getting along well over there. That's the level I do it. When I am really having problems, I sit and look at their pictures and talk. I tell them to not be silent and quickly respond. Then I say [laughing] that that is unreasonable because they are pictures. I have become strong, compared to the past.[44]

Being able to interact with deceased loved ones in the familiarity of their own home helps practitioners maintain a sense of intimacy and continuity.

Therefore, especially for a person who lives alone, talking to those at the altar, even while it is partially an "unreasonable" act, is a healthy activity. Consciousness studies suggest such imaginary interactions might help people survive the debilitating effects of loneliness. Gyokko Sensei, though, stressed, "if you don't know loneliness, you won't know the deepest flavor of gratitude."[45] These rituals do not prevent loneliness, but they do help practitioners continue to function, despite being lonely. Being in the home, such ritualized activities facilitate transforming the relationship of the living and dead in a manner that integrates the loss in a life-affirming manner. Family members continue to interact, so the divide between life and death is immaterial.

Many of my consociates explained how in times of need they turned to their loved ones at the altar, because they are the ones who understand them most. The women added that they had an even greater expectation for help now that their loved ones are dead, because they are Buddhas. Updates on developments in problems usually accompany the morning or evening greetings. Of course gratitude is duly expressed when their personal Buddha has helped solve the problem.

Laughter and joy are also part of this transformed relationship. Several women said they looked forward to summer so they could offer watermelons or autumn when the persimmon would be ripe, because their loved ones especially enjoyed those fruits. In this way, they could continue to feel connected through the passing of time. Or, when out shopping, many women said seeing a special sweet that a loved one favored reminded them of pleasant times together, so they would get the confection to offer on the altar in the evening "for dessert." Such simple gestures provide the living with a warm wash of fond memories that buoys them along in their lives.

Nagai-san explains how rituals at her home altar with her personal Buddhas even help her relive joys from childhood. She explicitly states how this does not occur at a temple, only at her home altar. "I don't feel too intense when chanting sutras at home. But at the nunnery [nisōdō], I feel that I am chanting seriously. At home, I just feel like I am conversing with the people who have gone over there. I remember my childhood being full of joy and abundance. So I want to return to that feeling [when I am at the home altar]."[46]

At first, after the funeral, just caring for the deceased through food offerings sometimes spurs a bereaved person to start caring for herself. If she has to make rice for the personal Buddha, then she is more likely to eat, especially if she lives alone. Furthermore, daily offerings of food and water, or tea, are an opportunity to greet the deceased. Fresh flowers offered on the home altar bring beauty and closeness to nature into the home.

Honda-san explained that before her mother's passing she had associated the smell of incense burned at a Buddhist altar with things that were old and gloomy. After her mother passed away, she found the smell of incense reached into the interstices of her heart and connected her with her mother. The smell of incense helped her through her grieving. She was twenty-five when her mother passed away. At the time we had this conversation she was fifty-six. Now when she burns incense she feels her mother's presence, bridging the gap between life and death.

When the dead are recognized as personal Buddhas, it enables the healing of the survivors. Through engaging in memorial and ancestral rituals, the living can find support and understanding in a way that is not readily available through other means, for these personal Buddhas in home altars are specifically focused on taking care of the living in a direct and intimate way. These mundane rituals belie the profound insight that grieving never ends—it just changes with the seasons. They also illustrate how healing is available in the home through the dead acting as personal Buddhas.

Personal Buddhas are at the center of domestic rituals. In addition to homemade rituals, many women engage in more formal and traditional rituals to help them heal and prepare them to meet the difficulties that inevitably arise. I think of these as "foundation" rituals. They are the base that keeps things stable. They revolve around the home altar: personal Buddhas, making offerings, bowing, chanting, and praying are the central foundation rituals. These women claim such practices enable them to keep a perspective on things and minimize the experience of despair and frustration that could so easily overwhelm them. Several of them describe their home altar as an anchor for the household. They describe it also as a harbor, a safe place to allow them to "be" with heart-wrenching and intractable situations. They tell me it is safe because their ancestors or personal Buddhas are intimate healers who listen with compassion. The women add that sitting at their home altar, however ornate or modest, enlarges their perspective on their experiences, especially in the midst of daily chores and tight schedules.

The Healing Dimension of Daily Rituals at the Family Home Altar

The family Buddhist altar functions like an attentive and compassionate person. One woman explains, "It is like a part of the family."[47] Moreover, upon the death of a loved one, the home altar is a physical location where

Home altar room

they can go for support. They are not left alone with a complete void. Hence, they can express and experience grieving with a deep sense of being understood, no explanation or excuses needed. This sense of being understood continues as a part of daily life for all but one of the women. Indeed, for those who have an active engagement with their home altar, each important event is recounted there. As one of the women puts it, everything the family has "received over the years we offer to the home altar."[48]

Understanding the centrality of the home altar in domestic Zen is illuminating. The home altar creates a ritual space in the home that most families can directly connect to several generations back. Those with contemporary stresses and challenges still find succor in its attending rituals. A Buddhist home altar not only provides the physical space for ritualized action but also creates a space of meaning. Delineating a space that is designed for thoughtful reflection and cultivating gratitude does not merely allow you to reflect and be grateful—it also inspires you to do so. It affirms that such activity is worthwhile and important, as important as activities that demand regular attention, like putting a meal on the table or hanging the laundry to dry. The Buddhist home altar also enables a space where the limitations of the passing of linear time are suspended, facilitating the passing of boundaries of life and death. The virtual space also protects you in a space where it is safe to feel otherwise terrifying emotions. Instead of such emotions immobilizing a person, when experienced in the safe haven of the home altar you can often feel their full force and watch as they transmute into empowering clarity or calm acceptance. Moreover, the combination of the three kinds of ritual space—physical space, meaning space, and virtual space—created by a Buddhist home altar provides a site to galvanize determination to overcome debilitating fears or release aversions, a place for "eustress." [49] Eustress is a term endocrinologist Hans Selye coined to describe a good kind of stress. [50] I would even go so far as to say a home altar is a place where (negative) stress can be transformed into eustress. Perhaps this is due to Gyokko Sensei's claim, "unlike people, you can rely completely on the Buddha." [51] Personal Buddhas understand one deeply, but they are not omnipotent. They cannot just make problems go away or grant you what you want. Yet, they do help you feel more secure and, therefore, more able to respond to problems with greater peace. "I don't feel that they will just take care of my problems. I feel that they look with warm affection. I do pray they help things go in a good direction." [52]

With one exception, all the women in my study are the primary caretakers of their familial home altar. For four of the women, this is because they are single and live alone. It is important to recognize even the women who live alone are still actively part of their families (whether alive or deceased), including parents, siblings, cousins, nieces, and nephews. They see themselves and make decisions about their lives in the context of their families' needs and concerns, and they maintain some type of altar in their homes as an expression of this connection. Another three women are widowed, but they, like the remaining four married women, have always been the person in their family who is most actively engaged with the altar. This responsibility for the home altar is in almost every case a personal choice. The exception is one woman who feels obligated to maintain the main home altar for her husband's family as a customary duty. This woman, however, has also made a less formal altar for her own family in an adjoining room. She does this, she says, because she does not feel the Honorable Buddha in the main household altar understands her like her own family does.

A balance between valuing family and personal needs is sought by each of the women. The home altar serves as a place of empowerment for the women, even as they are fulfilling a cultural duty to honor the family and patrilineal ancestors. Although from the structure of the ritual it can appear that women are subservient to their husbands' family, most of the women find it an activity that serves their own empowerment. It is not merely a one-way street in which the women are acted upon by males who place themselves structurally in a higher status. The women experience calmness, clarity, strength, and support from the performance of the rituals. Simultaneously being the filial daughter or obedient wife, the women reap the benefits of praying and chanting for themselves as they are serving others.

The women report their practice of making offerings at their home altar—like candle light, incense, flowers, and food—help them in immediate and specific ways. Yamaguchi-san explains how offerings at the altar are woven into daily life. "When you receive something, you first put it on the altar and ring the bell. Later, you take it down and have it."[53] Even her children make quick and simple offerings of incense, ring the bell, and ask for help before a test. The offerings require physical acts that take you beyond yourself. The focus is on what items and gestures might welcome and please a loved one, whether the image is of a particular Buddha or of a particular ancestor. Kawasaki-san explains how "when I get something nice, I offer it and say, 'Satako-chan [her deceased younger sister], here, have some.'"[54] Gifts and significant purchases are first placed on or near the altar for a time before they are used, eaten, or put away. It is an expression of gratitude that also creates the sense that personal Buddhas are in part the source of and participate in the family's good fortune. Such overt physical action prepares the mind for expanding beyond insular preoccupations and opening up to a larger experience of the moment.

Respect is inherent in the ritualized observances, especially when they are performed with a sense of familiarity and intimacy. Respect in this context includes respect for the Buddha(s) recognized in the altar as well as the myriad of people who have come before, those present now, and those in the future. Those who light a candle with this kind of respect belong to an expansive community that connects people across time. Not only do you feel part of something bigger, which has a buoying effect, but you have a sense of doing something meaningful, which affirms that you are important. Additionally, it requires focus and controlled use of small-motor muscles. Most days this is not a difficult action, but on days when you are worried if you are going to be around long enough to take care of your growing child, or if your child will recover from a serious illness, such refined actions can be a challenge. Calming down enough to accomplish the task can help keep things from spiraling out of control. Likewise, lighting a stick of incense to offer can have a steadying effect on the body and mind. You must be sure not to grip too hard, because incense breaks easily. Incense also adds the sense of smell to the visual stimulation of the light. A familiar smell—especially those associated with intimate connections to loved ones who lit incense in the home before passing on or associated with other times sitting at the altar feeling comforted and safe—can draw on the strength embedded in those associations. The aroma permeates the home, also affecting those not sitting at the home altar.

Bowing in front of an altar further calms and focuses the body, unleashing a cascade of internal responses indicating you are safe. Bowing is, in ethological terms, a vulnerable position. You are not able to see if there is anything coming to attack, hence you are not in a position to protect yourself. Volunteering your body for this position enhances the feelings of reverence and gratitude. It confirms it is a safe place, a place where trust and acceptance are real. Most commonly, bowing at an altar includes bowing with palms pressed together. Touching the hands together closes the circuit of the body, giving a sense of being stronger and more focused than when the hands are loose by your side. Moreover, the hands cover the location of the heart, likely making a human animal feel more protected and less vulnerable.[55] When done as part of a ritualized act, the physical posture of the bow reinforces the aim of feeling safe. Feeling safe, in turn, makes it easier to experience gratitude. Indeed, when you are afraid, thoughts of gratitude usually remain just that—thoughts. Feeling gratitude seems to require a relaxation of the heart, contrasted to the tightness that accompanies fear. A bow can help the body-mind trigger the cue to loosen up and accept whatever reality is unfolding. Accepting with a bow is not indifferent resignation. It is a posture of embracing the situation with thanks. Such bows are done at times of profound challenge and deep need. Bows are a frequent ritualized gesture of gratitude that punctuate a day of interacting with others and engaging in the common gift exchanges that attend respectful relations.[56]

After bowing upon receipt of a gift, gifts are then customarily offered to the home altar as a gesture of respect aimed at the giver of the gift and in recognition that you are part of a family, which includes the deceased. Kawasaki-san affirms this practice: "What we have received over the years we offer to the home altar."[57] It is a concrete way to tie a family together across generations, both living and dead. Such relationships are vital to experiencing healing, because at the home altar one receives a vital support (from the ancestors) that comes with no hidden strings, painful barbs, or ambiguous signals. Giving gifts to the home altar also increases your sense that you are karmically connected to a body of people, which helps to dissolve narrow self-concern.[58]

Chanting further expands the person by filling the mind and body with sounds that can, and often do, replace the narrow activity and focus of the mind. Unlike Logos-based traditions where the meaning of the chant is the focus for contemplative reflection while chanting, chanting for these women is rarely about comprehending the words. These women report that their chanting is not done with the motivation that it will directly address their emotional needs. Rather, the deep breathing and regular and rhythmic sounds facilitate an experience that serves as a break from the push and pull of emotions. After such a break, rejuvenation and clarity are gained through the expanded perspective of the chanting experience.[59]

The types of chants range from short mantra-like phrases to long sutras. Chanting at least the *Heart Sutra* once a day is a common practice. The *Jikku Kannon-gyo* is also commonly chanted, indicating an affinity for Kannon, the goddess of compassion. The *Kannon-gyo* from the twenty-fourth chapter of the *Lotus Sutra* is chanted when there is a special occasion, like a monthly death anniversary. Kawasaki-san regularly chants ten different sutras each morning. Her explanation of what she does includes some of the rationale she uses to determine what she will chant and when. It is clear that chanting at the altar is important, but she never loses sight of the other important things she needs to do during the day.

> Typically, my daily devotions (*omairi*) include the *Heart Sutra*. I start by sitting in front of the home altar, light the candle, then I light the incense. Then in front of the Buddha I say, "I am about to do my devotions, please accept them." Then I bow three times, reciting, "Refuge in Buddha, Refuge in Dharma, Refuge in Sangha." [She repeats it three times.] Bowing to the Buddha means bowing to the Buddha heart-mind in me, if I were to analyze it. I feel gratitude to the Buddha in me, to the Buddha who is here [in the home altar], and to Shaka-sama [the historical Buddha]. I feel like I am asking for forgiveness for the "self" that keeps me from reaching Buddha heart-mind. I will be receiving the gift of being able to chant the sutras, so I focus my heart on feeling that it please be moved in the correct direction. That is my feeling while I am doing the three bows.
>
> I do the sutras in the beginning of the Sōtō Zen devotional book. At first, I looked at the sutra book, but these days I don't. I chant with the bell (*chin*) and wooden drum (*mokugyō*). I do one section at a time. There are five. When I have no time because I am busy, I just chant the *Heart Sutra* and the

Kannon Sutra. For Ohigan and Obon I always chant from the first section to the fifth section of the *Shushōgi.* I don't chant it on the three days of Obon, but once through on one of those days. For Ohigan, it is actually the twenty-third, but the week before is considered the week of Ohigan, so sometime during that week I will do it.

After the *Kannon-gyō,* I chant the *Shariraimon,* and then I do a sacred phrase (*darani*) from Amida Nyōrai-sama's *Konpon Darani.* I also chant a part of the *Taihōkō Kegonkyō Fumonbon.* It is good for chanting to ancestors. Then I offer the *Myōshinge* that helps with all matters of the heart, then the *Isshinchōrai.* It takes me about an hour. If you chanted more slowly, like is proper, it would be more, but these days I am so busy I just spew it out. [She laughs as she speaks.] Honorable Buddha's eyes must be twirling with dizziness! It should take about two to three hours. I chant a lot of things, because I want to receive a lot of things! I figure that Honorable Buddha understands, so I think it's OK. Since I shouldn't just do that, though, I also go to Aoyama Sensei's to learn what I should do.[60]

Yamamoto-san also chants daily, but not quite as long. She has her own unique combination.

Every day I chant the *Heart Sutra, Ichimai Kishōmon* [Hōnen's "One Page Pledge"], "Namu Amida Butsu" ten times, and Obāchan's posthumous Buddhist name ten times while hitting the wooden drum, and bow to the sun, and end. Jōdo-shū says to do Namu Amida Butsu ten times, but I decided to do her posthumous Buddhist name ten times. I do it because she is an important family member. I give her dinner before we eat. I do it with a sense of gratitude to her. I want to help her do well crossing over.[61]

Her freedom with deciding what and how to chant indicates her deep sense of familiarity with ritual activity. She does not need to just do as she is told. She tailors her chanting practice to suit her specific interests and concerns. In so doing, she makes morning chanting a time of healing.

Gyokko Sensei does a significant amount of chanting, too. In particular, she has done extensive chanting of the *Heart Sutra.* "My mother did the *Heart Sutra* practice. She's from a temple of the Eihei-ji line. My mother's parent's home is Sōtō Zen. Among the rituals I practice that my mother taught me, is to chant twenty-eight rounds of the *Heart Sutra* for Fudo-san. That's his number. It's from India. Kannon-sama is eighteen rounds of the *Heart Sutra.* I've never confirmed this. It's just what we do."[62]

Gyokko Sensei has kept a detailed log of her *Heart Sutra* practice. She records who "told" her how many times she should chant each day, the number of days to do it, and what date to start. Among those that she records are Kanzeon, Jizō Bosatsu, Dainichi Nyorai, Fudō Myoō, and Toyokawa Inari. For example, one of the entries in her chanting practice journal reads as follows: "told" by Jizō Bosatsu January 15–February 4, twenty-four rounds [per day], 1964. She says she "hears" most of the instructions while at her home altar or when she is sleeping. Her motivation to engage in this chanting practice is evident in her following explanation. "I did fifty rounds of the *Heart Sutra* for three weeks. At another time, I did three hundred rounds [of the *Heart Sutra*] in one day for five weeks. Yes, I remember that I chanted even when I rode a train. I was determined. I chanted fast, very fast. It took effort. My mother was sick."[63] Another time she alluded to a time when her son was young. "Once I gave one thousand rounds of the *Heart Sutra* [in one day]. My son would fall asleep. That's the way he grew up."[64] Gyokko Sensei also does this chanting practice with others, too. "We do one thousand rounds of the *Heart Sutra*. We need about twenty people, then each person chants fifty times (simultaneously). If there is a child sick, then people gather. It's hard to get twenty people together. Most people don't have the values to do this. To have this done by a temple with the priests would cost ¥200,000 [more than $2,000]! So, I thought *we* should just do it. There is merit in doing one thousand rounds of the *Heart Sutra*."[65]

At times, they are actually in the same room together, but they also can be in their own homes and commit to doing the same number of rounds for the same number of days. She explains how they count in these situations. "Sometimes it is done with just a few people meeting together, and if five people do it for five rounds, that's twenty-five."[66] Once she even called me to tell me she was "told" I should chant ten rounds of the *Heart Sutra* for eighteen days. She added it would usually be eighteen times per day, but she thought that she was told it was just ten times for me, because I am busy. Doing just ten rounds of the *Heart Sutra* took more discipline, organization of time, and determination than I had anticipated! It made me appreciate her chanting practice much more after that. Perhaps that is why she was "told" I should do it.

Unlike Gyokko Sensei, another woman, Kawasaki-san, has a distinct preference to whom she chants. "I chant sutras to Kannon-sama for things. I like Kannon-sama more than Hotoke-sama [in this case referring to Sakyamuni Buddha]."[67] She is not alone. Many people indicate a preference for the goddess of compassion, because, in Japan, she is a more approachable

motherly figure. It is easier to expose your vulnerabilities to her. More than
one person has commented to me that Sakyamuni Buddha is "too perfect" to
relax around. For Kawasaki-san, however, all Buddhas are the same. "In my
head Birushana Butsu [Vairocana], Hotoke-sama [generic Buddha], and
Amida Buddha are all the same: I think they are all 'Namu Amida Butsu.' I
feel the same when I am facing a statue of Shaka-sama [Sakyamuni Buddha]
or Daibutsu [Great Buddha in Nara]. They are just different forms."⁶⁸ Despite this, she does admit to a slight preference. "When I have an important
matter, I think if I offer it here at home it has a direct line to the Daibutsu.
They are connected."⁶⁹ With more discussion, more of the specific ways she
selects ritualized practices for specific situations comes forth.

"I do believe in the power of 'Namu Amida Butsu.' At the most difficult times, I go to the doctor, but I think it is 'Namu Amida Butsu' that
works in a way you cannot see."⁷⁰ Kawasaki-san then told the story of her
son who was injured on the playground but did not feel pain. It turned out
to be a broken arm. The doctor was surprised her son did not seem to be
experiencing pain. She reenacted for me how she just kept reciting "Namu
Amida Butsu," inaudible under her breath, her lips barely moving. It is
clearly not the volume that matters. It must be the focus of the heart, but
asking her to explain her understanding of the mechanics of the practice
did not seem as important as her understanding of what the chant does.
She thinks chanting "Namu Amida Butsu" helps transfer the pain so you
do not feel it when you need the most help. After having explained some
of her most private practices and thoughts, she paused to reflect to me. "I
am seen as an odd person, because I am not so old and I rely on things that
you cannot see with your eyes. In an age where people rely on science, I
spend time working on polishing my heart. I feel I am always protected. I
don't tell a lot of people that I was healed by 'Namu Amida Butsu.'"⁷¹

I held my teacup in both hands as I drank in the honor she had bestowed
on me. It would be my responsibility to contextualize and frame the practices she does with all seriousness, yet she does not feel comfortable telling
those in her neighborhood. I felt her trust as well as her generous heart that
would share this in the hopes that someone, someone she never met, speaking a language she does not know, living in a country she has never seen,
might someday be assisted by her humble practices. Reserved for the deepest
of interactions in Japanese culture, we looked deep into each other's eyes. I
tried to convey with the purity of silence that I would treat her with respect.
Words did not have the gravity commensurate for the moment. Words are
not trusted as deeply as bodily action and expression in Japanese culture, for

there is a keen awareness that it is easy to say beautiful things without being genuinely sincere. The body, however, does not lie.

Gyokko Sensei also describes chanting "Namu Amida Butsu" more as a way of focusing and orienting her heart than as a deliberate chanting practice. She explained to me how she learned what to do in the face of life's vicissitudes. "Hasedera Kannon in Nara told me there are good things and bad things, and not just good things. When that comes to you, it is a matter of *how* you respond. *Tada hitasura* 'Namu Amida Butsu' (Praise Amida Buddha purely from the heart)."[72] Gyokko Sensei describes how she gains insight by attributing her insights to "hearing" the teachings of specific Buddhist figures—in this case, the Kannon of Hasedara in Nara. I understand her claims of "hearing" such teachings as a way of expressing her gratitude for being part of a complex interrelated cosmos. She respects it and is humbled by it. She does not want to diminish or distort it by claiming, "I think . . . ." It is not that she never makes claims to having her own thoughts. She does. Yet she distinguishes the difference between her own thoughts and teachings that come from a Buddha or bodhisattva. When I asked her to clarify how she heard the teachings, she answers matter-of-factly. For example, she says she was standing at the temple and heard the teachings. When pressed, she says she "heard" with her heart. It is clear that such details of "how" she heard are not something she cares much about or questions. To "hear" such teachings is just the way her mother raised her, although she does admit it is a gift to hear them. She attributes her ability to hear to maintaining a sincere and respectful Buddhist way of life. Chanting is one of the ways that helps her stay sincere.

Moreover, giving praise to Amida Buddha—whether things appear to be good or bad—helps her keep a broad perspective. It is easier for her and for others to balance on something broad. Conversely, it is easier to lose your balance with a narrow perspective, making any situation feel worse and limiting your ability to respond creatively. You suffer less when experiencing events with the sense that you are part of an expansive realm that includes you in its compassionate care, like Amida Buddha's. It makes waiting for each diagnosis, each call in the middle of the night, and each loss less frightening. Being prepared to face these situations with an immediate and simple act such as chanting "Namu Amida Butsu" gives you room and time to breathe. Not unlike practicing a fire escape route to increase one's odds of making it out of a fire safely, Gyokko Sensei has a "plan" for when "bad" things happen, enabling her to get to a safe place and prepare for the next step.

Chanting from the heart is a ubiquitous practice in domestic Zen. It is a basic tool for garnering the focus and energy required to respond to the inevitable vicissitudes of life. It is done alone or in a group—whether together or scattered in different locations—to magnify the impact. Multiple rounds are done in the event of significant difficulties or challenges. Repeating a familiar chant helps Gyokko Sensei, among numerous others, find her way back to other times when she chanted when she was calm, reminding her body how to feel safe again. Perhaps such chanting also stops the cascade of stress-responses that often accompany fear, a question for future research. For now, the ethnographic materials tell us that whether you are sitting in front of your home altar chanting clearly, standing in front of a Buddhist figure chanting under your breath, or running with a child to the doctor's office chanting only in your heart, chanting can have an immediate, practical, and positive effect on your healing. It provides the breathing room and steadiness of mind required to see what next course of action would be most helpful.

If chanting helps you breathe and focus, praying helps you feel connected and activates compassion. Zen nun Kitō Sensei teaches that prayer opens the heart of compassion. She explained that when you pray, you experience no-self (mushin). When you relinquish all, it is the realm of emptiness. But since we have form, she stressed, doing things that involve form are effective. Thus, praying with prayer beads in hand and incense lit at the home altar or in a temple can help people, although you can pray anywhere. She remarked, "To pray knowing you are heard heals you. You know you are heard because everything is interrelated." Kitō Sensei explained how prayers to Kannon facilitate this awareness of being heard and interrelated. After all, Kannon "hears the cries of the world." She even includes the bodhisattva vows as prayers, because prayer is not just for asking for things, but also for committing yourself to a certain kind of behavior, like being kind to a person with whom you have trouble getting along. In sum, prayer is a compassionate healing activity.[73]

For example, Honda-san has a continuing sense of protection from her deceased parents, her personal Buddhas. "People ask me if I am lonely because I do not have a husband, but I respond by asking, Why should I be lonely? I have not felt much loneliness. It is not so much I feel I can communicate with them [deceased parents]. It is that I feel they are taking care of me, protecting me. That is why I have become more cheerful. I am always being protected by them. They have become closer now that they have passed away. They are always with me now."[74]

For annual death anniversaries or even monthly death anniversary rituals, most of the women ask a nun to come to their home and chant at their home altar. This is a time for the women to open up to another understanding ear. Nuns are noted for their capacity to listen carefully. There are several conditions that have given rise to nuns serving this role. In a sense, the history of monks, but not nuns, performing funerals has resulted in an impression that monks are associated with death. In contrast, nuns serve people in a listening capacity as one of their most important contributions. Aoyama Rōshi said supporting the women in homes is the nuns' most important work. It was a surprise to me when she wrote that in the foreword to my book about Zen nuns' history and practices, adding, "We must exert ourselves unremittingly, because the children these women raise are the ones who will saddle the world on their shoulders."[75]

The way in which nuns offer their most helpful support of laywomen is listening to them after chanting sutras at their home altar. When tea is served after chanting, it naturally becomes a time and space where it is safe for a woman to show her vulnerabilities. It is in the privacy of her own home. Neighbors will only see a devout Buddhist, not question if a person is having emotional difficulties, which is something most Japanese are highly committed to keeping hidden. Hence, people rarely seek therapy. One woman who did, however, found talking with a nun more helpful. They all note how powerful nuns' listening is. The intimacy that develops in deep listening is healing. The power of listening is potent when the listener is a person, but these women have demonstrated they receive a similar benefit when the listener is their personal Buddha.

Increasingly in integrative medicine and Zen practice in the United States, meditation—not ritual—is seen to be the primary Buddhist practice that can be enlisted to help with healing. Japanese lay Zen Buddhists, however, do not often turn to meditation for healing. Instead, they turn to ritual. Their instinct is corroborated by research on altered states of consciousness. This research "suggests that the performance of rituals generates a different psychological experience from that of practice meditation. Ritual performance generates experiences of communitas. It rewards corporate religious activity in ways that meditation does not."[76]

Tending the heart-mind is a central concern in all domestic Zen practices. Ritualized activities in a Zen healing paradigm involve polishing the heart-mind. In addition to the ritualized activities of making offerings, chanting, and praying, any activity can be ritualized and done as heart polishing. Repetitive activities such as laundry, cooking, and cleaning are often done in such a manner in monastic and domestic Zen. Honda-san explains, "If a person does not find a place that she can heal her heart-mind, a place for her heart to be, then she will be very insecure and unstable."[77] Therefore, doing daily tasks in a manner that creates a space for working on your heart is not uncommon. Doing laundry can just result in clean clothes, or, when done with your heart-mind, it can also heal. Gyokko Sensei describes how she learned about how heart-mind helps. "Kōbō Daishi taught me that with Kanzeon you see the world—not through the eyes, but through the heart-mind. Listen not with your ears, but with your heart-mind. Then, everything will appear differently. Look deep from the heart-mind."[78] She went on to explain how perceiving through your heart-mind enables you to understand the relationship of things that do not occur in a "linear cause and effect" mode.[79] This more expansive and complex perspective of the heart-mind enables you to make connections and understand things from a wider angle. Indeed, Gyokko Sensei understands all things in the universe have a heart-mind. Accordingly, "all things in the universe communicate through heart-mind."[80] Viewing things in this light gives one room to breathe in the open spaces of the universe while making sense of current conditions, and provides the room to explore what actions and responses are most helpful in the context of intimate and cosmic relations.

Maintaining a clean or clear heart-mind is required to perceive through the heart, stresses Tanaka-san. By this, she means to not let things sit and fester or calcify into bitterness in the heart-mind.[81] She sees that all is born out of the little things in daily life. So, tending to how the heart-mind handles the things that come up in daily life, whether it be a recalcitrant in-law or a jealous neighbor, makes all the difference. She tries to keep her heart cleared so such things have nothing to get stuck on when they pass through. She notes how you can also see the ramification of little things when you keep your heart clear. She holds "this is the only way to improve."[82]

The general society's value placed on working with the heart is not as prominent as it has been in the past, according to these Buddhist elders. Among others, Gyokko Sensei explicitly noted that, especially since World War II, what is accepted as "normal" has changed. Before the scientific paradigm of measured proof became the common currency of "truth," people responded to a world full of things that could not be seen, but only sensed in the heart.[83] For these women, what is important is to act in the most healing mode, which for them does not turn on right or wrong answers. Rather, through her practice, Gyokko Sensei explains, "Buddha teaches discernment. Buddha doesn't give answers. It is very important to have discernment. There are so many things one must decide in a day. Experience is required to gain this strength."[84] Even as times change, a person changes as she gains an ability to discern more clearly and gain more strength. One of the aims common to these women is how to become strong enough to respond to a situation with a positive and realistic perspective. Nagai-san sheds light on her increased ability to interpret her life positively, even as she faces a decline in her health. "The thing I get from going to the nunnery is I must look with bigger eyes. I must find a way to make things work in the context of the fact that I am married with two children. My surgery is also a gift. I must interpret things in this way. If I did not have this injury, then I would still be full of energy and things would be even worse. The house would fall apart. So, I think this [decline of health] must be a gift from Honorable Buddha."[85]

She attributes her new ability to be strong enough to see her poor health as beneficial to the teachings she received from the abbess and the practices she has learned at the nunnery.

Offerings, chanting, bowing, praying, and polishing the heart-mind give the body something to do that facilitates loosening the grip of delusions. The commonality of these ritual practices is that the task is designed to interrupt, stop, and change the flow of thought and surges of emotion by engaging in actions that immediately and concretely direct the body-mind to the deeper values of caring and respecting. Engaging in these daily rituals are the primary practices of domestic Zen.

Offerings literally take the focus off you as you physically give something to another. This act is not only an expression of care for another but also helps extend your own foundation. When focused only on the small self, it is like trying to balance on a pinpoint, which is extra difficult when the winds of change blow or the ground begins to quake beneath. Chanting gives you breathing room to stabilize in the face of unwanted changes and visitors (like cancer). It is not coincidental that chanting requires breath, because physical and metaphorical breath is needed. Bowing with palms pressed together helps you gather and focus your strength. Many feel the same as Honda-san, who explains, "I feel centered when I am in front of the Buddha. My heart becomes calm. I suppose it is that I think the Buddha has power to help, and that is why I feel like I can feel peace there."[86] Even just sitting in front of the Buddha helps you feel safe enough to open up and experience gratitude. Praying helps you focus on what action will help and on what kind of act is most compassionate in a given situation. Each ritualized practice, no matter how brief or informal, helps polish the heart and heals.

The collective experiences of my consociates ranges from facing death through disease, the untimely loss of family members, infertility, and crippling chronic pain. These experiences have given rise to powerful emotional responses including paralytic fear, agonizing heartache, depression, and terror. Yet, that is only one side of the picture. The women carry themselves with calm dignity and display refined aesthetic sensibilities with kind hearts that do not betray their inner suffering. They are quick to notice the everyday beauty around them. Joy is contagious through their smiles. The fact they have descended into one or another kind of hell realm and emerged without cynicism, bitterness, or anger is a heroic achievement. The ritual practices of making offerings, chanting, and praying on a regular basis are the resources that fuel their resilience and strength. Though they appear to be simple rituals, requiring no officiant and done in the privacy of their own crowded homes, these rituals form the framework within which they take these tremendous challenges and weave compelling tapestries that empower themselves and inspire others.

Public Ancestor Rites that Heal

Obon

Obon is a summer ritual to welcome home deceased loved ones.[87] This ritual gives a heightened sense of togetherness unlike any other time of the year. Each family engages with Obon differently, but no one in Japan, even the high-tech and finance industries, are unaffected by it. During this time, many families have a nun or monk come chant sutras at the home altar, even those who might otherwise do little else for their ancestors the rest of the year. From August 13 to 15, businesses are either closed or operating with few employees, for many take leave to be with their extended family during Obon. In an ironic modern twist, people clog the railways to "return home" to the villages and towns where their ancestors lived—even if they were themselves born and raised in a large city like Tokyo—to greet the ancestors who are also "returning home" for a few days. Indeed, some people still engage in the tradition of placing at the home altar mounts on which ancestors can return. For those who return quickly, there are cucumber horses with corn silk tails and for those who

Obon offerings at home altar. Cucumber horse and eggplant cow mounts for ancestors to "ride" home on. Individual tea and rice-cake snack offerings.

return slowly, cows made of eggplants with chopstick legs and a stub of chopstick for the tail are provided.

In Kawasaki-san's home, they even boil thick *udon* noodles and wrap three around the middle of the mounts (like a saddle), to represent the river the ancestors have to cross to get back.[88] The river is the Sanzu no Kawa, akin to the River Styx. Kawasaki-san offers the details of her family's ways, which are more extensive than most engage in today, especially in an urban area.

> When we enter August, we go to the family plot, before the twelfth. All gather together and clean the gravestone and offer flowers and do the *o-segaki* memorial rite. We don't go back to the gravestone until the fall for the Ohigan memorial rite. When I was a child, I heard that Ohigan is when Honorable Buddha opens these large doors so that no matter how deeply someone has fallen into hell he can be saved. The lid to hell is shut except at this time. So ancestors at this time can be helped and everyone is happy. It is done twice a year, in the spring, too.

On the morning of the thirteenth, we clean and beautify the home altar. Then we bring the mortuary tablet with the person's posthumous Buddhist name forward. We set out the special plates and chopsticks made of a certain wood for the ancestors. We place the *o-dango* (spherical rice cakes) to welcome them. Water and tea are also placed in front of each ancestor's mortuary tablets to welcome them. In the case of our home, we have a Sōtō Zen nun come and chant the Obon Tanagyō.

We really look forward to the ancestors coming. It feels more lively when they are here. There is no sense of sadness. It's a nostalgic sense. During the first Obon (*hatsubon*) for Grandpa, when we lit the welcoming flame, there were two praying mantises on the bushes. One was thin and long, and the other had a big body. We laughed as a family and said although they are insects, these are Grandma and Grandpa! We don't feel sad. It is more like we feel nostalgic and happy to welcome them.[89]

On the eve of the thirteenth, a few of the women still engage in the practice of burning the welcome home fire (*mukaebi*). Most people just place a store-bought lantern or two by the home altar to light the way home. Kawasaki-san continues her explanation of what her family does.

In the evening, the whole family gathers and we light the welcoming flame. We burn three pieces of pine. We also burn little wood strips to make it easy to burn. Since pine has oil, it burns with a flare. We do it at the entrance gate of our home. The ancestors follow the light to come home. They say "I'm home," and we say, "We have been longing to greet you (*Onatsukashiku-gozaimasu*)." [Significantly they do not say "*O-kaerinasai*," which is reserved for greeting those returning home.] We leave the door open and keep incense burning at the home altar. Our family chants one round of the *Heart Sutra*. Then we stand and chant "Namu Amida Butsu" until the wood turns to ash. Then we say, "Welcome! Welcome!" "Please stay for awhile this year, too." My child says, "Come in (*Irasshai*)." [Also a phrase only used for guests.] My husband cleans up the ashes. My child says to them, "Please do as you please." Then I go in to the home altar and ring the bell and say, "Please be at your leisure."[90]

After arriving, the ancestors at Kawasaki-san's home are given dinner at the altar. They have an Obon menu that details what is served at each meal the ancestors will be served, including snacks. The family eats the same meal every year, completing the sensory experience of Obon. Kawasaki-san gives the details.

We have a set menu every year. It is all vegetarian food: kabocha squash, eggplant, and fried tofu. We give rice and tea along with the entree. When we finish eating, we clear their dishes as well, because they are done, too. After we clear the dishes, I put it in the refrigerator and anyone can eat it when they want. We also prepare a plate for ancestors that have no place to go. Mu-enbotoke-sama are Buddhas with no relations to care for them.

After we take the evening meal away, we keep water offered and chant. We fix the things that are served at Obon, such as watermelon and traditional sweetened red bean and sticky rice confection (*o-hagi*). We also serve snacks at 10 a.m. and 3 p.m. At those times, we especially give fun treats to the children who passed away. We eat at the same time. We also give the same to the Mu-enbotoke.

During Obon, I chant the same chants as I do on a regular day [about an hour]. After eating, we chant the *Isshin chōrai*. We place the dishes for the unconnected Buddhas Mu-enbotoke beside the horse (eggplant). The horse is on the edge of the straw mat. We put the Obon lantern out just during the thirteenth through the fifteenth. On the fourteenth, the ancestors are supposed to wake up early and go off somewhere. So you just give seasoned vinegar vegetables and tea. They are so busy they don't have time to eat. Where do they go off to? [said playfully]. Since they have not been here in this world in awhile, they say that they go visiting friends and places. Then when they come back, they have a leisurely dinner. On the fifteenth in the morning, they have the proper miso soup.

On the fifteenth, on the day they return, we take the food that had been offered to the Mu-enbotoke-sama to Nittai-ji temple after wrapping it up in the lotus leaf. When we wrap the leaf up at the end, we put in the chopsticks and plates and everything together.[91]

The final dinner offerings, flowers, mounts, and lotus leaf of the Mu-enbotoke's offerings are then all rolled up in the special straw mat that had served as the base for the Obon offerings. It is tied together very tightly at the ends and more loosely in the middle to make a boat shape. Since it is dark, Kawasaki-san instructs, "the sending off flame is to help the ancestors watch their step on their way back." She affectionately and politely adds, "Please return now (*Dōzo o-kaerikudasai*)."[92] Notably she uses the verb to designate people returning to their home, implying that is where they now belong. The remaining family chants "Namu Amida Butsu" and the *Heart Sutra* as the little "sending off flame" burns out in the aluminum pie plate set on the edge of the front porch. Afterwards, they take the "boat" to a temple that burns them in a bonfire to send them off.

The numbers of people [at the temple] are huge. Before there was a large flame. Now there is a tent and they accept the offerings and you write your name. Then they send them all off together chanting the names.

Before they were burned as they were sent down the river. Now, there are too many people. Before we walked and took our own lantern and lit the candle. We left notes to the ancestors. Now we drive and just light incense once we arrive. Nittai-ji temple has a lantern lit already. You light three incense sticks. Of the three incenses, one is for the ancestors, one is for our home's Buddha here, and one is for Sakyamuni. I might be wrong.

Then we eat shaved ice and drink a favored carbonated beverage (ramune) in the place set up for people to rest and have refreshments.

The feeling we have when we send them off at Nittai-ji is, "Please come again next year. Please protect us. We will get along harmoniously, so please be at peace." Instead of feeling sad, I feel that I am grateful that I was able to greet them with health. It is not much of a feeling of sadness. I have heard that those who have lost children or suddenly lost a spouse have difficulty when sending them off. In the case of our family, we are all calm because they went when they should go.

At Obon, I feel affection and warmth about the ancestors being close. At Ohigan, I am grateful for being able to do the memorial ritual for them. I feel refreshed. I feel good about myself for having been able to do the memorial ritual for them. I feel purified.

In contrast to my daily life where I think of myself most and there are things I haven't become aware of yet and still need to learn, I feel grateful for what my ancestors have given, so it is nice to do something for them through this memorial ritual.[93]

Children who grow up interacting with their grandparents as personal Buddhas find it natural to welcome them at Obon. Kawasaki-san was clearly moved her young child could still have a relationship with her grandmother. "My child drew this picture of a watermelon at nursery school and asked that it be offered to grandma at Obon. She also drew a cartoon of tea and other offerings at Obon with the caption, 'Welcome. You have honored us by arriving. Also, please protect us so things like fires, earthquakes, and lightning don't happen. Namu Amida Buddha. Nenpi Kannon Riki.'"[94] As a preschooler, she already has a sense that her ancestors protect her from harm.

Honda-san also grew up with these rituals in her home. As an adult, she recognizes how the Obon rituals have affected her perception of death.

Interacting through various rituals with family members who have passed on have clearly helped her reach this peace with death.

> I do ancestor commemoration rites with a sense of nostalgia. My father, grandfather, mother, and, many years later, my grandmother passed away. I have naturally lost my fear of death. I think that when I lose my life I will be able to see them over there. This saves me psychologically, even when I am in front of the Buddha. Obon is a time when it feels like I can talk with my ancestors. They feel very close. I can stand in front of the family grave and say, "I have returned." I also add that since I might join them in this grave, "Be good to me." The dark feeling has gone away compared to the past. I can go to Kōrin-ji Temple or the grave with a light feeling, with a sense of happiness that I will meet them, that I can thank them. I go to [the grave] on Obon (August) and for the vernal and autumnal equinox ritual of Ohigan every year. Sometimes I go on the monthly anniversary. I go [to the grave at least] four times a year. I want to have my own way of commemorating my ancestors. I used to just think of my mother at such events, but now I think of everyone.[95]

Her calmness over the deaths of a number of her family members is evident. The intimacy of being able to speak casually about joining them is notable, as is her sense of joy in interacting with them. It is also clear the rituals are the vehicle for this intimacy. Obon is a core ritual in domestic Zen, yet each person develops her own way of honoring ancestors.

Obon is not only a time to have the ancestors home for meals—it is also a season in which most people go to the family grave site and clean it extra well and make enhanced offerings. Engaging in these rituals at a time when many families throughout the country do so heals in a different way than the monthly grave visits do. There is a deepened awareness everyone is in this together. Everyone will die. This awareness is not done with a foreboding, but with a matter-of-factness that many find calming. Obon rituals are distinctive in that some are performed publically and others are performed privately. Rituals performed in concert with others have their own place in the healing experience of these women. Research has shown having witnesses affects the outcome of an act, for group rituals engage people in a broader community.[96]

Jizō Nagashi

In contrast to the nationally recognized and widely practiced public ritual of Obon, the other public ritual I will discuss is practiced by a more specific group of people. The annual, day-long Jizō Nagashi is a poignant rite currently performed only by Sōtō Zen nuns. Depending on the relationship of the participant in the ritual to the deceased, it can be experienced as a memorial rite, ancestral rite, or both. It is distinctive because participants ride in a large boat on a lake.

Jizō is an enlightened being (a bodhisattva) who guides people in the different realms of existence. The historical context for the origins of this ritual is unknown even to the abbess of the main Sōtō Zen nunnery (Aichi Senmon nunnery), who leads the ritual. She does know the nunnery started doing the ritual after World War II. She started doing it when she was fifteen years old, in 1948.[97] Historical origins are not the focus of concern for the women who lead and participate in this ritual. What matters is people can experience this unique form of memorial rite, which takes place partially in a boat in the middle of a large lake. They have woven it into the array of ceremonies that help people live with loss, a critical dimension of the nuns' practice, and of vital interest to lay participants. Refining the art of living with loss is not a uniquely Zen concern, for such concerns cannot be contained within conceptual and institutional sectarian boundaries. Life—and surely death—defy such categorization. Many laywomen who engage in this ritual do not indicate a loyalty to Sōtō Zen. Many I interviewed actually are formally affiliated with another Buddhist sect. Why do they join in this extensive daylong ritual? Is there anything Zen about it, other than the fact that Zen nuns lead and organize the ritual?

The ritual is done on July 7 every year. Although participants readily recognize its beauty and power, it is not a common ritual. Usually about 450 women participate, along with a few men. Fourteen chartered buses are typically needed for transporting them all. Buses numbered four and nine are not included, however, for these numbers have homonyms that mean "death" and "suffering," respectively. People from the greater Nagoya area ride in these luxury buses that are carefully calculated to arrive simultaneously at the designated temple and lake where the formal parts of the ritual occur. Some years they go to Lake Biwa and others to Lake Hamana. It is a one-day mini-pilgrimage. Communitas is fostered by treats passed around the bus along with stories of new aches and pains, new babies, and recent deaths.

The formal ritual is divided into two main parts. The first part is held in a Sōtō Zen temple. The focus of this aspect of the ritual is the reciting of posthumous Buddhist names. When one registers to participate in the ritual, the names of the dead that one would like to be remembered during the ritual are requested. The nuns then write each name with brush and ink onto a wooden tablet. In July, it is always hot and humid, yet the laity sit in tight formation around the center of the worship hall. The silence as Aoyama Rōshi makes the incense offering conceals the presence of more than 450 people. After chanting and ceremonial music of cymbals and bells, each nun receives a stack of the tablets. Raising one tablet at a time to the forehead in a gesture of respect for the Buddha represented, they intone each name, some voices loud, others soft, all overlapping.

Although it is a group activity, as the nuns chant each individual deceased's name, the women with whom I collaborated expressed they heard the calling of the name in their hearts in a way that made the dead feel present. Furthermore, in the context of hearing the name of your loved one chanted among hundreds of others, the connection between your loss and others' loss makes you feel that you are not alone but rather in a community of people living with loss. Being part of a community of grievers is healing, because it makes it clear you are not singled out in your pain. Death is a condition of life.

The second part of the ritual takes place at a lake with all participants riding on a large boat chanting and singing Buddhist hymns. Jizō Bosatsu's sacred phrase (*shingon*) is chanted quietly: *onkakakabisanmanesowaka*, over and over. The chant is like the musical ground over which the melancholy melodies of the pilgrimage songs ride. The beauty of the natural setting and the mixing of the sounds of chanting, singing, and the wind are conducive to experiencing a blurring of the realms of living and dead. This is a grieving ritual where people feel the connections between themselves, lost loved ones, and the natural world. Upon boarding the boat, each person is handed seven slips of rice paper about three inches by one and a half inches, with an image of Jizō Bosatsu stamped in red.[98] After the boat has reached the center of the lake, each person finds a place—whether among close friends or off to a quiet corner—to send off the slips. With mournful melodies as accompaniment, each slip is raised to the forehead before it is let go on its journey to flutter in the breeze and swirl into the lake. When the rice-paper Jizōs that symbolize a lost loved one dissolve into the water, the women experience a visceral sense of interrelatedness. In other words, in death you are transformed and liberated into the universe that supports all. In this moment, many people experience a keen awareness that one and all are what constitute the universe.

Sōtō women implicitly connect the experience of this ritual with Dōgen's insight into the primacy of Buddha nature. It is a conduit for people to experience their own Buddha nature as they recognize the rice-paper Jizō image as an expression of universal Buddha nature. It dissolves into the water—another expression of Buddha nature—as a poignant expression of their deceased loved one: a Buddha unencumbered by a body as it swirls, floats, and suffuses the beautiful interrelated expanse of the universe. Even though there is no evidence that Dōgen performed this ritual, the nuns perform it because they know intuitively it helps people experience his teachings, especially to know viscerally that all existents—yourself, your deceased loved ones, the deceased loved ones of others, and those living all around—are all Buddha nature. Such an experience is the pinnacle of healing in the Sōtō Zen Buddhist context.

The Jizō Nagashi ancestral rite brings those living with loss together as a community. It affirms the lives of the living as it honors the lives of the dead. In that affirmation, the ancestral rite functions as a healing rite. Publicly honoring your personal Buddha in a community ritual is part of the healing activity of many of these women. Healing or experiencing your Buddha nature is not the purported purpose for the ritual. It is formally a memorial ritual. Yet, in honoring the deceased, the living can experience their interrelatedness with all things—in other words, they can experience their Buddha nature. They are not usually cognizant of this in a cerebral manner, but their bodies understand. Intellectual understanding of interrelatedness does not heal. It is only when interrelatedness is experienced that it can heal. The most intimate healers are dead loved ones, personal Buddhas who know you best and who are with you everywhere all the time, no longer restricted by the forces of gravity or the limitations of space and time. What enables healing is to cut out the delusion that you are an isolated, independent entity. This healing is actualized in the Jizō Nagashi.

No One Is Alone

Rituals in the home, at a temple, and on a lake offer a glimpse of the way in which the living interact with the dead in a manner that helps the living heal from their loss. Ancestral rites function as healing rites for all twelve of my consociates. Indeed, in their healing paradigm, several rituals are employed that are not usually recognized as healing rites. It is only in seeing how a ritual is used and how it affects someone in the context of her life story that the healing power of numerous rites becomes visible.

On the surface, funerary and memorial rituals mark the passing of time. Yet, when these rituals help people heal, they do not engage in a linear concept of time. Healing happens in the present moment, a concept of present that is not flanked by the past and the future. It is a present moment so full that nothing else exists but what is occurring in the moment. As funerary and memorial rituals facilitate this experience of time, conventional divisions of life and death make no sense. It is not a denial of reality. It is experiencing reality as healing. It is awareness of the vastness of space-time and a vision of intricate interconnections that make up the universe.

This expansive perspective often generates gratitude and a peace with the vicissitudes of life. Death helped Honda-san gain a larger perspective on how to live. "I think the reason I don't panic about life and things is having seen my mother's death. I realized there is nothing to gain from making undue distress."[99] The fundamental assumption is she thinks she is not living an independent life based solely on her own power and effort. She, like the other women, see they are alive because the myriad interconnections in the universe work together to generate and support life and death.

Death is not some distant and abstract phenomenon. Gyokko Sensei even laughs at how she has reached an age where she jokes with her siblings and friends about "who will die first." She is also more interested in what she calls "*kokoro no furusato*" or, less poignant in American English, "hometown of the heart-mind." She says you need to prepare for your own death. She even had a formal photo made in anticipation of it being put on the home altar.[100] It's as if she is looking forward to helping others more freely when she, too, can become a personal Buddha. This is healing of the highest order.

Rituals in honor of their dead facilitate expansive awareness, for there is an intimacy found in their relationship to the dead who are now "Hotoke-sama" (personal Buddhas). The various ancestral rituals unleash the healing power of their "own" Buddhas by creating an experience of direct interrelatedness with everything in the universe. That is why they say, "I am in humble and grateful receipt of healing [by the universe]" in the gratitude tense (*iyasaremashita*) and not in the "lonely" form of "I am healed" (*iyashita*).

Funerary and mortuary rituals help these women experience healing: the rituals are designed to reveal how death dissolves the distinctions that delude many into seeing themselves and others as separate entities. At first, it seemed counterintuitive that Kakuzen Rōshi taught death is a powerful perspective from which to begin healing. Having worked with these women, I began to understand more deeply the rituals of death. I finally understood what he meant. Feeling safe with death unleashes the bonds of fear that entraps one in delusions, desires, and suffering. The rituals involving personal Buddhas illuminate the reality that, even in death, no one is alone. This is healing.

CHAPTER 4

Domestic Zen
Living Esoteric Wisdom

Medicine and sickness cure each other, and the entire earth is medicine. What is the self?

"*Hekiganroku:* Case Eighty-seven," translated by Stephen Addiss

Zen in the daily life of a family is creative and flexible. Unlike its monastic counterpart, which thrives on control, discipline, and impeccable cleanliness, domestic Zen is at home with the chaotic, emotional, and messy lives of people struggling with their families, health, and jobs. This sphere of Zen has not received much scholarly attention. One reason is researchers can gain relatively ready access to Zen texts and many monastic institutions, while the practices performed by individuals and families in their homes are, by their very nature, hidden from public view. Vulnerability reveals this hidden side of Sōtō Zen, the nonpublic spaces where most people dwell. Moreover, domestic Zen practices are transmitted orally through largely informal networks of personal relationships. Thus, they are not recorded in the written documents Buddhist scholars typically examine. As a result, the private Zen observances performed in the home have largely escaped scholarly notice.

The contours of domestic Zen as experienced and created by my consociates comes out of the Japanese cultural milieu where aesthetic preferences, an intimate sense of connection to natural phenomena, and the concept of relational self are woven together in a distinct manner. It is difficult to ascertain how much is Buddhist influence, because "religion" and "culture" are not indigenous Japanese concepts and, hence, their boundaries are indistinct, especially after fifteen centuries of all manner of interaction. Among cultures, though, it is clear Japanese culture falls along the spectrum of those that are more highly ritualized. This dimension of Japanese culture lays the foundation for the dynamics and sensibilities of domestic Zen. Daily activities are performed with a level of importance also found in explicitly recognized religious practices. This is unsurprising in a Zen context, for Aoyama Rōshi teaches, "Religion is daily life."[1] Without bifurcating "sacred" and "profane" realms, as is found in several other cultures, concrete everyday activities are ultimate.[2] Therefore, cleaning floors and cooking food can be done as supreme acts of importance. With this context, meaning is abundant in daily life.

Highlighting the activities and experiences of women takes us to the core of domestic Zen: often women are the center of the family, especially when it comes to daily life tasks, crises, healing, and ritual practices. Their practices draw on several sources and traditions due to the nature of Buddhism in the home versus in the monastery. In a monastery there are relatively regular schedules and predictable events, because the monastery intentionally minimizes outside influence in order to maintain its function for monastic training and practice, whereas in a family unanticipated events arise because family members are engaged with various people and entities outside the family. The women, in responding to the needs of their families, must be flexible and creative. Therefore, domestic Zen is inherently less formal and codified than monastic Zen. The practices the women adopt or create are based on the necessities of their lives and do not reflect a concern for observing or maintaining the doctrinal and institutional boundaries of Zen or even of Mahayana Buddhism. It is natural that Zen in a domestic context includes rituals and practices from a spectrum of sources. Women's ingenuity is evident in the fact these practices are rarely dictated from above. Since all are Buddha nature in a Sōtō Zen context, no institutional qualifications are required to create rituals. In fact, homemade rituals are some of the most effective.

Many of the practices and rituals are not even explicitly aimed at healing. Therefore, examining the intent of the ritual vis-à-vis the performer of the ritual is not a fruitful way to explore the efficacy of these rituals. Understanding the cosmology of the ritual, however, is illuminating. In the Buddhist context, there is no linear relationship of cause and effect. With everything interrelated, a linear line of influence is impossible. Hence, an explicit healing ritual is almost nonsensical from a Buddhist frame of reference. Yet, employing the category of healing ritual helps us see dynamics that are central to the women who engage in and create domestic Zen.

Domestic Zen is based on Dōgen's teaching that "practice is enlighten-ment." Ritualized behaviors in Sōtō Zen are practices. For example, when you cut carrots without waste, you are enlightened. In other words, practice is ritualized activity done in accord with wisdom and compassion.

Some of the rituals included in their domestic healing activities are known but have not been examined in this light. Others I describe here have not previously been documented. Embodied engagement with these rituals provided me with a chance to see what rituals people participate in, but em-bodied engagement in rituals alone did not yield understanding of what the rituals mean in the context of family life. Intensive and extended conversa-tions spanning hundreds of hours provided crucial insight into the ways rit-ual practices help women cope with the vicissitudes of their lives.

Most of the information comes from stories told over cups of tea. Nel Noddings agrees that, "stories are powerful research tools. They provide us with a picture of real people in real situations, struggling with real problems. They banish the indifference, often generated by samples, treatments, and faceless subjects."[3] The information I received is not drawn from teachings and practices delineated in scriptures or sectarian documents. The informa-tion is raw. Even as it is embedded in the specificities of a particular context and time, often the vulnerabilities, anxieties, fears, and hopes tap into human emotions and concerns that are more generally experienced.

My consociates' stories are rare because these women have lived through a period of rapid change in Japanese culture. I saw this as an op-portunity to hear their experiences before the wisdom embedded in their lives is no longer at hand. I have deliberately chosen to focus on these posi-tive experiences with healing. This research fits into the stream of research that studies positive dimensions and dynamics, such as those explored in positive psychology[4] and studies on "resilience in the face of adversity."[5] An examination of the positive aspects is a choice to focus on the "ritual masters" of the Zen Buddhist home to learn what they do. It is an exami-nation of what the women chose to share with me about their healing ex-periences and practices.

Rituals of Daily Life

The needs and limitations of daily living have given rise to a complex array of activities my female consociates have creatively included in their prac-tices. In seeking answers to their problems, they found solutions in ritual practice. These women did not merely find solutions to just get through a crisis, but, on the whole, found power and beauty in living out their daily lives. Each woman has her own distinctive combination of ritual practices. Some are explicitly recognized as conventional Zen practices and others go beyond institutional Zen boundaries.

In addition to Zen Buddhist practices, the larger Japanese cultural context needs to be kept in mind to understand how ritualizing daily activities is a "logical" and "natural" focus for these Japanese Buddhist women. Boyd and Williams stress how "ritual reveals our activities to be comprehensible."[6] In other words, ritualizing daily activities like cooking, cleaning, and hanging laundry is an indication that mundane and necessary activities are highly valued with a significance beyond the literal benefit of nutrition and cleanliness. These activities help orient the women. Ritualizing daily actions helps them integrate multiple emotions and worries into their lives. In a sense, it tames them or "normalizes" them by associating them with the familiar, concrete, and positive elements of their lives. "It is by means of ritual that we seek to provide for ourselves an integrating vision so that we can see particular activities and conflicting demands as aspects of a harmonious whole which is our 'form of life.'"[7]

Kawasaki-san was looking for guidance in seeing meaning in common daily activities. She found Sōtō Zen helped her more than any other religious tradition with which she was familiar or engaged. In particular, the teachings of Aoyama Rōshi gave her a way to find the meaning she sought. "Her teachings are so wonderful! It is not about miracles, but daily life. When something happens in your life, you can't rely on miracles. Tōdai-ji temple is all about the things you can't see with your eyes—the unusual power and mystery of miracles. Aoyama Sensei is about being in this, receiving this, about how people to people relate well. To live in gratitude (*ikasareteiru*) is the base. *How* to live is stressed."[8]

Kawasaki-san had religious experiences that are associated with esoteric Buddhist practices, but these logic-defying events did not address all her concerns and needs. She wanted a way to live with daily challenges and be nourished by them, not overwhelmed. Seeing all events as integral facets of her life enabled her to feel an energizing life force course through her common activities and concerns. Kawasaki-san says,

> It is only Aoyama Sensei that teaches more about how to live your life. It's in the hearing of the teachings and then noticing things in daily life while raising children or cooking and then realizing what the teachings meant. And

then hearing more teachings and seeing how they are a part of your life, repeating this over and over, noticing and becoming more aware of things bit
by bit. This is how a home-dweller [layperson] learns. This is what and how
she teaches. While doing work, while living in the child's world, teaching
with this context is what is helpful.[9]

Sōtō Zen is particularly conducive to a home-dweller's practice because
a pragmatic impulse courses through domestic Zen. It stresses doing basic,
necessary tasks. The approach does not bifurcate mind and body, so polishing the floor polishes the heart. In this mode, doing daily chores is religious
practice.

Everyday things, however, are not all pleasant and routine. Scary things
come up, like a cancer diagnosis, deaths of loved ones, serious injuries, and
lost dreams. Ritual enables you to respond to these more-intense events by
giving you a controlled, predictable, and safe space to face dangerous things
and wield powerful forces like actualizing Buddha nature, speaking with
the dead, and ingesting substances that yield results beyond reason. Engaging in rituals when lost or confused can help you see more clearly what course
of action or thought is best. A ritualized activity can also function like a mirror that reflects how you are doing, whether you are apathetic, guarded,
scared, or in harmony with the deepest dimensions of your condition.

One of the main findings of my study is the joy and peace women attain in their daily lives through ritual practices. Rituals serve as conduits
for keeping them in touch with the interrelated nature of existence and
provide a foundation of stability and clarity that enables them to experience joy, even in the midst of constant change. One of the women, Gyokko
Sensei, says she engages in numerous ritual practices to help her accomplish her ideal that all should be done with a heart-mind of "lightly,
lightly" (*sararisarari*) with a sense of things flowing along and not getting
snagged on resistance, resentment, past disappointments, fears, or even hopes
for the future.[10] Her approach corresponds with the medical concept of
allostasis, or "stability through change," which "promotes adaptation."[11] In
Gyokko Sensei's effort to let things flow, she is in constant motion to find
balance in all circumstances. She gains stability by making adjustments to
her emotional responses and physical needs. When her knees hurt, she
walks slower. When her anger is aroused, she breathes deeper. When her
fears are triggered, she chants the *Heart Sutra*. In so doing, she lives in the
moment and maintains enough clarity to not lose sight of what is important, even as troubles arise.[12]

Indeed, there is a vast array of rituals women have found effective in helping them deal with life's most challenging events. In such moments, the womens' questions are far from *kōans* (questions designed to awaken nondualistic insight into the nature of ultimate reality) such as, "Does a dog have Buddha nature?" The women cry out questions directly from the messiness and misery of their intense situations. In their homes, they report that rituals help them when they serve on the frontlines of depression, dementia, and death.

The following six real-life situations include a range of rituals and practices my consociates employed as they faced difficulties. Their bravery is tremendous, as exemplified by their willingness to submit their vulnerabilities and pain to academic scrutiny. I applied critical analysis to uncover the women's thinking patterns and to explore the dynamics of their practices. These women stress how these practices empower them, so, accordingly, my study highlights the ways in which these rituals have been effective in their lives. The vignettes from Zen Buddhist women's lives are framed as a response to six questions that illuminate dynamics and details of domestic Zen.

Ingesting Healing Power

What nourishes in a "domestic Zen" kitchen?

I had no idea such a practice existed in the relatively tame, refined, and reasoned quality characteristic of most Japanese Buddhist rituals with which I was familiar. Had I heard Gyokko Sensei correctly? Did she really tell me to eat the syllable printed on rice paper? At least the paper is made of rice, I thought, making it a bit more palatable. It tasted like incense! What had I expected? The paper had been imprinted with the *bonji* (syllables) mandala, purportedly carved by Kūkai, the ninth-century Shingon master and pan-Japanese Buddhist leader. No less, the ink used was made out of water drawn from a well and consecrated in the Mizu Tori ritual. I had stood out in the cold midnight air watching the observable parts of the solemn ritual to draw the water that had flowed from a sacred spring many miles away. This ritual has been performed every year for more than 1,200 years. The rubbings of the mandala of syllables had been on the altar in the Nigatsudō of Tōdai-ji temple for the Mizu Tori ritual. After two weeks of nonstop incense burning, it is no wonder they tasted like incense. I did not even know what the syllables meant. It was clearly not about the meaning of the written word.

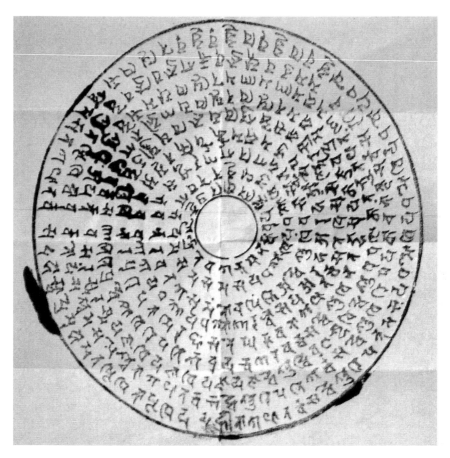

Bonji mandala

Nobody I asked could read the syllables, called *bonji*. They were powerful Sanskrit-based seed syllables (*siddhams*), and reflect a root connection to Indian Buddhism. It was all about the meaning invested in the word, the history of its making, and the rituals that attend it. On several occasions, to calm my worried heart, Gyokko Sensei told me I must rip one syllable off and ingest it with a heart focused on wisdom and compassion. I was then to chant the *Heart Sutra*. She said the course of action in accord with wisdom and compassion would become clear. She was right.

My inauguration into the healing balms a Zen kitchen can cook up was eye opening. I had never really considered the full range of possibilities. In addition to the syllables on rice paper, sacred Mizu Tori water, Kannon medicine, special approaches to cooking, and a host of teas are on the menu. Three of the ingestion-based practices actually come out of Tōdai-ji temple. The women do not even comment on how they just move freely among different sects' practices. Once I directly asked Kawasaki-san about where Tōdai-ji fits in, and she explained, "Tōdai-ji is everything. It is now called Kegon, but all sects are included."[13] After reflecting awhile, she offered, "I don't know much about the history. All I do is humbly receive the benefits and say thank you! [Laughter.] It's about 1,200 years old. When people do the ritual, it is for family health and domestic safety."[14]

Practitioners of Tōdai-ji-based teachings are quite engaged with the mystical dimension of Buddhism. There is a lot of talk about spirits—direct communication with Buddhas, bodhisattvas, ancestors, trees, flowers, dolls, and animals. The types of teachings offered through this communication ranges from things like Fudō Myōō (Buddhist god of fire) teaching a woman how to wash windows more efficiently, to Kannon (Buddhist goddess of compassion) explaining how to deal with intense family conflict.

The practice of ingesting *bonji* syllables was the biggest surprise.[15] I had not known there was such a practice in Japan. Each *bonji* syllable contains the seed of a particular energy understood to be embedded in the image. Kūkai, early ninth-century founder of *Shingon* esoteric Buddhism in Japan, brought them to Japan. The women who engage in the practice of ingesting the syllables believe that Kūkai is the one who carved the *bonji* syllables into a mandala now held within the Tōdai-ji temple complex at the Nigatsudō temple where Kannon is enshrined. The *bonji* mandala is formally called Sonshōdarani. More than four hundred *bonji* syllables form concentric circles making up the sacred image. A limited number of rubbings of the purportedly 1,200-year-old woodcarving are made each year in conjunction with the annual Mizu Tori (*mizu* means "water," *tori* means "to take") rite held in the spring. The sacred water drawn during the ritual is used to make the ink with which the images are pressed on rice paper. Many scriptures are chanted to endow the rubbings of the *bonji* syllables with mystical dharmic power (*hihō*).

Two women enthusiastically shared the details of how they ingest *bonji* syllables. They explained how you swallow one when you are very sick or very troubled by some problem. Gyokko Sensei demonstrated as she said, "I rip them up this way."[16] The ritualized paper is so precious that Kawasaki-san said that with several in her family, they sometimes even just take the parts of the paper without a *bonji* syllable. They do not want to waste it, and they figure that the paper was consecrated in the same way. It is better than nothing when the situation is not dire. Sometimes you just swallow one, or sometimes you ingest one a day for several days, depending on the seriousness of the issue. They claim this has helped them heal from physical illnesses, reduce pain, and clarify emotional problems. Gyokko Sensei told me, with a sense of warning, that she doesn't "take it unless I am 'told' to do it by Hotoke-sama (Honorable Buddha)."[17]

In March of 1999, these two consociates with deep connections to both Sōtō Zen and Kegon Buddhism invited me to attend the Mizu Tori ritual at Nigatsudō of Tōdai-ji. Not only was it a rare opportunity for me, it was even a rare event for them. Tōdai-ji is widely considered the most important temple to the nation, and ten thousand people regularly attend. A man close to the head (kanchō) of Tōdai-ji was our host, so we were able to walk past the throngs of people—most just hoping to catch a glimpse from a distance—directly to the base of the temple. We were showered by the flying sparks of fire as the monks ran along the perimeter of the raised temple with huge wands designed to purify. It was the last night of the ritual, so there was extra intensity in the air. People were actually aiming to have a spark land on them. There were plenty to go around. Many commented how it was surprising no one was hurt by any of the sparks, adding to the mystery of the moment. The climax of the ritual, the drawing of water from the sacred well, occurred at 2:00 a.m. We were escorted into a tight space where we could view the monks chanting inside Nigatsudō. Through the lattice, we could see the sincerity on their faces, thinned and polished from the austerity of the ritual—fasting with little rest. Cramped in the tiny dark space it could have been any century over the past millennium or more. The ritualized "physical language" dictates the motions must be extremely slow to display the appropriate level of respect.

Water purified and consecrated in the Mizu Tori is another ritualized element that supports healing. One of the ways the water helps healing is by being offered to Kannon, since she helps others heal.

> The Mizu Tori water is offered to Kannon-sama. It is given for Kannon-sama to drink once a year. Kannon does the work of the Daibutsu [Great Buddha in the main hall of Tōdai-ji, Dainichi Nyorai/Mahavairocana Buddha]. She hears the prayers of people. Kannon is like a part of the Daibutsu, not a separate being. It is not just the size of the statue. It is the sense of being expansive. It always seems like the Daibutsu is present, no matter where. It is so big—not the statue size. It is the power of the Dharma. I get giddy and happy (waku-waku) when I get close to the Daibutsu Great Buddha.[18]

The temple also lets people give donations to receive a small bottle of the water drawn at the ritual. It is really just a few drops of the sacred water added to a small vial of regular water. Nonetheless, it is treated as a precious fluid that gives access to the power of Kannon, the Great Buddha, and, in turn, the Dharma of the cosmos. Once I was given the opportunity to ask a priest who has been one of the few to perform the ritual in Nigatsu-dō about the powers of this water. He jumped up and got a plastic water bottle. He found another empty water bottle and proceeded to pour half of the water into it. Perfunctorily he handed it to me. He explained how at the end of the ritual, each of the priests receives a bottle of the water that has been mixed with water used in this ritual for more than 1,200 years, making it exponentially more potent than the vials available to the general public. The lack of attachment to such a rare Buddhist treasure was stunning. The display of the Buddhist virtue of generosity was in itself healing.

The ingredients for health include water deemed empowered with the compassion of Kannon. The compassion is instilled through the fasting, chanting, and prayers of the priests. Kawasaki-san said she "started doing the Mizu Tori for family safety and health about thirty years ago, maybe more."[19] No studies cite statistics on this practice, but these women do not rely on statistics to decide which practices to do. They rely on personal results. Gyokko Sensei explains, "You only need a little of the Mizu Tori water, because, after all, it is a matter of vital energy (*ki no mon*). You take it when you don't feel well. It really works."[20] Kawasaki-san explained to me how her family ingests the water. "We drink it in the kitchen. We put a little in a cup. Or I put a little when cooking the rice we all eat. Just one drop at a time. The drop contains the prayers. If someone has a cold, I put it in their tea."[21] If she burns herself or has a headache, she drinks a drop in her tea. She clarifies, "You do not put it on the spot that hurts. You drink it."[22] These are examples of how the kitchen is part of the "sacred" space in domestic Zen. The analgesic powers of Mizu Tori water is also legendary. "When Grandpa was old and hurt all over because he was injured in the war, the doctor said that there was nothing more he could do. There was no medicine to take the pain away. I asked him if he wanted some of 'the' water. So, he had it about three or four times, and the pain went away. He died without pain. He would tell people who came he did not have pain."[23]

She goes on to reiterate another time she was surprised how effective the water was. As she explains, it is clear she is amazed at the efficacy. It indicates she does not consider faith in the healing power of the water as the reason it works. "I cut my foot and it got infected. I drank, saying 'Namu

Amida Butsu.' It never hurt. I had to go get intravenous fluids on an out-patient basis for a couple months. When once I saw the actual cut, I was shocked at the raggedness of the cut. But I never felt pain. I drank one drop in my tea on days when there was to be some treatment. I took a drop saying, 'Please give me favor' (onegaishimasu). It never hurt."[24]

Adding a chant while drinking the compassion-empowered water can help with acute pain.[25] Humbly asking for the water's favor also seems to help its efficacy, perhaps by opening your heart and mind to the possibilities that defy straight scientific cause-and-effect verification. In another example that involved a surgery on her son, she explicitly states, "There might be other reasons why these things went so well, but I think it shows how there is more than just your own power at work."[26] Herbert Benson, M.D., found those who had a sense there was something greater than themselves at work had statistically significant improvement on several health measures, including faster recovery, shorter hospital stays, and better health for a longer period after surgery.[27] Studies might be harder to do on practices like Mizu Tori due to their domestic nature, but at this point, the possibility for research is open. Firm conclusions that such things are ineffective cannot be made, especially with numerous accounts to the contrary.

Tōdai-ji's Mizu Tori water does not have a monopoly on healing water. Among other locations in Japan, Yawase Kannon's spring is famous for healing, too. Kitō Sensei took me on a one-day pilgrimage to this site in Inazawa City, Aichi Prefecture. At this site, the water is freely available and there is little ritual involved in procuring it. Usually people first go to pray, facing the figure of Kannon at an opened altar area. Many also often write special prayers on forms available for that purpose. People are known to bring several vessels in order to transport the Kannon water home to friends and family.

Another aspect of Kannon's healing power is the medicine, called Kannon-yū, which has been distributed through Tōdai-ji since the ninth century.[28] It is known to be effective for curing colds, diarrhea, dizziness, and a host of other ailments. As she hands me a packet, Kawasaki-san explains, "Kannon-yū tastes good when you are sick. It's good for the stomach and helps kill the bacteria. It's for fevers or diarrhea. I take Kannon-yū and go to sleep well. Kannon-yū is not so strong."[29]

Umemura-san, a trained dietician, holds that "feeding the heart-mind nutritiously is important."[30] Although no one else used the exact same phrasing as Umemura-san, all the women do things everyday to nourish their heart-mind. Nourishing the heart-mind and nourishing the body are intricately intertwined, and the care is a fundamental part of domestic Zen. What nourishes is different for each woman. Taniguchi-san says she has learned, "You need to love yourself, because you can't depend on the love of another forever."[31] One of the ways she loves herself is to eat three meals a day and walk an hour. The abbess teaches her nuns and laywomen to eat with the awareness that the universe is supporting the meal. She also stresses the purpose of eating is to help all.[32] Honda-san does treat eating in this way. "Eating is the most important thing. I try to get a good balance."[33]

Morning is a ripe time for ritualized actions. Embedded in daily activities like greetings and cooking, they help a person stay aware that they are supported. No task is seen as "mundane." Knowing you are supported helps buoy energy, which is critical for maintaining a clear perspective. Gyokko Sensei shares what she does: "I was taught you should start each day with saying 'Good Morning' to Jizō or Kannon-sama, just as if they were a person. Since I worked, I was sleepy one morning when I was making breakfast, and I dropped something. It woke me up. I heard a voice say, 'That's OK!' I looked around to see who was talking, and that's when I realized that Buddha has a sense of humor. Buddha taught me humor is necessary for human life."[34]

Eating is a way that can help people feel more connected to the earth and the rhythms of the seasons. Ritual foods are made from the foods in season at the time of the ritual, often made only for that ritual. Special foods made in accord with the ritual calendar imbue those foods with deepened significance. Pausing to prepare and eat white spherical rice-flour cakes (*dango*) makes enjoying the autumnal full moon a special event, helping one feel connected to something even beyond the earth. One of the most graphically ritualized foods is called *toshikoshi soba,* directly translated as Year-Crossing Noodles. The long noodles are eaten with a sense of gratitude that one can cross into the New Year and with a hope for long life. Gyokko Sensei regrets, however, it is harder to feel the specialness of an event these days, because "now you can get any food whenever you want."[35]

Increasing accessibility due to modernization, however, is not all bad. Kawasaki-san is able to go to a local traditional medicine shop (*kampōyaku*) to procure tea usually only available to mountain ascetics (*sennin*) who are known for their miraculous powers. The tea is called *shōjusen.* It is made of red pine needles (*akamatsu*) ground up into a powder. Kawasaki-san explains why she likes it. "It's good for cleaning the blood. Mountain ascetics used to drink this. I had my daughter drink it since she was little. She never stayed home from school because she was sick. She's in high school now."[36] She explained that it helps prevent fevers and colds and helps with heart problems. Some people add it to other teas. All of the other women have their favorite health teas (*kenkōcha*).

Gifts have ensured the writing phase of this project is similarly enriched by an assortment of healthy tea. As per my method to engage in any activity my consociates deem helpful for me to understand their healing paradigm and practices, this book is also fueled by *bonji* syllables, Mizu Tori water, Kannon water, and Kannon-yū. My consociates thus offered a glimpse of the daily activities that help invigorate and sustain families as they face various challenges. The mind and body are inseparable, and these women show us how they respect and care for their hearts, minds, and bodies in potent ways that take place quietly in their kitchens.

Conceiving and Raising Children

What might a Zen Buddhist woman do in order to deal with the trials of conceiving and raising children?

As she had done for more than three decades, after finishing the breakfast dishes, Nogawa-san went to the talisman-adorned and ornately carved Buddhist altar that had been in her [husband's] family for generations to perform her morning ritual of offerings and chanting. She placed a cup of tea in a mug on the altar for her personal Buddhas then lit the candle and a stick of incense. The small room had begun to fill with the aroma of incense when she glanced at the small clock placed between the incense burner and the bell. Noting the time, she called out to her husband to take out the garbage, because they were due to collect it any minute. She then struck the bell and put her hands together in prayer, bowing as she quietly chanted "Namu Amida Butsu" three times. Next, she chanted the *Heart Sutra* from memory. Today she would also chant the whole *Kannon Sutra*, because it was the twentieth anniversary of her having decided to adopt her sister's child as hers [since her sister's family already had several children]. Today is a private anniversary, a chance for Nogawa-san once again to give thanks to her personal Buddhas for assisting her in becoming a mother.

It is not surprising a child was adopted within a family, because this is the pattern of more than half the adoptions in Japan.[37] It is also common that Nogawa-san would have such intense interest in becoming a mother. Mothers are deeply respected in Japanese culture, although one of the reflections on motherhood I heard was particularly unanticipated. Aoyama Rōshi, a spiritual teacher of Nogawa-san, said she thinks "women are designed to be mothers."[38] Her explanation of what being a "mother" means is revealing. It is "to care and teach with understanding." She further elaborates that women's bodies have an advantage over men, because women's bodies have wombs, which "are a place of deep peace, pure compassion, a source of life, like the ocean is the womb of earth."[39] The abbess Aoyama Rōshi's definition is expansive and includes all women, not just those who are biological mothers. This is a striking example of how expanding your perspective is healing. It heals all women who live with the social judgment they "should" be mothers and chose not to have children, or those who wanted to become mothers and, for one reason or another, have not.

The abbess continued with another unanticipated view: "Everyone wants to return to the womb. It's instinct to return to your place of birth. Even fish do it. When Dōgen was dying, he returned to Kyoto where he was born. He was returning to his mother."[40] Her last statement was clearly meant as "returning in his heart-mind," because Dōgen's mother passed away when he was a child. That one who has become famous for articulating his penetrating insights into the Dharma in the end is remembered as one who wanted to return to his mother underscores the value Sōtō Zen, especially its female adherents, places on motherhood.

Numerous rituals in the domestic Zen repertoire revolve around the activities of motherhood: conceiving, birthing, raising, educating, protecting, and healing children. It is no wonder, then, that among others, Zen temples that offer ritualized wooden plaques onto which one can write prayers (*ema*) include a steady stream of prayers for a healthy child. Since this is a ritual practiced in public, it is commonly known. Nogawa-san, not constrained by sectarian boundaries, also engaged in the private rituals of ingesting *bonji* syllables and putting drops of Mizu Tori water into her tea. Ingesting such "sacred" substances proves she is not alone in dealing with a difficulty. This calms her so stress does not exacerbate difficulties. Perhaps engaging in such ritual practices helps her relax because, as Driver points out, "ritual brings . . . the not-yet into the here-and-now."[41] Not only are *bonji* syllables efficacious for helping one become a mother as in the adoption case above, but Gyokko Sensei explains how they are also helpful for safe delivery of a baby. Speaking with the authority that comes with experience, she counsels, "People who are pregnant should start taking *bonji* syllables about ten days before birth. The women who took them had smooth births. These have been in use for hundreds of years."[42]

Yamaguchi-san looked me in the eyes. She seemed to be making sure I was listening with my heart-mind. I could tell she wanted to share something she did not talk about much. "I had a miscarriage," slipped quietly off her lips.[43] The gravity of her pain was evident in the fact that at our last meeting a week before she related her agonizing experiences involving the birth of her first child, the birth of the daughter who was soon to be married.

> I didn't attend my father's funeral because I was eight months pregnant. Everyone said I should not go for concern that I might lose the baby. At first, I didn't care. I was so sad. I loved my father, and I thought anything would be OK for the baby. Grandma (*Obāchan*) begged me not to go to the funeral. I had very complex feelings. I wanted to go, even if I miscarried. Then she begged me. She said the people who die will not come back but the baby is just starting. So, I thought, she's right. If I went and I miscarried riding the train, then it would be killing that child. In Japan, they say the eighth month is the most important month. [Japan counts gestation as ten months.] My father died of a car accident. She was worried I would have too much of a shock. It was a sudden death. Those are hard. He was sixty. I cried by myself a lot. My water broke, and I had to be in the hospital for two months. Since my father died, I thought I will do whatever I can to give birth to this child. Being in the hospital that long I saw a lot of things. It became ever more clear to me how precious life is.[44]

Yamaguchi-san has three children, all grown now. Two of the rituals she included with these births were, not surprisingly, for enlisting protection. "I had an amulet (*omamori*) when I was pregnant. It made my heart feel strong. I was happy my friend brought me the one she had when she gave a safe birth. My husband did the calligraphy congratulations/celebration (*kotobuki*) for the cloth wrapped around the lower abdomen (*hara-obi*) of pregnant women. I think it is about how you hold your heart and energy that is the most important."[45] Part of the power she felt from the special amulet for "safe birth" and the especially long white cotton *obi* cloth worn under clothing to help support the life growing inside her womb came from the fact it connected her to people she loved and trusted, helping her heart to feel strong. Even the fact such items exist is testimony to the fact she is not alone in her fears and hopes. She joins countless women who have sought support and connection to a greater power as they clutched a "safe birth" amulet. These ritualized items may seem small, even insignificant in the grand scheme of things. Yet, in ushering in a new human life, they connect women to potent sources of power that help them as they transport a fragile life across the dangerous threshold between the primordial waters of the womb and life with its mysteries, challenges, the possibility of a mother's healing love, and eventual death.

It was not until Gyokko Sensei became a mother herself that she realized she needed healing. It was then she began her earnest practice of chanting the *Heart Sutra*. Gyokko Sensei also ingested *bonji* syllables to help her heal from her childhood experiences of being a "received child." In her case, it was not an adoption within the family. She was given to another family when her father wanted to remarry after his first wife's passing (Gyokko Sensei's birth mother). His new bride made the condition she would marry if the four-year-old child (Gyokko Sensei) was not part of the package. Gyokko Sensei was old enough to remember needing to move away. Although her new parents welcomed her with genuine warmth and she was their first child, Gyokko Sensei said she always felt she had to be on her best behavior. She knew she was different from her siblings. In her late sixties, she is able to say, "I would not have felt so happy if I had not practiced [Buddhist rituals], especially since I was sent to live with another family."[46] Now she says she "feels gratitude."[47] It was her "new" mother—who herself had been raised in a Sōtō Zen temple family—who guided Gyokko Sensei in these healing practices. Gyokko Sensei exudes respect for her mother, and it is clear her life has been profoundly enriched by engaging in the practices her mother taught her.

When dealing with the injury or sickness of a child, among many Japanese Buddhist mothers, one popular short mantra-like chant is from the twenty-fourth chapter of the *Lotus Sutra*. It summons the power of Kannon, the goddess of compassion: "Nenpi Kannon Riki."[48] In times of acute need, like while rushing to the hospital after a child has broken an arm on the playground, or when a high fever has spiked in the middle of the night, chanting this mantra continuously under her breath helps the mother keep her wits about her. The mothers who have done this say it helps them not feel alone or desperate. This then helps them stay focused on what they can do to assist, rather than being distracted by fear and immobilized by a sense of helplessness. Whether Kannon is understood to actually come to the aid of the child or whether just invoking her helps remind a mother she is not alone in the universe is not something the women have tried to clearly distinguish.[49] For them, it does not matter. For them, what matters is it helps them get through difficult times. Raising children is a series of difficult times. Even though children grow and most gain increasing skills that enable the mother to take a step back and breathe, all of the mothers had a story to tell of how they doubted their abilities, worried if they were doing the best thing, and spent a lot of time trying to ensure their child grew up safe.

One of Kawasaki-san's proudest accomplishments is that her son "*never* missed school due to illness."[50] She did everything she could to help him keep his health.

> With my child growing up, I was always saying, "Kannon-sama, please help!" I was always chanting the Kannongyō! I did it more for getting help with things in my actual condition than for my ancestors. In the end, it is something that does help with actual conditions and is for ancestors, so it made me chant it even more fervently. At first, since it is long, I only chanted it when I was given the opportunity during rituals. Now I chant it smoothly.
>
> There were several times my son woke up in the middle of the night with a fever, and when I fervently chanted "Nenpi Kannon Riki" he fell back into a peaceful slumber. In the middle of the night, it happens. In the day, he's out playing cheerfully, and then at a time when there's nothing you can do at 1:00 or 3:00 in the morning he wakes up crying. Whether I understand or not, I just fervently chant. But then it passes without having to go to the doctor.
>
> There are lots of times when there's nothing you can do. The most terrifying time was when he was about four and he was cleaning his ear with a bamboo ear cleaning stick (*mimikaki*). I was thinking it was dangerous, and I warned him to be careful. My husband called for help to carry something heavy, and I went for just a minute, and in that short time he pushed the stick into his ear.
>
> There was a scream. I felt my vital energy (*ki*) collapse. The ear is one of the worst places for pain! I was so scared, I just chanted, "Nenpi Kannon Riki, Nenpi Kannon Riki, Nenpi Kannon Riki." It was late at night, around 9:00, so we took him to the hospital by car. When we arrived, he just jumped out of the car!
>
> Another time he was almost hit by a car. He was about five or six. At that time, it [Nenpi Kannon Riki] helped, too. A woman who sees things that cannot be seen with the eye thought he had been hit, too. But she saw Kannon-sama stand in front of the car to stop it.

The time it takes for children to grow up is full of terrifying moments. It is not a matter of reason. From others' perspective it might look foolish for me to chant, but the reality is he is OK.[51]

Of course Kawasaki-san is not alone with her doubts and fears. Gyokko Sensei tells of a time when her daughter was in kindergarten. The nature of her concerns differed since Gyokko Sensei worked outside the home. "A lotus was blooming in the mud. No one knows what kind of lotus will bloom from the mud. To put it simply, I couldn't do a lot for my children because I worked. The regret lingered. But then I was taught by Buddha [by going with my daughter's school field trip and seeing the lotus blooming in the mud] when the environment is not all good, a lotus will blossom."[52] Mud is a necessary ingredient for bringing out your wisdom and compassion. Therefore, children do better in an environment where there are challenges. This lesson nagged at the heart of this working mother who turned to chanting and listening to the universe's messages.

A child must experience failure to learn and grow strong, yet it requires copious amounts of patience not to interfere with this vital process. Gyokko Sensei sums it up in a pithy statement: "The practice of the parent is to be patient."[53] At such times, imperceptibly chanting your favorite mantra—whether it be "Namu Amida Butsu" or "Nenpi Kannon Riki"—can be a lifeline to the requisite strength required to observe in silence.

The doubts of parenting weigh heavily on mothers' hearts. Raising children undertaken as part of a "practice" to polish their hearts helps them weather the storms and navigate through troubled waters. It is a long journey. It is full of tears, fears, and humility. Umemura-san uses the word mother harbor (*bōkō*) to describe what she thinks a mother should be. She says with palpable pain as she ponders her thirty-something daughter's problems, "I was not enough of a 'mother harbor.'"[54]

Kawasaki-san's following reflection is as if she is responding directly to Umemura-san, but it did not happen this way. That it sounds like it could be is testimony to the shared heartaches and experiences of mothering. "The measuring stick you use on yourself is not accurate. It's too limited. If you use your own measuring stick, you get either too proud or depressed. So, just chant the *Heart Sutra* and follow the light of Kannon. It is a matter of how far you can bow your head and just be 'Namu Amida Butsu.' When you are 'Namu Amida Butsu,' you are in the air after jumping off."[55] By this, she means you are taking action and doubts do not restrain you. You act with your whole being and move with the awareness that you are supported.

When dealing with more extended problems like keeping lines of communication open through the vicissitudes of adolescence, chanting at the home altar when children were in earshot was a favored approach.

> I guess, putting your hands together is a good thing. In the morning when the children are leaving, after I have finished making the lunches, I do the *Heart Sutra*. I beat the wooden drum (*mokugyō*), and they each come out one by one. [The altar is right off the front door.] If they know there is this kind of lifestyle somewhere, if it remains with them somewhere, when they are confused or something, there is a home to which they can return (*kaerubasho*).[56]

Not only did chanting in the morning when the family was up and about help the mother maintain some perspective on the situation, but it also cultivated a mood in the home that gave a sense no one, including the children, is alone in dealing with difficulty. It broadened the perspective of any given problem. Chanting at the home altar enables the mothers to model a method to work through difficulties that did not require direct intervention with the child, which is not only not always possible but also not always advisable. The sounds of the bells, chanting, and wooden drum accompanied by the smell of the incense is impossible to ignore. It is a way a mother can express she cares and is willing and trying to help. It does not invite a battle of competing wills or jockeying for power. It invites a reflective and calm approach to sorting out the situation.

The Hana Matsuri, or Buddha's birthday ritual, in April is not performed specifically for helping to raise a child, but it is one of a few very child-friendly rituals held at a temple. A special altar covered with flowers is made with a baby Buddha statue. The offering is sweet tea poured over the image. This ritual is also taken as an opportunity to present the Buddhist teachings more didactically to children. Ogawa-san admits, "When I was a child, I thought making offerings and doing things at the home altar were just forms. So, I didn't like them. I didn't understand the meaning or the heart they can be done with. I understand now."[57] Of course, children will not experience rituals in the same way as adults do, but performing them as children can have a deep impact on their adult lives.

Trying to give children fun opportunities visiting new places means a parent takes on extra responsibility. In addition to the general cautionary and preparatory measures, Yamaguchi-san took extra insurance. She took an amulet to help protect the children in her charge. "I have a Buddhist carving of Amida Nyorai, my protective Buddha, I carry with me on important occasions. When I was the head of the PTA and we took the kids to the sea for a field trip, I took it with me praying that all the kids would get safely home. I kept it in my purse."[58]

Umemura-san is refreshingly honest. She is polite, kind, and comfortable in her own skin. She lives passionately, finding ways to heal from the various challenges she had in her life, including being given away as a child. Heartache and confusion colored her early life, and becoming a mother herself has meant more heartache, too. Yet she carefully tends to her heart, lest it not be open to beauty.

> At first I thought that Kannon-gyō—[she chants] "Nenpi Kannon Riki"—was a stupid sutra. Why are people so grateful? When the mother who raised me was hospitalized for days—we [Umemura-san and her sister] chanted the *Heart Sutra* quietly, since she [mother] had no consciousness and we didn't want to disturb others. It was pouring down rain on the day I left to return home. When the plane went above the clouds, it was *beautiful* up there, even though it was terrible rain below. And I thought, why is it so beautiful? I thought, oh, when you just look down low, you see rain, but above the clouds it is always like this, clear and beautiful. I thought this must be what Hotoke-sama's [Honorable Buddha's] view of the world is, seeing both. This thought penetrated my heart. Then I began to think, how can one live without "Nenpi Kannon Riki?" If you chant this, then you will be rescued. Who will rescue you from the storms? "Nenpi Kannon Riki" teaches that Kannon will help you see this world. It is the same with "Namu Amida Butsu."[59]

Raising children is not over when the child reaches eighteen. For some, it continues to be a daily matter with a child in their thirties and forties living at home with their parents. Gyokko Sensei goes even farther: "Even if you die, you are still a parent. You still look after your children."[60] This was a pleasant image, but it did not prepare me for her next observation. "When you came, I could see that your mother's spirit (*rei*) was with you."[61] Part of a thoroughgoing concept of interrelatedness is an expansive view of parent-child relationships that defy Newtonian views of the world.

This panoply of ritual practices enlisted by mothers to assist them in their role of caring for their children is diverse. There are rituals that are directed to specific problems and general concerns as well as rituals that address a variety of emotional needs. Such rituals are an integral part of a complex strategy to foster the health and well-being of the family. These rituals place the mothers at the center of the home, connect them to the greater community, and are a conduit for directing powers perceived in the Dharma to protect and nourish their families.

Ritual Health and Home Insurance

Is there "ritual insurance" to protect against uncertainties and fears?

Nogawa-san made sure to prepare dinner in the morning, something that would be quick to just heat up and serve, because she knew she would be returning home late that day. It was the day of the annual Daihannya ritual held at a nun's temple. She never missed going. She wanted all the help she could gather for her family. There was no immediate crisis, but she knew that in any given year things would come up to challenge her and others in her family, whether an illness, a big decision about what to do with their modest family business, or issues with their daughter. She always went to popular rituals like this early. This was her way to show respect for the importance of the ritual and to secure a centrally located seat. Many other women of similar age arrived early, too. Most kneeled down on the tatami mats, while others chose chairs.[62] Eventually every available seat and spot on the floor was filled and the nuns filed in to sit at the small sutra tables placed in rows that ran perpendicular to the main altar, leaving the middle section directly in front of the altar open for the lead celebrant. A *hira*-style taiko drum with its large round head, about six inches deep, was hanging in its ornate flame-motif stand. This drum, reserved for the Daihannya ritual, creates an intensity of energy rare in a Zen temple.

The lead celebrant walks in with vermillion silk robes and a gold brocade surplice (*kesa*) draped over his left shoulder, holding a long white-haired whisk that only the highest in the room may handle. With measured steps, he approaches the altar and offers an extra long stick of incense, indicating the specialness of this ritual. All the nuns and the head celebrant bow deeply, three times, as the large bell (*keisu*) is struck. The first sutras are chanted with the monastics standing. Offerings of sacred water sprinkled about from a leafy branch and lotus petals (made of paper) are strewn in the direction of the laity. The excitement in the worship hall is increasing as the conversations of the laity settling in intermingle with the monastics chanting. The *Heart Sutra* begins, the purported core of the *Perfection of Wisdom Sutra,* as the drum beats a rapid rhythm, raising the intensity dramatically. After a few rounds, each nun holds up a sutra book. Collectively, they will open each page of this six-hundred-fascicle sutra, which requires several dozen sutra books to contain it all. Each sutra book is raised, first to the forehead in a gesture of respect, then high above the head, letting the accordion-folded pages flow down in a graceful arc of fluttering pages. A sacred phrase is shouted out energetically, a ritualized "reading" of the sutra. (Unleashing the protective powers of the sutra does not require comprehending the words contained within the sutra.) This is repeated in the cardinal directions. A high-pitched bell punctuates the cacophony of sound: the drumming (DONdoko DONdoko DONdokodokodokodoko DONdoko DONdoko DONdokodokodokodokodoko), each nun shouting out the sacred phrase at her own pace as she begins to open each sutra book, the names of laity being called out to get in the queue to receive the blessings directly from the main sutra book. It is obvious the main sutra book is special because it is covered in silk brocade and is five times thicker than any of the other books, which are covered in a simple dark-blue rice paper.

It is finally Nogawa-san's turn. She kneels in front of the altar to make a granulated incense (*shoko*) offering. As she crouches, she shifts over to face the Zen master in the center, the lead celebrant. She returns his shallow bow with a deep bow, placing the tips of her fingers in a triangular point and touching her forehead to the floor, the most formal and respectful bow, reserved for such important occasions. While bowed, the Zen master takes the large sutra book and aims the corner into a pressure point on the top of the fleshy part of the shoulder.[63] She remains bowed as he does the same to the other shoulder. He mutters some chant under his breath, barely audible in the flurry of sounds filling the worship hall. She raises her body high enough to bring her hands together and bows slightly, palms pressed together, before standing up to allow the next person to come and receive her blessing. The *Heart Sutra* is again being chanted by the whole group of monastics gathered. The sutra books that have been "read" are being gathered and new ones distributed. Laity continue to file through to receive blessings to take home to their families. Nogawa-san stays for a while longer. Given the number of people still waiting, she knows that it will take at least another hour. She decides to return home to serve her family dinner, bringing the protective powers of the Perfection of Wisdom into her home for the new year.[64]

Women take on the role of transmitter of blessings from the temple to the home. Unsurprisingly, they constitute the largest population at any given ritual held at a temple. Almost all the women with whom I consulted invoked the powers unleashed at various public and ceremonial rituals. The three rituals explored here are Daihannya, Setsubun, and Hyakumanben. We will also take a brief look at pilgrimages, including Shikoku, the Eighty-eight Temple circuit, Kannon *meguri* pilgrimages, and a much less famous route to relics of the Buddha outside Nagoya. These rituals are for generalized protection of family members and the home.[65]

Daihannya is mostly done shortly after ringing in the New Year, and Setsubun is done on February 3 or 4. These temple rituals are rich with sounds and colors. Hyakumanben is rarer, and the women engaged with it are among the organizers. They hold it once a month at a group member's home, and they invite a priest from their temple to officiate. Most of the women have been on one pilgrimage or another. I will highlight a few of the more poignant experiences here.

The Daihannya ritual is the most dynamic of the rituals performed inside a Zen temple. Among rituals, it is an "artistic masterwork" that moves the body through visual, aural, and physical sensations.[66] Participants feel that the power generated by the drums and unleashed through the cascading sutra pages must be strong enough to protect them and their families. Ritual scholar Schechner asserts, "Rituals embody cognitive systems of values that instruct and mobilize participants. Their embodied values are rhythmic and cognitive, spatial and conceptual, sensuous and ideological."[67] The cognitive system embedded in the Daihannya is interrelatedness and emptiness. They are two sides of the same coin. Interrelatedness stresses the connections that constitute us, and emptiness stresses the fluid impermanence of all these relations. In this cognitive system, value is placed on acting compassionately in the present moment, with recognition that it requires powerful support to do so. Engaging in the ritual first washes your being with thunderous vibrations, shaking loose attachments that constrain a person from manifesting her full capacity to act compassionately. The deafening sound pushes out the past and the future, only allowing focus on the present moment. You are compelled to be fully present in mind and body, releasing the hold that regrets (past) and worries (future) might have on you. The abbess Aoyama Rōshi, who leads the Daihannya ritual in various temples with which she is associated, teaches, "You cannot be fully healed if you are thinking of the past and future. You must be oriented to here and now."[68] "Here" is understood to be the expanse of the universe, not some arbitrary pinpoint of space. "Now" is likewise the fullness of events occurring in the universe, not some mental focus on events of your own choosing. Bowing down awaiting your turn to receive the direct force of the scripture on your body connects you unambiguously to the wisdom contained within as it acknowledges that you cannot do anything alone, only in community, only with the myriad inter-relationships that buoy, support, and nourish a person.

One of the powerful aspects of doing rituals in public among many other people is that you become a part of a community of people who are also seeking out support. It helps you not feel alone in being overwhelmed by the sometimes rugged terrain of life. It also quells the temptation to feel singled out and sorry for yourself, because you see that others, too, carry burdens in their hearts and pains in their bodies. The ritual event facilitates making connections and expanding perspective enough to inte-grate what is going on in a manner that helps the women do what needs to be done. These seasonal and periodic "insurance" rituals fortify them with the extra support that is not only deeply appreciated, but also is relied on. No matter how good a life appears to be from the outside, there are invari-ably quiet turmoils that wrench hearts and strain stability.

In contrast to the serious and dramatic ethos of the Daihannya ritual, the Setsubun ritual ends in a carnivalesque free-for-all of goodies thrown and grabbed with unabashed enthusiasm. The ritual marks the end of winter and the beginning of spring. The primary concern is to ward off bad things and welcome good things into the home. The ritual must be renewed each year. Two of my consociates took me to a temple they fre-quent. They were both "lay ordained," so they wore robes and chanted up in front with the priest. Kawasaki-san says with awe, respect, and shyness, "On that day I am given the humbling opportunity to sit up front and humbly wear the respectful monastic robe [*koromo*]. I chant sutras I don't know."[69] Evidently, she understands that the text is not as important as being present. Here is how she explains the day's events:

> On February 3, at the Setsubun Mamemaki, we receive this talisman [*o-fuda*] for health from the temple's head priest. The ritual of throwing soybeans [*mamemaki*] is usually something a shrine does, but some temples do it, too. This talisman is from Nigatsudō where priests from all over the nation gather and recite prayers for people's families. There is a ritual for burning the talis-man [from last year]. They chant the *Rishu-kyō* [*Adhyrdhaśatikā Prajñāpāramitā Sūtra*] and *Sangemon*. There is always a monk from Tōdai-ji present. The rit-ual of throwing beans is in the evening. It lasts about an hour. It is full of grandmothers [*obsāsan*] and grandfathers [*ojīsan*] from the neighborhood. Kids are everywhere from the neighborhood. There is no place to sit. At 11:00 a.m. is when we chant formally. At noon, there is a meal. There is no formal procedure. You just eat when you do. It's made by the neighborhood people:

real family food. Then we chant the *Rishu-kyō*. At about 2:00 p.m., the ritual of throwing soybeans is performed. Chocolate and rice cakes (*o-mochi*) and candy are thrown, then there is a lottery where everybody wins. The things that you win are tissue paper, saran wrap, a teacup. There are no big prizes. It's about from 11:00 a.m. to 4:00 p.m.[70]

This temple's version of the ritual is particularly child-friendly. The children have a direct and visceral experience of receiving good fortune, because in addition to the traditional soybeans, candy is also thrown toward them. While the throwing occurs, loud shouting fills the air: "Fortune in. Demons out" (*Fuku wa uchi. Oni wa soto*).

Gyokko Sensei gives me a version of the "Fortune in" chant. She uses pictograms with the same sounds (like homonyms), but the pictogram meanings create a resonant but more explicitly Buddhist meaning.

> *Fu ku wa u chi*
> 不苦者有智
> Those who have wisdom will not suffer.
> *O ni wa so to*
> 遠仁者疎道
> Those who are far from compassion are off the path.

She clearly enjoyed the festivities, even finding a punned verse that captures the seriousness with which she holds Buddhist teachings and practice. Everyone wants suffering and demons to leave and fortune and compassion to come, but Gyokko Sensei does not forget to remind us of the power we have to gain wisdom and act compassionately. The ritual for her is a chance for her to renew her practice, even as she fully engages with the belief that the ritual helps make it happen. This is another example of how ritual gives you a sense you are not alone. Not only do you join others who also do not want suffering and seek happiness, but there is a collective sense that even beyond the immediate community there are forces that will help if you are open to them. It comes with the underlying warning that not all things are helpful, and those things should be cast out. Top on the list are the demons of greed, ignorance, and hatred. These three poisons block generosity, wisdom, and compassion. Yet amid the exuberance of treats and simple gifts, positive qualities and actions can always be invited in. On the eve of spring, a season of new growth, the ritual of throwing beans brings a community together.

Hyakumanben literally translates into "One Million Times," referring to a metaphorically large number of times to pass the prayer beads around. It is a rare ritual, and I was excited to learn about people practicing it on a regular basis. This group of people includes two of my consociates. They perform the ritual on the twenty-seventh of every month in the home of a relative who lives just outside the Nagoya city limits. Gyokko Sensei assures me, "It's just among family [broadly construed to include long-time friends], so it's fine [that I join them]. We do it in the Buddhist altar room. The prayer beads are made of sandalwood. There are 108 beads. You focus on what you care about as you pass it around."[71] The ritual began with about fourteen of us sitting around the large string of prayer beads that had been neatly placed into a circle on the tatami floor. An altar had been placed in the center. A purple-robed priest lit a very long stick of incense and the chanting of various sutras began. Once the sutras were complete, "Namu Amida Butsu" was repeated about a dozen times, then one of the quieter women bowed down with her head to the floor. She began to speak in a voice of authority and strength that I had not heard from her before. The powerful quality of her voice and the extreme reverence in her body language were unparalleled by anyone else in the room. Everyone sat quietly with hands held with palms together, even the priest. The conjugation of the verbs she used was not common in even polite contemporary conversations. It sounded as if we had been transported back in time. I was also disoriented by the perspective of the voice(s) she used. At moments, it was the clear and confident tone of a master and at others it was the profound humility and gratitude of the recipient of the wisdom. Some of the "teachings" included admonitions to be in harmony with people from different parts of the world and to let go of attachments that bind and constrict. After nearly thirty minutes, she raised her head, looking a combination of humbled, pleased, and amazed. The others gave her subtle nods of approval. I had not known channeling was part of the ritual. Apparently, it is common in this group. I later learned this was only the second time this woman had been "chosen" to be the vehicle. She was channeling no less than Amida Buddha, and she was deeply honored. She indicated surprise as well, seeming to stem mostly from her humility. After a moment of moving out of this extraordinary phase of the ritual, we raised the prayers beads and slowly began passing them while chanting "Namu Amida Butsu." As the tempo increased, it transmuted into "NamAmidabu": the sound made when crossing the lips of those intimate with saying it over and over and over and over. When the one extra large softball-sized bead landed between your two hands, you raised it to your forehead in reverence. Some closed their eyes,

Hyakumanben prayer bead passing ritual

others focused on the beads passing in front of them. It was a delicate dance of rhythmic motion passing the beads. Adjustments in speed, tension, and timing were constantly made to accommodate someone using one hand while wiping her face (of sweat from the activity), shifting her body (due to legs falling asleep with two hours of sitting on them), or moving her arms to get a little reprieve from the steady and rigorous movement.

Being among the youngest by decades, I came to appreciate the commitment required to engage in this practice. After just thirty minutes, my arms were tired from passing the beads in sync with those around me. During the last twenty minutes of the hour of passing, the tempo accelerated to a furious pace. The volume of the chant concomitantly rose to a feverish pitch. A split second of one person not being completely focused on the present moment of bead passing would cause the whole chain to go into contortions, everybody making the necessary adjustments to get it back on track. We were clearly all in this together. Each person's actions affected each one of us in a different way. Everybody had to respond as one organism to maintain the rhythm. It

Ritualized clothing of pilgrim, with bureau-
top home altar in partial view

was such a physically driven group practice that made interrelatedness an immediate and visceral reality. The power of this coordinated motion went deeper than (inherently dualistic) words can reach to make one experience the nature of our intricate interconnections and impact on each other. Being part of the chain leaves one knowing at a cellular level support is there, responding to subtle changes and needs. Words are not necessary here. Everybody understands, is rejuvenated, and is empowered to face the illness, loss, or troubles she brought with her.

Gyokko Sensei knew I wanted to understand what happens when someone channels (enters *sugari*). She explained to me very matter-of-factly that "when we *sugaru* (implore, lean on) we become empty (or zero; *mu*) and Shaka-sama (or whomever) comes through. An oracle message (*otsuge*) then happens. My mom did these things, and I just followed her."[72] Gyokko Sensei does not elaborate, in part because she says it is not the kind of thing that happens in a rational or controlled realm. She explained it is part of an invisible power, and she respects what the eyes cannot see. In terms of the dynamics of the ritual, the channeling helps you feel not alone and in awe of the potential for power in the universe to support, guide, and understand. Yet, the height of the ritual was clearly the last twenty minutes of working as one organism to move the prayer beads in an unending circle like a swirling cyclone of compassion, loosening attachments that gripped you in suffering and sweeping out obstacles that obscured the view of your interconnections.

Circles are a common shape in numerous rituals. Formally, it is a shape that gets its strength from being a continuous whole. It embodies an expansive perspective that includes all of the 360-degree angles and the infinite increments in between. It is stable and perfectly balanced even when in rapid motion and tossed about. These qualities are often sought when someone goes on a pilgrimage, whether the route itself is circular or a circle is formed between your home, the site, and return to home. The most famous pilgrimage in Japan is the Shikoku Eighty-eight Temple pilgrimage. It involves an essentially circular path around the island of Shikoku, following in the wake of the Great Buddhist Master Kūkai, who was born on that island in the eighth century.[73] People have sought to "walk with Kūkai" for centuries, bringing their fears and hopes with them.

Umemura-san decided to go on the pilgrimage after her children were grown adults. She wanted to integrate numerous things more deeply into her heart. She had lost several loved ones, including the mother who raised her and a Zen nun with whom she was exceptionally close. She was also unsure how to proceed with mothering her adult children. One of her children had not yet become independent, even though he was into his thirties. So, Umemura-san donned the white garments that transport you to the liminal space of the pilgrim and started on her journey, taking train and boat to the island and then walking as much as she could. She stopped to get her pilgrim book stamped at each temple, affirmation to herself that she had really been there. She chanted the *Heart Sutra* at each temple and drank in the natural beauty of the landscape, as she felt increasingly able to breathe deeper and touch places in her heart that had gone dry with neglect. This pilgrimage was a courageous act of recognizing that she needs to nurture herself, too. The beauty surrounding her soothed worn places in her heart, softening the calluses she had developed with each pain, enabling her to be more flexible and less resistant and to accept her own life. Although she did not have time to go to each temple, she did complete the circle from her home and back. The circling enabled her to bring her opened and softened heart home. She knows that her journey continues, but going off to a far side of the circle enabled her to see her home life from a larger perspective. The perspective gained on the pilgrimage works like one of Seurat's pointillist paintings that appear to be blended and whole when viewed from afar, yet appear as separate dots when seen up close. In a sense, it is like two views of reality: at once

Temple seal in pilgrim book

interrelated and discrete. The pilgrimage enabled her to see the wholeness again, and she returns to her pilgrimage book of stamps to refresh her perspective. The feel of the book on her hands, the smell of the paper, and the vermillion stamps guide her heart back to the wholeness she experienced on pilgrimage.[74]

Pilgrimages to Kannon, goddess of compassion, are also frequently undertaken by those seeking healing.[75] The most famous route is to one hundred temples. Two circuits of thirty-three temples and one circuit of thirty-four temples begin with the Saigoku Pilgrimage route, followed by the Bandō section, and end with the Chichibu portion where one additional temple is added to complete the one hundred. The design of thirty-three temples in a route represents the thirty-three images of Kannon, including the Eleven-Headed Kannon, Horse-Headed Kannon, Thousand-Armed Kannon, and the Child-Rearing Kannon, a unique and most stunning lifelike version of Kannon breast-feeding a child. Unsurprisingly, it is a favorite among those wanting children. It is located at the Sōtō Sect Temple Kinshō-ji, number four on the Chichibu route. Kannon is most fondly seen as a compassionate mother figure, so it is natural that pilgrimages to her are found throughout Japan. Kannon is a nonsectarian figure, and, accordingly, temples from several sects are commonly found among the temples on any given pilgrimage route. Interestingly, on the Chichibu route, twenty of the thirty-four temples are Sōtō Zen.[76]

Kitō Sensei, a nun who many think of as a living Kannon, has done the whole pilgrimage. Even though she found strength at each of the one hundred temples, for someone who is always listening to everyone else's cries, she found she needed to do something more. She does her own pilgrimage to take her the extra distance required of one who gives of herself freely, leaving only a few hours of sleep a night, decade after decade. When she is with you, she is completely present, and you feel she understands everything that quivers in your heart. She never intimates that she has other places to go or people to see, yet she is constantly moving from one person to another from early morning and into the night, every single day of the year. She gave me a glimpse of what she does to draw ever deeper into her well of compassion, though she is too humble ever to call it that. Her personal pilgrimage draws on practices that reach back to India and stretch down highways leading out of Nagoya.

Ever since Kitō Sensei was a young student-nun, she has helped out at Tōgan-ji, a Sōtō Zen temple in Nagoya. The current head of the temple is her teacher's disciple. The temple is rare, not just in that it was important even in Oda Nobunaga's day when he was working to unify Japan in the sixteenth century, but it has an Oku-no-In—a most sacred place reserved for those willing to make the extra effort to journey to it—with relics of the Buddha brought from India. This Oku-no-In is significantly farther from the temple than most. It is on the top of a small mountain in Shitarachō of Kitashitaragun, which is eighty kilometers (about fifty miles) from Tōgan-ji in Nagoya. This is the same distance between the bodhi tree where the Buddha was enlightened and Vulture Peak in Rajgir, India, the mountaintop where the Buddha is purported to have given the *Lotus Sutra*. A Sōrintō pillar marks the spot where the relics are treasured on the mountaintop outside Nagoya. Kitō Sensei decided to walk the distance between Tōgan-ji and the Buddha relics enshrined in the Sōrintō pillar at the Oku-no-In. In her mind, it was a pilgrimage to the Buddha.

She originally did this ritual to test herself. She thought that if she could do this pilgrimage, she should go to India. She became the first and only nun to tend the Japanese Temple in Bodh Gaya, India, something she did for four years (1970–1975). Most who come to run the temple are monks, and most stay only a year or two. She was there before there was even a building, sowing seeds of compassion that enabled a smooth opening for Japanese pilgrims who came to Bodh Gaya to see where the Buddha was enlightened. Japanese pilgrims are far wealthier than the Indians in the village, so establishing warm and trusting relationships with the locals was vital for the Japanese temple.

Moved by the powerful energy of Bodhidharma, she embarks on her twenty-four hour pilgrimage in October, a time when Bodhidharma is especially remembered in the Zen ritual calendar. She wears saffron-colored robes, the color monastics wore in India, because, she says, "they are better for walking in the night than black. I can be seen more easily in saffron."[77] Changing from Japanese black robes to the Indian saffron robes makes her feel closer to the Buddha, too. It is evident in her voice and in her gait. She has done this grueling pilgrimage more than ten times. Once before she went to India, once at the original site in India from Bodh Gaya to Rajgir, and annually since she returned to Japan, some years twice. Foregoing her daily footwear of sandals (*zōri*) and socks (*tabi*) for a pair of tennis shoes, she would set out late in the afternoon so she could make it to a bus stop with a wooden bench and covered roof that she knew about more than halfway along the pilgrimage route. She knew if she made it to the bus stop before dawn, she would make it to the top of the mountain peak in time for sunset, even affording her a little time to sit and rest on the bench. All along the way, she chanted the *Heart Sutra,* almost as automatic for her as breathing. She admits to occasionally pausing the chant to shout, "Hotoke-sama, *tasukete!* (Honorable Buddha, help!)" The fuel required to walk up and down low-lying mountainous roads for nearly fifty miles—stopping to rest only once—is more than the body usually has stored. It is the extreme energy demanded that necessitates she draw on deep reservoirs within. Her extra stores of fuel come from the frustration and pain she has carefully kept from everyone. It is a potent fuel, because it was generated out of compassion. Now she must be sure to be compassionate to herself, too, and burn it all off. The effort propels her up to the Buddha. She admits that as she aged she would call out more frequently. It also gradually started taking closer to twenty-seven hours. All the long midnight hours walking alone seems to have cultivated an intimacy, a sort of pact of solidarity between those who have experienced something intense together. Her ease with the Buddha is reflected in her ease with herself.

There is no distance, no fear, no doubt, only acceptance. This vastness of acceptance is the source of her boundless compassion.

In 1990, just as the dog-tooth violets (*katakuri*) were in bloom—notable because the plant is made into a starch powder commonly used in Japanese cooking—Kitō Sensei took me with her on this pilgrimage. Our journey was nothing like the one she usually took. She arranged for a young man who helped at the temple to drive us most of the way. We just hiked the last mountain peak. Atop it, we built a fire to boil water, and she whisked tea (*maccha*) for us. Even this extremely abbreviated version of the pilgrimage was a rare opportunity to hear some of the behind-the-scenes stories of rituals and thoughts a "living bodhisattva" turns to when she seeks support and understanding.

Caring for Elders

What might a woman who practices Zen turn to when she is the primary caretaker of her completely dependent and demented elderly mother-in-law?

Yamaguchi-san reflected back to an earlier time in her marriage.

When Grandma [*Obāchan*] first moved in, I vowed to myself I would make a home that was better for having my mother-in-law live with us. I wanted a home where being with her was special. I wanted to bring out the best that comes with this situation. Grandma was a very devout Buddhist. She chanted at the altar every day. It was good for everyone to sit behind Grandma and chant the sutras on special days like Obon (summer ancestor rites) and New Year's. She was the leader. It was the only place where she was leader in the house. She taught us all many things. I was grateful that my children grew up in a home with three generations.[78]

Bringing out the best in a situation helps everyone. The children could absorb the wisdom embedded in the ritual mastery of Grandma while Grandma was treated with the respect commensurate with her age. Three generations under one roof living in harmony is the traditional ideal family in Japanese culture. Yet, the aging process is not always so rosy. To hear these women tell it, the challenges of caring for a person who gradually degenerates over several years are cumulative. The realization an elder is no longer capable of doing something on her own is slow arriving, because of the desire on everyone's part for the person to be strong and healthy. It is also a matter of respect when you are caring for an elder. It is often imperceptible when the power shifts and the younger generation needs to be assertive and take the lead. There is no formal ritual recognizing this change that requires all parties to cultivate a new identity. In the shuffle, dignity, pride, and confidence are often lost to the elder, while patience is often lost to the caregiver.

Such was the case of Yamaguchi-san. Everyone in her three-generational home called her mother-in-law "Obāchan." This affectionate term for grandmother was natural, because she filled her role as eldest female in the home with reliable and endearing warmth and kindness. Her daughter-in-law, Yamaguchi-san, brought her own refined sensibilities with her to the marriage, and deeply respected Grandma's profound level of attainment. Grandma had been a model of the quintessential embodiment of elegance, grace, and kindness. She spoke in the most respectful form of Japanese (*keigo*) all the time. Yet, on her lips, unlike the way in which it might sound on the lips of others, it was not out of place in the kitchen or at the family dinner table. Her humility was not put on for public appearances. It reflected the core of her beauty and strength. Yamaguchi-san explains the dynamics and thoughts that led up to her breaking point.

> At her core, Grandma was a beautiful, respectful person. It was just the aging. After age ninety, she was no longer able to hear the views of others. [She lived to ninety-eight.] She would say her own ideas. She would no longer accept what others said. When that started happening, I thought she was getting old. She had not been the kind of person who pushed her wishes. That's when I started thinking it was hard. Since I was born after World War II, I received the U.S.-based education, and I had a different idea about the mother-in-law/daughter-in-law relationship. She was a Meiji person, so we were very different. It was hard for me to just agree to everything she said. For example, [in Grandma's view] the soft, leafy part of the spinach is for men and the stems are for women. I was raised equally, and not set aside because I was a girl. Since Grandma had not worked and had lived in the mountains when she came to live with us, she was like a transplant from Meiji. She was pure! She trusted people and was extremely polite. She has many wonderful qualities, so I could not mention the parts I didn't get along with. My conscience would hurt, so I said nothing. I wrote in my diary, with fervor. She is a person who you can respect. I wanted to be round. I thought

that's what I had to be: a woman is to be beautiful, which means not saying anything bad about anyone.

If I got really angry, I would be the odd one. If you think about it, it would be silly for me to be angry. She would get angry at me if she got an idea of something [that I knew was not true]. I would sometimes pretend to do as she said, and then she would relax. At first I would get angry. Then I got used to it, and I could just play along with ease. Sometimes I would take Grandma out to Ōsu Kannon [a traditional shopping district] so both of us could get a break. It would help us both when we got irritated. She trusted me completely. We'd argue, but she would hold my hand when we went out. I was encouraged by people who would tell me that I was doing well taking care of her. This helped me continue.

However, I would get so sleep deprived, because she came to wake me up about once an hour every night. She would turn on the light and come upstairs. She was confused about time. She was worried that if I didn't get up, I would be late getting everyone to school and work. She'd come back, having forgotten that she already came. She would come on Sunday, too. Sometimes I would put something so the door wouldn't open. She didn't realize it was intentional. She thought something was jamming the door, so she used her strength to try and open it [laughter]. I can pray for her every day, because there were mostly good times. I still feel that I wish I had done this or that for her. But, I could not have done any more than I did. It was really hard.[79]

As Grandma aged, she went from a refined mode of being to refusing to change her clothes soiled from toilet accidents, even when her grandson's friends complained about the bad smell in their home. The Shinto-based focus on purity makes such a predicament untenable. After several years of this, tensions and stubbornness reached seismic levels. A sharp butcher knife was drawn and aimed. Threats targeting the old woman's last ounce of self-respect were fired. The daughter-in-law exercised the tiny remainder of respect for her beloved mother-in-law by leaving the house. Although leaving a demented ninety-seven-year-old woman alone in the house was not necessarily safe, it was safer than if she had stayed. She had exhausted her patience years ago. Now her own grip on reality had snapped. Desperate, she knew she had to get help for herself. She went to the person she knew would be able to help, a Zen abbess, and confessed that she had held a butcher knife up to Grandma.

The abbess Aoyama Rōshi listened deeply and did not judge her. She showed that she understood how these situations could be so difficult. Instead of using words for explicit ethical instruction, she employed listening and silence to empower the daughter-in-law in the ethical and arduous activity of continuing to care for Grandma. She has seen numerous people wrestling with this kind of situation, people who are otherwise polite, caring, and conscientious.

In John Traphagan's study of aging in Japan, he articulates the social dynamics of aging well. "In the process [of senility or forgetting basic assumptions about behavior that define one as human], one can also lose the symbolic and social capital that is associated with being a normal, culturally competent, human being."[80] The rituals of being culturally competent in Japanese culture are not only numerous, they are often subtle. Indeed, subtlety is the mark of a culturally refined person. With the Japanese population living longer than it ever has before, there are few rituals for responding subtly to the ravages of dementia. This directly collides with the deep rituals of respect for elders. As family after family struggles with this, Rachel Remen, M.D., a physician committed to holistic health, puts her finger on the problem. "The trust of process that comes from personal knowledge and experience is really the foundation of helping and comforting one another. Without it, all of our actions are driven by fear. Fear is the friction in all transitions."[81] The transitions of aging compounded by the transitions of a society that must adjust to the new heights of aging are fraught with fear. It is, however, less the fear of dying than it is the fear of living without respect. It is not common knowledge how to live with both respect and dementia. There are no rituals passed down that target this specific situation. Yamaguchi-san has grappled with how to find balance in this fragile relationship that changes imperceptibly with each dawn. Having completely lost her balance, she redoubles her determination to find a way.

The *Guide to the Bodhisattva Way of Life* offers helpful insight into one of the critical components of treating those suffering from dementia with respect: vanquish anger.

> Unruly beings are as (unlimited) as space:
> They cannot possibly all be overcome,
> But if I overcome thoughts of anger alone,
> This will be equivalent to vanquishing all foes.

Yamaguchi-san knows that she is the lynchpin. She is the one who must make the adjustments. She takes to heart the teachings of the Dalai Lama, that "the only factor that can give refuge or protection from the destructive effects of anger and hatred is the practice of tolerance and patience."[82] The question is *how* to be patient when a solid night's sleep is elusive, the stench is repulsive, and communication is strained beyond function. The abbess Aoyama Rōshi made it clear that the caregiver must not neglect caring for her own mind, heart, and body. Simple rituals can be lifelines. Respect and patience are embedded in the rituals she suggested. By performing the rituals, you act respectfully and patiently. The method is to perform the ritualized behaviors enough to become facile at transposing the elements to suit any situation.

A vital aspect of performing the rituals effectively is to do them in what the abbess calls "circle time" (*ensō-jikan*).[83] All points are starting and ending points that only occur in the present. Time does not run in a linear one-way line from past to future.[84] Each moment is complete. This is the key to liberation from regrets of the past and fears of the future. They do not exist in the present, and they can only cause suffering if you focus on them. She says, "One step. One step. [Your] purpose is one step now."[85] For motivation, she adds, "A fool is one who is not aware that she is already a Buddha. Move like water," is her suggestion on how to not lose focus on the present.[86] In a subsequent Dharma Talk, Aoyama Rōshi develops the theme of "Heaven and Earth" and stresses that it models how to be in the present. She adds to an audience that included a number of elderly Japanese women, "Aging is something given by the power of 'Heaven and Earth,' and we must live manifesting that nature."[87]

These kinds of teachings, along with personal counsel, helped Yamaguchi-san return home to her family with a new sense of possibility. She also started practicing the rituals the abbess Aoyama Rōshi suggested, including regularly wearing prayer beads around her wrist for a constant reminder to be present in "circle time." She began chanting at the home altar as Grandma had done every day. The chanting builds in deep breathing, calming the heart, mind, and body. She also started doing scripture copying of the *Heart Sutra*.[88] With each careful stroke of the brush, this practice also has a calming effect. Since the brush reveals the heart, copying the scripture also enables her to see herself move into the present as frustrations melt away. It is not uncommon for the strokes at the end of the sutra to look more fluid and graceful than the strokes at the beginning of the sutra. The steady hand required to brush the intricate characters of the *Heart Sutra*—many of them not in common use—helps keep the mind focused on the present. The immediate feedback of the brush will expose whenever the mind wanders away from what is right in front of it.

Now when she hangs the laundry she tries not to think about anything else, and just cooks when it is time to cook. In addition, she tries to see the beauty in the moment and have fun. One of her fondest activities when her children were younger was to make a snow bunny for the breakfast table on the rare times when there was snow, complete with nandina ears and red berry eyes.

The full story cannot be recounted here, and there were difficulties yet to face, but Yamaguchi-san had a transformational experience in being heard by the abbess. Being heard yet not judged on some abstract code of moral conduct that knew nothing of her struggles was the key to her healing. Precisely because the abbess did not put ethical behavior on center stage, she was able to help the woman behave more ethically. The abbess encouraged basic ritual practices that helped her sustain her equilibrium. Although they are simple rituals, integrating them into her life helped her maintain balance within herself and with her family, including Grandma.

Along with Yamaguchi's experience, others have noted that these ritual activities help reduce stress and its attending negative effects. Moreover, as with other rituals, these, too, seem to help increase "eustress," or stress with positive effects.[89] "Post-traumatic growth" is also an area receiving increasing attention, and it may help contextualize Yamaguchi-san's newfound ability to find her balance at home.[90] The shock of losing the person she knew herself to be—thoughtful, helpful, and caring—and finding herself holding a butcher knife aimed at her beloved ninety-seven-year-old grandma jolted her to recognize she needed help. The support of the abbess and Yamaguchi-san's own engagement with daily ritual activities gave rise to an increased ability to see from an expanded, and, therefore, steadier perspective. Meanwhile, she was able to not lose sight of her deep connection to a woman who behaved nothing like the refined Grandma she used to cheerfully and readily respect and admire.

A dozen years after Grandma passed, while sipping tea together, Yamaguchi-san drew me a picture Aoyama Rōshi had used to make the point about living in the present moment. It is a simple line drawing of a Japanese-style ghost with undefined hands reaching out in a coveting motion, long hair trailing, and floating above the ground. She explained, "The hands are reaching for the future, the hair drags the past along, and the feet are not touching the ground."[91] She then writes, "Cut off before and after, just here."[92] With a joyful smile she quietly adds, "Aoyama Rōshi said I was good at being in the present now."[93] Her joy comes from knowing she has worked hard to get here and that Aoyama Rōshi knows how difficult it has been. Her matured approach to life is, "Have fun now, take care of yourself, and then you can take care of others and not build up stress."[94]

Surviving Loss through War, Suicide, and Homicide

What might help a Zen Buddhist who struggles with applying the concept of nondualism to her life?

Nagai-san was still in elementary school when her two eldest brothers left the family, saying they had found jobs in a nearby village. A neighbor, however, found them under a bridge, having starved to death. It was World War II, and food was scarce. They only said they had found work so the rest of the family might then have enough food. After her parents died a natural death, Nagai's older sister committed suicide. That sister had been mentally unstable for several years, and her parents had been committed to caring for her at home. Later, her younger sister remarried after a terrible divorce. She met her new husband through an arranged marriage (*omiai*). Not long after returning from the honeymoon, her sister confided that the relationship with her new husband was not going well. Nagai-san advised her to give it time, because all new relationships required an adjustment period. A few days later, detectives called my consociate. Her sister had been killed—by her husband.

Nagai-san's daughter is middle-aged, physically healthy, intelligent, yet still living at home. Her daughter does not seek employment, companionship, or even to come out of her bedroom in the daytime. As Nagai-san ages, she worries about what will happen to her daughter in the future, her own older sister's choice weighing heavily on her heart.

Nagai-san is the epitome of refined grace and aesthetic movement. Her smile is warm. Her care for others is immediate, yet she conceals such losses in her heart. Just one of these tragedies would be tough to integrate into your life, but she carries several. Her generosity in offering to be part of this research on healing rituals is a tremendous act. She is still working on integrating everything that has happened in her family. She is also weary from it all. Still, she gathered her courage and approached me on a January evening in the lobby of a Japanese taiko drum concert we both happened to be attending in Nagoya. She recognized me from the Sunday that I spoke about my research at teatime at the nunnery. I had passed out more than sixty name cards, asking people to contact me if they would be willing to help me learn about the healing practices they have found helpful. Nagai-san walked up and bowed, introducing herself to me. She continued, "Back in June, I thought I should call you because I have all these problems. Then things just happened naturally. I feel it is my younger sister who is leading the way. This is a mysterious connection. We just coincidentally meet at this concert. I thought I should call you. But I had surgery and forgot. So, this is really a sign that I should do this. I hope it is useful. There is nothing better than this."[95]

Since Nagai-san had thought so much about whether or not to share her experiences with me, we get a rare glimpse into her inner thoughts that led her to agree. Her hope that opening up about her vulnerabilities might help another person is a testimony to the depth of her compassion. Even with all the trauma she has been through, it is remarkable she has not lost touch with what she values most. She admits it has not been easy, and her journey has taken her in several directions. For her, there is no rest until she finds a way to resolve all the losses, anger, fears, and regrets.

That we met is a mystery to me, too. It underscores how field research is dependent on some serendipity and that it is a qualitatively different mode of research from research in the laboratory or library, where there are greater possibilities for control. Encounters in the field can open up avenues that the most carefully designed research agenda cannot match. Of course, when working with human experiences in a holistic way, the only way to proceed is to be open. Sometimes you are fortunate and someone like Nagai-san comes along and introduces herself.

At our first meeting in her home, Nagai-san serves me tea as I face her home altar and traditional alcove (*tokonoma*) where a beautiful flower arrangement and painting are displayed. It is evident she has prepared the room for meeting with a guest. After some polite talk, it is clear she is ready. She has thought about this, and now she is prepared to reveal her deepest vulnerabilities, her raw pain, and unadorned fears. Were it not for Aoyama Roshi's encouragement for people to help me with this research, I cannot imagine gaining such deep trust so quickly.

Nagai-san launches in. "My deepest motivation is I want to get help. I don't have the strength. I want to relax as soon as possible. I don't care about polishing my heart."[96] I am stunned to hear such a devout Buddhist woman admit to not caring about polishing her heart. She appears to be the definition of "polished heart." It dawns on me that it must be that her misery runs so deep even the decades of polishing have not been enough to release her suffering. Although polishing your heart is an ideal aim, Nagai-san teaches me through her experiences that there are times when just being able to relax into your circumstances is a laudable aim. She shows me that healing does not necessarily mean improving yourself or becoming a "better" person. Sometimes it is most important to just be—to be OK with what is, and to breathe deeply. That is her quest.

Nagai-san sharing such intimate details of her heart with me is, in effect, her oral memoir. As I listen to her, I see her doing what Toni Morrison explains is the process of writing a memoir. Morrison elucidates it as "a process of gaining access to interior life—a kind of literary archeology: on the basis of some information and a little guesswork you journey to a site to see what remains were left behind and to reconstruct the world that these remains imply."[97]

Nagai-san's eyes reveal the losses that occurred when she was in primary school have taken a toll. Her family lost everything in the war, and they had to move to a cooperative farm. No longer did she have bows for her hair and a home filled with nice things. They worked the land, yet it would not yield enough to fill everyone's belly. Her two older brothers had gone off "to work," never to return. The sacrifices of war even for those not serving in the military were heart wrenching. Yet, she reflects, "there are so many more people who have suffered more through the war. So, I am not as badly off."[98] Later, she elaborates on her memories. "In an inexplicably mysterious way, only the good things are left. I wonder if people are designed to forget the bad things. Like when I remember the days on the farm, I don't think of how hard it was to live so meagerly and roughly. What comes to mind is that the flowers bloom in spring and the barley grows so green. We planted a peach tree to sell the peaches in the market, and I remember the beautiful pink blossoms. The birds were chirping all around. The air was good."[99] Time has enabled her to look from a larger perspective, and she can see others suffer more than she does. This is an indication she has resolved this suffering in her heart. She realizes that memory can serve to protect, letting old wounds heal.

A wound that has not fully healed, however, is the loss of her elder sister through suicide. Once their parents had passed on, the eldest living brother became the new head of the house. His wife did not want the mentally unstable sister around anymore. Mentally unstable though she was, she could still tell when she was not wanted, so she left the only way she knew how. The wound of losing her older sister has reopened fear for her own daughter's future. She does not want history to repeat itself. She wants her daughter to be able to support herself, because Nagai-san will not be able to take care of her forever. Although she does not spell it out in direct terms, it is clear what she fears. Nagai-san volunteered for a suicide hotline for more than a decade. She says it is for her sister, but I come to sense she has a larger burden in her heart.

There is one thing that nags at me most. I don't know if it is appropriate to talk or not, because I don't want you to become upset. Is it OK? Will your heart not be hurt? She [Nagai-san's youngest sister] married an oldest son, so this was not a good fit. She divorced after two years. She was just twenty-four. She decided to leave her [two-year-old] son there, because it was better for her son. She returned home, but she often disappeared to Tokyo to catch glimpses of her son. When she was thirty-nine, she wanted to marry. She went to a place that arranged marriages. In March of her thirty-ninth year, she met a man and they were married in May. He came from a good family with a good education. He liked horseracing. They went on a ten-day honeymoon. At the end of July, she wanted to discuss something with me. She wanted to divorce. I asked her, "Why do you want to separate from a man who seems on the outside like a man from a good family and good education? Shouldn't you try to endure it a little more?" Then on Saturday, August 1, a phone call came from the police station of Meitō-ku. I thought it must be a mistake. They wanted me to come to check and see if it was my sister. No, the phone call came on the fifth. Her neck was strangled and she was killed, my younger sister. Are you OK?

My younger sister had received some land from my father, so she had some money. He sold the land and gave her the money because she would have to be on her own now. He, "the other" [new husband], had his eyes on that money. He had loans from his horse gambling, some hundreds of thousands of yen. He looked like a good person, but he wanted to gather money to be rid of the gambling debts. That's what I think. Until then, there was a woman he had lived with who worked in a bar. But she had the eyes to see what kind of person he was, so she escaped. But my younger sister did not have the eyes to see through a man, so she thought he was a good man. She was a little lacking in her ability to see him clearly. He graduated from Chuo University in architecture. His younger brother had gone as far as being on the board of directors of a company. His father even received a commendation of some kind from the emperor. So the son had been raised as a spoiled boy [botchan]. Then he went off on that path.

Then me, my other younger sister, and my younger brother had to work. So, the three of us went to take care of the things afterwards. "The other" [new

husband] had been taken off [to jail] immediately. So, the room had been left
as it was. My younger sister played the *koto* (traditional stringed instrument).
We had been given lessons, and my younger sister had degrees in both *koto* and
shamisen (another traditional stringed instrument). So we took her *koto* and
shamisen, and the important items. The rest, clothes, furniture, all the rest, we
had the funeral home take. Everything was new. We looked through all the
things to see if there was anything important, and we found in a drawer on the
very bottom a picture of the baby son she had left in Tokyo.

[In the courtroom] I saw those scenes only on television. I never thought
that I would experience it myself. He [the new husband] came in with his
hands cuffed, and they let him loose as he sat down. His parents were sitting
directly behind him. When I saw that, I really thought with a deep sigh that I
was glad I was on the victim's side—that I was not on the side of the criminal.
Our burden was heavy, but their burden was greater, because they were the
criminals.

After a year of court, in March he got an eight-year sentence. That's short
isn't it? Eight years. The court ended and then one week later we held the one-
year memorial service. Then I came down with insomnia. Through September
and October, I couldn't sleep at all. From December, I had a ringing in my
ears. I thought it was odd. Then when I went to see an internist who special-
izes in nerves, the doctor said that when you were under stress you were okay.
But when you could relax a little, then the symptoms emerge. Ever since then,
I have not been able to get rid of the ringing in my ears. This has been more
than ten years. But it does not go so far as to make me dizzy, so that is good.
But the cause is that. I used a lot of nerves in that whole incident.[100]

Learning of this gruesome death and its torturous aftermath in a year-
long court case—after having just learned of her older brothers in the war
and her older sister's suicide—gave me profound respect for how well
Nagai-san is doing. A testament to her healing, despite having to relive
the erosive tragedies as she recounted them to me, she expressed concern
for what hearing such events would do to me. She even called to check on
me again that night. Her journey to find peace, wholeness, and healing
took her through different religious traditions. She began with Zen, but it
did not help her. She was exposed to the meaning of the *Heart Sutra* and
its teaching on emptiness, but, try as she might to apply them to her experiences, it brought her no relief or warmth. It made logical sense, but it did
not help her with her pain. "The home altar in my house is Sōtō-shū [sect].
I personally am not fully into Sōtō-shū. I can't understand it yet. It talks

about how you must find the self by the self. It is easier for me to understand Christianity and Jōdo Shinshū. It says that you can rest here. I want to receive the gift of being able to rest. I am so tired of all my confusions that I want to lean on something. But Sōtō says that you must do it on your own."[101] Although her family was in the Sōtō Zen sect, Zen's "Self Power" approach was beyond her.[102]

Nagai-san felt there was no place to go for deep problems in Buddhism. "They just say to keep your posture straight."[103] She began to envy a Christian friend who was able to find peace after her son had committed suicide. Her friend was able to lean on the Christian God and feel she and her son were cared for. Nagai-san tried to believe in the Christian God's power and feel embraced by the love. She had an experience that helped her change her perspective. She still sounds surprised as she reveals to me that, "it was the words of a Catholic nun, not a Buddhist, who helped me most."[104] Nagai-san said, "I wanted to depend on someone. I wanted to receive strength. I wanted to be saved. Sōtō Zen is too strict for me. I am tired." The Catholic nun said to her, "The tired, please come to me [referring to God]." The nun made her feel good by saying that her sister was closest to God. Despite this helpful shift in perspective of her sister, going to church and reading the Bible did not help her. She desperately wanted to relax and lean on this God, but her desire and rational efforts to comprehend the salvific teachings were not enough. She thought it was probably because she was a Buddhist at heart and that she was not suited to Christianity. She thought that perhaps Amida Buddha might be able to help her because of "Other Power." She tried to chant the *nembutsu* ("Namu Amida Butsu") and lean on Amida's power, but to no avail. She did not feel any personal connection to Pure Land Buddhist practices of relying on Amida Buddha. She wishes she had the connections, but, in the end, she does not feel like it suits her.[105] Eventually, Nagai-san circled back around to Sōtō Zen, but entered it from a different angle.

There was some event at the Zen nunnery and I was passing by. I had been there for something before. Then I suddenly thought, what if I discuss this here, what kind of response will I receive? So, I went in and I explained the situation and wanted to have the eternal memorial service [*eitai kuyō*] done. Aoyama Sensei said that yes, we will receive your request. So, my younger sister's ashes are in the Sutra Pavilion.

It was the *Sankaiki,* Heisei 1 [1989]. Ever since then I have gone there. Whenever I pass the Sutra Pavilion, I put my hands together and say,

"Satako-chan, I've come again."[106] [tears] You know in the main worship hall in the back how they have the mortuary tablets there. My younger sister's mortuary tablet is there. So, I can't part from the nunnery. I have a karmic connection. My legs just head me in that direction. As the years pile up, when I put my hands together, it is more and more that I feel gratitude toward my sister. If there was not this kind of absolute connection, I would still be swimming in loss. I might have gone to church. I would probably not have come to the nunnery so regularly. I feel like my sister is pulling me here. She is guiding my path. Lately, I tell her thank you when I put my hands together, "Thank you Satako-chan." If it had not been for this, I might still be wandering.

I have been going to the nunnery for ten years, and I still don't feel like I have been saved or found peace. If I had not gone to the nunnery, though, I would be more unsettled. Because I have attended, I have experienced a kind of peace. I don't feel like I am all healed. I am better off than I would be if I were just on my own, though.[107]

Going to the nunnery is not a panacea and healing is not necessarily a state one attains. It can come and go. Feeling more peace, however, is something to be grateful for, and Nagai-san thinks her connection with the Zen nunnery helps. She participates in numerous activities there, including scripture copying, various rituals, and the monthly Sunday Zen gathering for laity where participants practice Zen-style eating and sitting, and where you listen to Aoyama Rōshi's Dharma teachings.

Nagai-san also tends to her home altar, making offerings and chanting, yet it does not help her heal. The fancy altar in the formal tatami room is for her husband's family. In an act of courageous creativity, she made an altar in her home just for her family. It is not in the main room, and it is not made of gilded and lacquered wood. It is a space she cleared off a bookshelf. The accoutrements are clearly not where the healing power comes from. "When I am in front of the home altar, I feel protected by my deceased family members. I don't feel it is from the Buddha."[108] Part of the wisdom of home altar rituals seems to lie in the intimacy experienced when with your personal Buddhas.

I was trying to find a way to give repose to the death of my older sister, and I went into training for the suicide hotline. Then just as that ended, this happened to my younger sister. The things that I have walked through. . . . Gradually, I feel things flowing. When I sit in front of the home altar, I greet Father

(Otōsan), Mother (Okāsan), Satako-chan (her younger sister), Oneisan (her older sister)—who died at seventy-five and had lived in Saitama—and my other older sister who committed suicide. All five of them. "Are you OK? Are all getting along well?" That is what I do when I do the memorial rites.[109]

She counts five deaths, but it is really seven members of her immediate family who have died: three by natural causes and four by unnatural causes. Since she was so young when her two oldest brothers died, she does not have a sense of a personal relationship with them. She has lived most of her life integrating their loss. She has many newer deaths to grieve now. Discussing this is emotional. As a person, I empathize. As a scholar, I hope I am not going too far. She has exposed a tremendous amount to me. In a quiet moment, I look at her and say, "I am sorry for causing you to remember such painful things." She returns my look and steadies her gaze into my eyes, "That's okay if it is useful, if it can be used as data for something."[110] Then she

Home altar for birth family
(not spouse's family)

looks down at her hands. It is clear that she is determined to help others any way that she can, but she aches to be helped herself.

As her pilgrimage to various religious traditions bears testimony, she does not wait for something to come to her. She does not stop seeking ways to experience peace. In addition to seeking a place where her heart could find peace, she has approached her healing in a holistic way. "I have been interested in Eastern medicine. I did yoga for ten years. Blood, water, and vital energy (ki)—if these three flow freely, then this is the foundation of health. So, you need to drink water and it must flow. Blood must flow and not get stuck. Same with your vital energy."[111]

Nagai-san realized it was important to not let her vital energy get stuck. In addition to yoga and drinking notable amounts of water, going to the nunnery, doing scripture copying and Buddhist figure copying (shabutsu), and tending her home altar help her get "unstuck."

Some have suggested that myths and rituals try to resolve unwelcome contradictions, but that in real life they do not get resolved away. Working intensively with these women for more than a decade, I have found their ritualized activities are not relegated to the perimeter of their daily lives. They are integrally woven into their lives. Their rituals are a mode of resolving and healing. The rituals actually help diminish suffering. They accomplish this by ritualizing the way they move their body and focus their thoughts. Ritualized behaviors draw on the wisdom of those who have suffered and sought healing. The experience is real. Ritualized behavior is as much real life as is nonritualized behavior. Some ritualized activities are a lifeline to deceased loved ones. They can help you find your way home when you are lost, in turmoil or in flux, and when you are confused. Many ritualized activities have become traditions because people have rather reliably been able to experience peace and relaxation while performing them.

The ritualized activities Nagai-san has done all along have given her enough breathing room to continue her pursuit of peace. This is notable, given all the trauma and loss she has experienced. Significantly, her ritualized practices have helped keep her resilient and open to seeing from different perspectives. Yet, the deep peace she was seeking was elusive. "I want to relax. If the figure of Shaka-san (Sakyamuni Buddha) were more clear, then maybe I could give all up to him. I want to feel that relief."[112] She finally had a breakthrough, or what might be called a post-traumatic growth spurt.

On Saturday evening, March 6, 1999, Nagai-san called me and told me that she had finally found relief. The key was that she could finally feel emptiness. It was no longer cold. It was no longer abstract. It was warm and full of life. The catalyst for this sudden expansion in her experience of emptiness was viewing paintings of the *Heart Sutra*. With an excitement and joy I had never heard from her, she told me about a single-artist exhibit of Iwasaki Tsuneo's called "Seeing the *Heart Sutra*," which was at the Nagoya City Museum. She had gone to see it earlier that day and the next day was the last day of the exhibition. The images went to the center of her pain and began to dissolve all the knots away. The paintings used the Chinese characters of the *Heart Sutra* to form the line of an image. The images depicted in the paintings included ducklings swimming in their mother's wake, lightning bolts, waterfalls, bubbles, atoms, and ants. It was the artist's intent to visually "explain" the meaning of the *Heart Sutra* through the images. A devout Buddhist, research scientist, and creative artist, Iwasaki's paintings are the first to transform the practice of scripture copying into not only an exquisite art form but also a profound mode of teaching.[113] He tried to show *how* "form is emptiness and emptiness is form" (which is the main teaching of the scripture) by taking everyday items and making them scripture. There is no dualism or hierarchy. It is all part of the same "stuff," poignantly depicted by ants, atoms, Kannon, and bubbles all composed of the same characters of the *Heart Sutra*. Everything is interconnected and empty of independent static existence. Things transform, but nothing is ultimately lost. Nagai-san "got it." Through his paintings, emptiness had become transparently obvious to her in the multiple forms of everyday life. She finally felt deep, deep peace, because she could feel embraced by everything around her. She was no longer alone in her struggles. She could feel support everywhere: In the air she breathed, she felt buoyed by the love of the people who have died. In the ground holding her up she felt supported by those who love her, even in their death, because death is not an end. Death is a transformation that unleashes energy to sustain various cycles of life.

Perhaps Nagai-san was predisposed to experience emptiness through the form of calligraphic images because she is an avid painter and practitioner of scripture and Buddhist figure copying. These practices had helped refresh her mind, but they had not helped unravel the knots that held her back from a deeply visceral experience of emptiness. Viewing Iwasaki's paintings of the *Heart Sutra* was the key to loosening the hold desperate loneliness and unrest had on her. In these paintings, she could "see" with her whole body-mind that she was not alone in the universe. She could comprehend with her body-mind the connections transcending time, space, and matter that had always embraced her. She could feel compassion in its pervasive expanse as well as feel its intimate connections in concrete details and events in her daily life. She knew that somehow her family was not suffering. This shift in perspective has provided profound relief. It is still difficult not to worry about her own daughter, and she still experiences sadness. She has stopped her decade-long volunteering at a suicide hotline, because she no longer feels death is something to be avoided as long as possible. She is uncertain if thinking this way is compassionate or not. It has also left her unclear as to what is the "helpful" thing to do. However, Nagai-san continues to be as compassionate as she can to those she encounters. Having finally experienced herself as integrally embedded in a supportive environment has brought her enough peace to feel whole as she tends to daily needs and concerns.

Terminal Diagnosis and "Miracle" Cloths

What might a Zen practitioner do when given a terminal diagnosis?

Doctors told Kimura-san, a humble and devout Zen Buddhist woman in her late sixties, her cancer was beyond their treatments. Her petite frame and gentle humility belied her inner strength. She fully believed that the traditional cleaning cloth (*tenugui*) given to her by the Zen abbess would heal her. To Kimura-san, this was no common *tenugui* cloth. Unlike the hundreds she had used over her near seven decades of life, this one had the calligraphy of the abbess and the image of a figure with palms pressed together in gratitude and respect (Gasshō Dōji) commissioned by the abbess printed on it.

It is important to know that the exchange of *tenugui* cloths is ubiquitous in the gift-giving culture of Japan. Everyone must give and receive gifts so often that practical gifts are preferred, food and cleaning supplies like soap and towels being among the most common. The abbess had these *tenugui* cloths made so she would have something useful to give to people. She thought that many might not actually clean with it, but might use it for special occasions handling special dishes. She did not imagine that they would be used for healing. Kimura-san, though, believed that the *tenugui* cloth had the power to heal her body. She lay in bed with one cloth on her pillow and one on her legs, the location of the cancer. Now, more than ten years later she is still farming her organic garden and mixing medicinal herbs for everyone's ailments from mosquito bites to arthritis. Doctors can find no traces of cancer in her body.[114] She has a twinkle in her eyes as she leans over and touches me on the arm saying, "It's true, Paula-san. That cloth healed me."[115]

Cleaning cloth with calligraphy by Aoyama Shundō: (left) "kindness and protection (*aigo*)," and (right) "expression of harmony (*wagen*)." Painting by Sakuma Ken'ichi, Gasshō Dōji (Child with Hands in Prayer).

Albert Einstein once said, "There are only two ways to live your life: you can live as if nothing is a miracle; you can live as if everything is a miracle." Kimura-san clearly chose the latter. She is unapologetic, although she is aware, like Flannery O'Connor, that, for some, "mystery is an embarrassment to the modern mind."[116] Mystery and healing miracles are not common fodder in institutional and text-based Zen, either.

The *tenugui* cloth Kimura-san claims healed her of cancer is the usual oblong shape, about sixteen inches wide and thirty-eight inches long. It is made of rather thin white cotton fabric, with brushwork printed in black and gray. The abbess Aoyama Rōshi commissioned a highly regarded Buddhist artist, Sakuma Ken'ichi, to paint two of his famous Gasshō Dōji images (figures with palms pressed together in gratitude and respect) facing each other. One sits on a lotus and the other is resting on clouds. Above the images, Aoyama Rōshi did calligraphy, renowned for its beauty and power. Above one side she brushed, "expression of harmony" (*wagen*), and above the other side she brushed, "kindness and protection" (*aigo*). Together, the images and calligraphy encapsulate the approach to life and its vicissitudes the abbess both teaches and manifests.

Kimura-san is one of the most devout laywomen affiliated with the Zen nunnery in Nagoya. Her presence at all manner of rituals and activities, including scripture copying, Sesshin, and Sunday Zen gatherings, would be missed if she did not attend. Her ever-present smile, kind words, and gentle nature are a reliable part of the community. At home, in addition to her substantial organic garden, she tends her elaborate home altar, located in its own room of her generations-old house. The large gate at the front of the property informs any visitor that there is history here. The manner in which she and her husband renovated the house indicates their deep piety. In preparation for the changes to the home that had been passed down to them, they copied the *Heart Sutra* one thousand times. They imbued each brush stroke with prayers for the safety, health, and well-being of the occupants of their home. They rolled them up and put them into the rafters under the new roof, imbedding compassionate protection into the very structure of their home.

Their aesthetic values are also evident, because from the outside the new and old parts of the house blend together seamlessly. Although Kimura-san thrives on hard work, the modern bath, laundry, and kitchen space inside makes daily chores more efficient. Of course, efficiency and hard work go hand in hand when done in a Zen mode.

Cotton *tenugui* cloths are staples for cleaning all Japanese homes and temples. Kimura-san uses multiple *tenugui* cloths countless times a day, every day of the year: to dry dishes, dust furniture, wipe counters and tabletops, cover her head from the sun while working out in her garden, bathe her body, then when she launders them and hangs them to dry. Indeed, it is not overstating it to say that *tenugui* cloths are an essential part of Japanese culture.

Yamaguchi-san, another of my consociates who received one of these *tenugui* cloths from Aoyama Rōshi, offers her thoughts. "As you age, I think it is increasingly important to be mindful of your facial expressions. I think what harmony refers to is like in the poem by Aida Mitsuo: 'Just your presence in the room makes it brighter.' I think [the writing on the *tenugui* cloths] suits women, especially. It is about bringing to life the special qualities of women. I like the words, but it is hard to actualize in daily life. I do try hard to do it, though."[117]

In discussing how to live according to these teachings, Aoyama Rōshi recognizes it is difficult, especially when we are upset or angry. Once she recommended people bow to each other with palms pressed together before starting to argue so they would have better arguments. Although her recommendation was met with laughter, everyone knew she was right. When discussing the power of the Gasshō Dōji with Sakuma Sensei and his wife, she said the great thing about bowing with palms pressed together is that it makes you focus and draws out the healing power in yourself.[118]

Kimura-san quietly embodies the teachings in the *tenugui* cloth. She respects the Zen master Aoyama Rōshi so highly her heart was open to the possibilities of healing. Her heart also flooded with pure gratitude, which enabled her to deeply connect with the powers of kindness in the universe. She felt the cloth on her pillow and legs protected her in such a fundamental way she felt utterly safe. Feeling safe enabled her to experience how inextricably interconnected she was with everything in the universe. These are all qualities that constitute healing in a domestic Zen paradigm. That they are also associated with a cure for a cancer diagnosed as terminal is extraordinary. Inspired by Kimura-san, others in the community also began seeing the cloth as imbued with healing power.

Yamaguchi-san recounts what she did and thought after being diagnosed with cancer.

I was told I might have uterine cancer. Aoyama Sensei wrote this [a poem about illness being a treasure from the Buddha] for the time that she was hospitalized and about to have an operation because she might have cancer. I don't think it is easy to think of cancer as a gift from the Buddha. But if it happens, to settle your heart, you need to do things. Things you must do for your children, and so on. So you need to live well when you can. If you've had a scare, you can see clearly the things that are important. Even if the body is sick, it does not mean the heart-mind is. You must keep the heart well. When I was waiting for the diagnosis about which level of cancer, 1, 2, 3, or 4, I was hanging the futon outside and a butterfly came. They have very short lives compared to humans. Even if they are going to die that night, they fly around with so much joy. I actually don't know if it's fun. It could be a lot of hard work to fly around, but it looks like fun! I thought, the butterfly's life is so much shorter, yet it can fly around. The same is with fireflies. They live fully until death. So I thought, I too must live well when I can. I didn't fall apart and cry at the time. I have thought since a long time ago that I would die once, so dying is not so bad. I thought dying in my fifties is a little soon, but when I think clearly, I think it is what it is.

When I was given the anesthesia, I said many things to the nurse. I said that I was really scared. When I was doing daily activities, I was fine. When you're in the hospital, you ride along with the flow of the hospital rhythm: this test, that result, next thing, meal, etc. I was happy to leave the hospital. I went home and waited for a week. I was fine while doing daily activities. The morning I was to get the results, my feeling got heavy. I wore the prayer beads Aoyama Sensei gave me the whole time, even during the operation. I had the *tenugui* cloth, too. My feelings about them were, "Please save me!" Aoyama Sensei told me to say the *Heart Sutra* when there was nothing more to be done. When I got out of surgery and woke up, I thought, oh yes, Aoyama Sensei said to chant the *Heart Sutra*. I was fading in and out, and people would come in and out. So I kept starting over and forgetting where I was [in the chant]. I only got through the whole sutra once. But it really saved me from thinking of other things. I felt Aoyama Sensei's presence with me. It gave my heart rest to have someone who knows the truth nearby who gave me a hand. I wanted someone to know my weakness, and I trusted her. I did everything she told me. I had the prayer beads, the *tenugui* cloth, the book she gave me, and I did what she said. She was a place I could go to like a birth home for my heart (*kokoro no furusato*) where I could get support. My mother and sister were with me, too.[119]

Here is a more detailed explanation of just how the *tenugui* cloth helped her when she was in the hospital to have surgery to remove the cancer.

I put the *tenugui* cloth on the pillow where I rested my head in the hospital. In Japan it is common to have a cloth wrapped around the abdomen (*haramaki*), so it helped me feel settled putting it there, too. Somewhere in my head was Kimura-san's story. I couldn't think my cancer disappeared because the prayer beads and *tenugui* cloth were there, but it made my heart feel safe. That is what I felt when I received it from Aoyama Sensei. It could have been anything. I did want something I could physically put on my body, although I can't distinguish clearly what is heart and body. It is like an amulet, something I could hold on to. It could have been anything. If I had not received anything, I might have asked for something. [We laugh.] People told me you don't die from uterine cancer, but people do. It is a cancer. I felt like I could die in peace with it [having the things from Aoyama Sensei]. I felt like I had done all I could. Afterwards, it is just the results. . . . As I went to sleep with one *tenugui* cloth on my pillow, Aoyama Rōshi's prayer beads on my wrist, the other *tenugui* cloth wrapped on me, my sense of things got big. I could just let it all unfold and sleep well. I did have a feeling that having her prayer beads made me feel like I was not alone.[120]

Unlike Kimura-san, whose cancer was treated as far as allopathic medicine could go before it disappeared, when the surgeons went in to get the cancer they had found through a biopsy of Yamaguchi-san, they could not find any. Yamaguchi-san was aware of the qualities she experienced: peace, acceptance, expanded perspective, and of not being alone. Having the ritual items she viewed as imbued with healing powers actually touching her body was clearly a critical element in her having a healing experience.

In these cases, the method of healing was not "traditional." It was not even intended by the maker and giver of the cloth. The only observable conclusion is that the meaning with which the receivers of the cloth endowed the cloth had an efficacious power when it was placed on their bodies. They say their doctors have no other explanation, either. Regardless of the "true" mechanics of this unpretentious ritualized use of the *tenugui* cloth, the gratitude, joy, and health these women experienced is genuine.

Larry Dossey, a medical doctor who studies the role the mind plays in healing, says that miracles "are really debates about worldviews."[121] If the lack of known scientific explanation were not seen as reason to dismiss a case, and if instead it were seen in terms of the possibilities for research on "miracle" experiences, especially with diseases like cancer, it might provide information that could help others.[122] He further suggests, "rather than focusing on high-profile sites such as Lourdes," it would be informative to examine "people's everyday lives."[123]

Miraculous in its own way, Honda-san experiences healing even though a cure for her chronic condition is elusive. She lives with pain in her leg that is at times immobilizing. At those times, she especially appreciates living in her tiny studio apartment, because everything is close at hand. Most of the time, though, she manages with a pronounced limp that results in her swaying from side to side as she walks. Like the majority of people in Japan, she does not own a car and takes public transportation, which increases the time she is subjected to stares and being treated as though she is unintelligent. A taxicab ride is reserved for critical times, due to the toll it takes on her modest means. When she does need to go out for groceries or other errands, she plans her route around how many stairs she will have to climb or descend in train stations, subway stations, and buses. She knows which courses are the easiest on her legs and weighs that against which way is the fastest. Depending on how many places she needs to go, she calculates how much is reasonable for her legs to handle that day. What is her secret to living with intense chronic pain that limits her ability to move around freely, and yet experience healing? One clue is that she practices scripture copying, yet she has never asked for relief from her pain in the "prayer" section allotted on the sheet.

> I have learned a lot of things from this illness. Illness is not something you should throw away! I understand this at this age. If I were younger, I would not have thought this way. I would have regretted the illness. The pain is real, but it does not require patience. I have never asked for it to go away. I feel grateful that I have been able to have a good life. Trying to be "patient" builds up stress. Pain is pain, but I don't feel I need patience. I have had this since I was about twenty-seven.[124]

The level of acceptance achieved by Honda-san was difficult for me to comprehend. Despite her relentless chronic pain, she is grateful for how much she has learned from it. She seems to live with a wide perspective and is advanced and disciplined in not taking a narrow, self-pitying view. She says she does not even need to try to be patient. She just accepts the pain is pain. She does not even wish it were gone. "It is what it is." Such non-resistance to her pain, even with the limits it puts on her activities, requires a rare level of resilience and a keen ability to maintain a steady and expansive view. She considers herself healed, because she does not wish her life were any different from what it is.

Reflecting on Honda-san's definition of healing made me think of a Zen kōan. Zen Master Tōzan was asked about getting rid of the heat. His response was to advise the questioner to go to a place where there is neither heat nor cold. Transposing this kōan to address healing encapsulates Honda-san's experience. "How do you get well? Go to a place where there is no illness or wellness." Physician Ornish's distinction between disease and illness is helpful here. "Disease is the physical manifestation of biological dysfunction. Illness is your experience of that process and your relationship to it."[125] Honda-san manifests the answer to this kōan, her intense chronic pain notwithstanding. She lives in the space where there is no illness or wellness when she accepts her situation and lives with it without complaint or longing. Seeing life through the conceptual lenses of either illness or wellness provides an incomplete and limiting view of reality. To focus on either illness or wellness is to separate the self from its vast interrelated context. By seeing herself fully embedded in the universe, Honda-san has accepted her situation as her "Genjō Kōan" (responding to actual conditions in a manner that does not generate suffering).

Kimura-san and Yamaguchi-san also found that place. In their cases, they were fortunate it also coincided with a cure. Kimura-san tailored her homemade ritual in a manner, consciously or not, that moved her mind and touched her heart in just the right way to help her feel cared for and supported by a vast web of compassionate power. The abbess Aoyama Rōshi had not envisioned her gift of a *tenugui* cloth would become a healing balm strong enough to dissolve cancer. Kimura-san also had not anticipated her use of the *tenugui* cloth would become a healing ritual practiced by several members in the community.

Domestic Zen as Ritual Domain

These up-close and personal images demonstrate that the practice of Zen in a domestic context is complex, ritualistic, and focused on the health and well-being of family members. The empirical information reveals the concerns, practices, and characteristics of domestic Zen. Most notable is that women are at the center of this realm of Zen. The range of circumstances in these illustrations is representative of the range of concerns among the women's families. They include health-focused ailments from common colds and chronic pain to terminal cancer diagnoses. They also include all stages of life from infertility and child rearing to the care of senile elderly grandparents, and to the trauma and grief over the loss of loved ones. In order for these women to respond to the complex and changing needs of their family members, including themselves, they engage in a range of practices that enables them to stay strong, even as they enter the eye of a storm. It is critical for these women to find ways to sustain themselves, for they undergird their families and seek to support their deepest needs.

The practices of domestic Zen incorporate a range of activities, including attending to the home altar, artistic expressions, household chores, participation in elaborate temple rituals designed to protect the family, eating *bonji* syllables, and applying a healing *tenugui* cloth to cancer. The practices that revolve around the home altar include chanting, offerings, bowing, and praying. The sound of the bells and wooden drum reaches family members who are not directly involved in the rituals. The incense also wafts throughout the home. These help create an atmosphere that invites people to remember that life is meaningful and that we are not alone. These nonverbal cues remind people there is support. The most common chants are done when under duress or on the run: "Namu Amida

Butsu" or "Nenpi Kannon Riki." These chants make the women immediately feel they are not alone, even as they feel helpless to take pain away from a child who broke an arm on the playground or clear the confusion of an elder. Such a practice is woven into the fabric of their daily lives. They do not take extra time, money, or energy, and they can be done while rushing to a doctor or cleaning up after toilet accidents.

Another issue this ethnographic study illuminates is that their practices engage in multiple ways of using text. Texts are not only read, but are used in eight other ways, including as body, food, comfort, instrument, and medicine. Chanting is mostly done as a mode of meditation, not contemplation and reflection on the meaning of the chanted word. Chanting has calming and clarifying effects. In the case of the rice paper *bonji* syllables, the text is eaten like a nourishing food. In the Daihannya-e, the text is treated as a body—an important body—indicated by dressing it up in silk brocade. Also, in the Daihannya-e a mantra is used as an instrument to unleash the protective power of the text as it is opened in all directions. Likewise, reciting "Nenpi Kannon Riki" functions as an instrument to elicit the power of Kannon, helping to calm and comfort a person in time of need. Medicinal properties of the text are found in the text being used to heal through touch, as in the Daihannya-e and the *tenugui* cloth. Further medicinal properties of text that target the mind were found by a woman for whom rational discourse could not reach deeply enough into her consciousness to help. Viewing text, in her case, painted into pictures resulted in a radical shift in her perception of reality. This occurred not after years of *kōan* practice, but rather was precipitated by multiple deaths in her family. The spectrum of uses of text revealed in the practices of these women illuminates a significant feature of their priorities. It underscores their concern for that which is effective in the cessation of suffering over and against that which tries to explain it. It reveals their wisdom that cognitive knowledge alone does not have the power to heal. Bodily experiences are the primary conduit for healing.

From a sociological line of analysis, these rituals mediate between the intimate relations of the inside (*uchi*, private) and the anomic relations of the outside (*soto*, public).[126] From a Sōtō Zen Buddhist line of analysis, the rituals are activities that manifest Buddha nature. Since everything is interrelated, ultimately there is no "inside" or "outside." In conventional reality, however, such distinctions are helpful.

A framework for seeing the motions and changes that occur in ritualized activities draws on Brian McVeigh's insights. He notes, "Rituals reveal a society's fears" (death, illness, having no children), "fault lines" (strains of

caring for elders), and "points of tension" (marriage and other family relations).[127] In marking changes and transitions, rituals redefine identities
and boundaries. Rituals around birth are clear markers of constructing,
whether it involves constructing a couple into "parents" and parents into
"grandparents," or a child into "older sister" or "older brother." Aging with
dementia often involves a particularly painful and challenging reconstruc-
tion of relationships, responsibilities, and identities, but there are no regu-
larized rituals for acknowledging this major change. Mortuary rituals are
particularly obvious in how they deconstruct by honoring the death of a
person, and reconstruct by recognizing the deceased as a new Buddha.
With a new death, a home altar is constructed or reconstructed to add one
more to the "ancestors."

As we saw, one woman reached her limit before developing her own
repertoire of ritual practices to support her with the changes in her family as
her mother-in-law aged. Women attend several rituals held in temples, usually as representatives for the whole family, or at least with the motivation to
help the whole family. For example, the Hana Matsuri (Buddha's birthday)
is explicitly for receiving support with children. Daihannya-e and Setsubun
are for receiving protection from calamity for the family and blessings for
health and well-being. The most esoteric of the practices include ingesting
rice-paper *bonji* syllables and sacred water from Nara's Tōdai-ji temple. The
most physically demanding of the rituals is the small group Hyakumanben
that requires each person to act in concert with all others to pass beads
around, encircling all in a flowing current of compassion. The most "magical" and ingeniously homemade of the rituals is transforming a traditional
Japanese *tenugui* cloth into a "healing cloth" that "miraculously" made cancer disappear. Even though these practices span a wide range of activities, a
commonality among them is they foster a visceral sense of belonging to a
vast network that both supports and is worthy of support.

These practices imbue Zen laywomen with steady, even corporal,
awareness they are connected and assisted, even as they sometimes feel
inadequate and overwhelmed to "make it all better." As these women attend to the regular needs and demanding crises that arise, such practices
as meditating while seated in silence seem out of place, impractical, and
unhelpful. Rather, the types of practices found in domestic Zen are done
amidst the sounds of water running for the laundry, dishes, and baths.
They are done with the aroma of food cooking and incense burning. Adding Mizu Tori water to the rice the family will eat for dinner is seen as much
of a key ingredient in nurturing the family as are soy sauce and seasoning

(*dashi*). It is because these practices are woven into the demands of daily family life that they are practical and effective.

Characteristics of domestic Zen include the flexibility to meet specific needs and the creativity to weave religious practice into daily life. Flexibility and creativity are necessary for family life, because the needs of families are complex and changing. Many needs cannot be scheduled or anticipated. Domestic Zen is different from monastic Zen primarily because it is driven by such different needs and circumstances. Therefore, different practices are required. Domestic Zen is full of homemade rituals and supplications for assistance. It does not run like clockwork. It is created anew every day. It is full of tears, dirty laundry, and expressions of frustration and fear. Yet, its most striking characteristic is that domestic Zen is propelled by an attitude toward the vicissitudes of life that hones in on the positive and the affirming.

My consociates' practices unfold within a Zen Buddhist worldview, but their interest is rarely institutional or philosophical. It is practical. Their practices are simple, accessible, inexpensive, portable, direct, and immediate. Years of disciplined practice are not required to perform or participate in these practices: they are accessible, even to the busiest person. Many can be done at home or on the run. The most important thing to these women is that the effects of a practice are immediate and direct. From calming down in a moment of crisis to being compassionately embraced despite tragedy, to being healed after a terminal diagnosis, these women have found empowerment for themselves and their families in their domestic practices. These women are conscious to take time in their daily lives to listen to their hearts. Whether it is chanting sutras for an hour or just quietly gazing at the trees while hanging laundry, they lead ritualized lives that make healing a daily activity.

CHAPTER 5

The Healing Power of Beauty

肉眼の見る所は限りがある.
心眼の見る所は無限である.

The places the eyes of the flesh see have a limit.
The places the eyes of the heart see have no limit.

GYOKKO SENSEI, AS RECEIVED FROM THE BUDDHA

Beauty is the center of the Japanese women's practices and locus of their healing. Indeed, the highly ritualized and aestheticized dimensions of Japanese culture are brought together in their way of healing. All ritualized activities the women engage in as part of their healing have an aesthetic dimension. The ones I highlight in this chapter focus on the explicit creation and appreciation of beauty. The types of aesthetic practices in which they engage include calligraphy, painting, poetry, music, flower arranging, and tea ceremony. They draw on the long traditions each of these arts has in Japanese culture, where aesthetic refinement is a mark of virtue. While cultures have distinct aesthetic sensibilities, the role of beauty in human culture is pervasive. The Dalai Lama's thoughts about the role of beauty correspond to the function beauty plays in the healing way of these women. He elucidates, "Often it is through the expression and appreciation of beauty that we unlock the compassionate potential in the human heart."[1]

The aesthetic practices the women cultivate as part of their healing activity are designed to help a woman polish her heart-mind. For these women, it is important to find ways to keep their heart-minds clear and to stay in tune with their bodies. Therefore, a practice that reaches a sufficiently deep level of body-mind harmony is necessary. Some of the practices in which the women engage are more explicitly aimed than others to train the body to move as one with the heart-mind. There is no more refined an example of this than the tea ceremony. All of the aesthetic practices, though, become more potent sources of healing the more attuned and mindful the person is. This became evident in the process of analyzing the aesthetic activities as a mode of healing. Often the healing qualities of the practices are directly linked to their artistic elements. These aesthetic practices help the women integrate mind, emotions, and body.

Japanese culture has focused on cultivating the senses to experience beauty, especially the beauty of impermanence. The key is to appreciate the present moment as beautiful precisely because it is ephemeral. The contemplative arts can be experienced as healing insofar as they direct your attention to the present activity with full body-mind engagement. Each motion is carefully prescribed to be the height of respect and efficiency, every gesture meaningful. When done with no extraneous motion or waste, the mind-body-heart moves in attunement with the environment. Doing so can feel cleansing as you tap into the rhythms and energy of those with which you are interacting, including implements like brushes, bowls, and water. When treating everything with which one comes in contact with respect and awareness of interrelationship, one feels respected in return and supported by a vast web.

The qualities of beauty that heal correspond to the principles of the paradigm, the way of healing, discussed in Chapter 2. Experiencing interrelatedness is achieved through complete body-mind engagement with a meaningful activity in the present moment. To experience this not only nurtures the self, but gives rise to a sublime joy in living. Being fully present requires having an open and accepting heart, which in turn cultivates gratitude because you can see from an expanded perspective. Seeing clearly and deeply is the root condition for acting with compassion. Beauty heals because it is an immersion in immediate and positive sensorial, somatic experience of the present moment.

In the following sections, I analyze each type of aesthetic practice based on the way of healing paradigm. My interpretation of each practice is based on deep conversations with the women spanning a dozen years, extensive embodied knowledge training, and participation in the activities with the women. How beauty heals is distinctive for each aesthetic practice, yet the shared worldview—concept of body-mind and understanding of healing—permeates them all.

Calligraphy

Brushed calligraphy is an art that visibly mirrors the heart-mind of the brush holder. Therefore, from the beginning of writing Buddhist scriptures in Chinese characters, there was a dimension that the written word was not just a conveyance of meaning but also an indicator of the qualities of the one who brushed the characters. The art begins with making the ink. To prepare the ink, a solid ink stick is dipped into a reservoir of water drops pooled in a stone, carved and polished expressly to serve the calligrapher. She holds the ink stick in her hands as she presses down on it and draws droplets up from the pooled water to the silken smooth flat surface of the stone. Gentle, slow, rhythmic rubbing and light pressure yields a finer solution. An erratic, rapid motion and heavy pressure produce a viscous solution. The viscosity of the ink is vital for expressing the calligrapher's state of being. Thick ink takes patient determination to make, and therefore indicates stamina and power. The ink quality will even distinguish different kinds of power. Power that erupts out of angry frustration makes rough, uneven ink. The power of steady confidence and strength makes smooth, even ink. Too much water and only brief rubbing of the ink stick on the stone surface results in thin ink, often an indication of fatigue, despair, or fear. Even as she rubs the ink stick into the water on the ink rubbing stone, she can see the quality of ink that is produced. The reflection of her heart-mind in the ink might nudge her to slow down and relax, or ignite determination to persist.

How deeply the brush is inserted into the ink and how much is stroked off along the smooth surface of the ink stone determines the quality and character of the color with which the hairs of the brush are swathed. Each hair of the brush is a delicate instrument that attunes to the subtlest reverberations of emotion and the slightest turn of thought. These guide it in moving the ink across the paper. If the woman holding the brush is sad and tired, or impatient with her pain, it is all laid bare on the page. If the brush is moved by deep gratitude for having one more day to live, or softened by compassion, the flow of the brush reveals a deeper quality of movement. The brush only records what occurs in the present moment. Therefore, a line of characters reflects the sequence and shifts of emotions and thoughts as they move across time. At each moment in this aesthetic practice, the woman receives immediate feedback on the condition of her heart-mind. Hence, she can make decisions and adjustments along the way. In the course of writing a long page, she can gradually find a stable peace.

The aesthetic practice of calligraphy has been ritualized in Japanese Buddhism as scripture copying. Buddhist scriptures have a wide range in length: only a few undertake the longer ones, such as the *Kannon-gyō* chapter of the *Lotus Sutra,* while the majority find the *Heart Sutra* most amenable to their spiritual needs. The meaning of the scripture is not the central concern: rather, it is the sense of familiarity it engenders and, quite practically, its relative brevity. The *Heart Sutra* is a perfect length of scripture to brush. It is long enough to give time to shift and adjust the calligrapher's heart-mind with keen focus and observant attention, yet it is not so long that it leads to carelessness or lassitude. The characters are also sufficiently complicated, requiring even the most educated in modern Japanese to slow down in order to accurately produce the intricately complex strokes for the characters that are seen only in scripture today.

Although many people practice scripture copying at home, numerous temples designate a special time for copying the *Heart Sutra.* On the third Saturday of each month, the nunnery where my consociates practice scripture copying holds this aesthetic ritual practice. Entering the nunnery's worship hall, facing the altar, incense wafting through the air, and sitting beside others who are similarly engaged enhances the efficacy of the practice. People come and go over the course of time from 1:00 through 5:00 p.m., most taking an hour to write. A nun offers a few simple words of consolation and encouragement to those arriving, since it is safe to assume most everyone holds something in their heart when they come. Without prompting, Kawasaki-san enthusiastically offers to me that her motivation for doing scripture copying at the nunnery is, "I love hearing Kitō Sensei's talk. She speaks just for five minutes right at the beginning. I go so I can hear her. What she says sinks in deeply."[2] She amplified at another time. "Kitō Sensei is a teacher who says things that make me feel relieved and safe."[3] Among a broad range of heart, health, and living advice, Kitō Sensei has said things like, "Eighty percent of sickness is due to stress. So take time to walk and chant. They are vital to your health."[4] She also offers advice that "in the morning you should rise with hope. When going to sleep, fill your heart with gratitude."[5] When she is done speaking, the silence of the worship hall fills with the hopes and fears of all present, a palpable quiet that undergirds the determination to cease suffering.

Kitō Sensei

At the end of the scripture, there is a space on the thick rice paper designated for a prayer, your name, home address, location at which you are engaging in this ritual, and the date. Once you are done writing, you offer your
script at the main altar. Loose incense is there for you to offer on the burning
coals as you bow with palms pressed together. It is clear that those who lin-
ger in a long bow have a deep current running through them. Along the side
of the worship hall, a low table is set up for the event. Here, a nun sits on the
tatami in formal style, with legs folded under (*seiza*), to record the participation, accept the donation to the temple, and pass out *Zen no Tomo* (Friend of
Zen), a magazine filled with accessible Zen teachings.[6] This is not the nun's
main purpose, though, especially in the case of Kitō Sensei.

As each person approaches individually, Kitō Sensei sees and listens
to what she has brought with her in her heart-mind. Few people discuss
matters explicitly or with any depth. Silence is everywhere, and everyone
respects it. It is rather an approval implicit in the air. By being completely
present with you, she affirms and embraces your whole being with no
judgment and no hesitation. You feel seen, understood, and accepted. As
Honda-san puts it, "I go to scripture copying because for that time, that

one hour, once a month, I feel understood. It is due to Kitō Sensei's presence."[7] It is a private interchange, yet all the women explained to me how
they felt healed just being in her presence. They do the scripture copying
practice to be near her as much as they go for the experience of the actual
practice. Indeed, Kitō Sensei is living testimony to the power of one who
embodies compassion. Those who are present at the end join together as
the nun in attendance leads in chanting the *Heart Sutra,* complete with
the steady beat of the wooden drum and sonorous gongs of the large bell.

The fullness of the aesthetic practice of calligraphy as a healing activity becomes clearer through the voices of the women's scripture copying
practice. Nagai-san provides me with a deep context for her scripture
copying practice. "I would not have gone so deep into Buddhism if it had
not been for the war and all. I started with calligraphy because I wanted to
find something stable. People's feelings change, so you can't rely on them."[8]
So she finds the practice helps her gain stability. She emphatically stresses
that the healing power of calligraphy starts with making the ink. "It is
important to mix your own ink, because it is the time that you quiet your
heart so you can do calligraphy well. Also, there is thick and thin ink, to
match your feeling at the time or the content of what you are writing."[9] An
indication of the seriousness with which she regards this aesthetic practice
and a testimony to the healing it has helped her experience, Nagai-san
copied an extensive scripture, the *Kannon-gyō,* which is Chapter 25 of the
Lotus Sutra. In addition to the length augmenting the challenge, instead
of the usual black ink, she used precious gold ink. The gold was a genuine
challenge that intensified the aesthetic practice enormously. She was deliberately seeking an intense experience, because she was trying to regain
some modicum of peace after her sister's murder. She had the gold
Kannon-gyō framed and displays it in memory of her sister.

The brush and ink are critical insofar as they help the women face
themselves clearly and polish their own hearts, yet the people with whom
you engage in the practice can augment its healing power immensely.
Honda-san's explanations of her experiences with scripture copying are
evidence of this. "Kitō Sensei puts my heart at ease. When she is there,
people wait in line to be near her. She is like medicine for the heart. That
is the most important thing for humans."[10] What I am most intrigued to
learn about her scripture copying experience, however, is that it is at scripture copying where she has a quality of experience more commonly associated with seated meditation. "I can become tranquil and experience '*mu*'"
(zero, or emptiness).[11] What she means by *mu* here is that she feels so

thoroughly integrated into the fabric of reality, supported, accepted, and safe, that she has no sense of being a distinct entity, and so finds a condition where suffering ceases.

It is striking that a ritualized aesthetic activity that takes one hour to perform and occurs just once per month could have such a deep impact on someone. Honda-san's experience is so potent, though, that although she lives with often debilitating chronic hip pain, she impresses on me how, "no matter how painful it was, I went by taxi to participate in the scripture copying ritual. Kitō Sensei is like the goddess of compassion, Kannon-sama. There were two times in twelve years that I did not go, when I threw out my back and when I had surgery."[12] It becomes clear to me that were she not to go to the scripture copying ritual and have a time to become empty, and spend those healing moments near Kitō Sensei, her pain would be unbearable.

Scripture copying practice as an aesthetic mode for healing is also effective in helping women work with emotional challenges and frustrations as they seek to be less angry and more peaceful. Noguchi-san leads me through her experiences of scripture copying and how they have helped her change. It also tells us how her engagement with the practice has changed over the years.

> Now in the prayer section on the scripture copying paper, I always write "Peace on Earth." However, during the first year I asked for "peace in my heart." That was at a time when I got angry just looking at another person's face. It has been numerous years, though, since I have asked for anything for myself. I sometimes ask for help if a friend is sick. I go because it is fun. If I just see Kitō Sensei's face, I am happy. That's enough. A few times, I have done scripture copying at home when I've come home from a night vigil the first night of someone's death (o-tsuya). I pray for their Buddhahood. I want to put something into their coffin. I have also just written a few times just to do it. When I am writing I feel calm.[13]

Scripture copying helped her dissolve her anger that her life did not go as she had hoped it would. An engagement was broken because she got sick. Although it was not a life-threatening or chronic illness, it was enough to stop the marriage arrangement. Scripture copying helped her expand her focus and cares. She has since lived a healthy life and she is comfortably single into her retirement years.

Both scripture copying practice and aging are helpful in taming the demons within. Honda-san confesses it was harder to tame her demon when she was younger, because it was easily stirred up with thoughts of negative self-perceptions. Now she does scripture copying when she is angry. It helps her find peace. She lets us in to her thinking about all this.

> Aoyama Rōshi says that we all have a demon and a Buddha in us. Sometimes my demon jumps out, and I must calm it down. Going to scripture copying helps. In the end, though, it is that I must win over myself. I must defeat my own demon. If I do not, then bad things happen. I try to make Buddha come out first. It takes discipline. I couldn't do it when I was young. When I got angry, I would think, "Oh I am a bad woman." I would be upset with myself. Now I can find peace in my heart more.[14]

Proof that she can find peace in her heart now is evident in how she reasons through personal responsibilities in the face of what does not appear fair.

> If you think your problems are caused by other people, or that they are other people's responsibility, that is more difficult to live with and painful. I don't like that. It's more difficult and painful if you think of yourself as a sacrificer or a victim. If you feel gratitude, you can begin to see many things. I really think that gratitude is a miraculous medicine. And then your heart becomes light, and other things begin to feel better, too. I sometimes think that my legs becoming bad is a good thing. I have become able to feel all kinds of different things. It is very interesting to see things from the perspective of having bad legs.[15]

Honda-san attributes the aesthetic practice of scripture copying to helping her grow in a range of ways. She does not indulge in self-deprecating thoughts anymore. She finds taking responsibility for whatever happens less painful than other alternatives. Most stunningly, she also feels gratitude for her chronic pain, because it has helped her expand her perspective.

These women show us how the aesthetic practice of calligraphy heals. Engaging in this ritualized activity of body-mind helps them focus on the present moment where they can gain stability and clarity. It draws open their hearts to accept even undesirables as it exposes the quality of their heart-mind to themselves. In turn, it then helps them cultivate gratitude and expand their perspectives. A critical dimension of the potency of this healing ritual is not insignificantly the peace and security that comes from a visceral experience of interrelatedness when they enter the orbit of Kitō Sensei's embodied compassion.

Painting and Drawing

Painting a copy of a Buddhist figure is the religious practice of Buddhist figure copying (*shabutsu*). Drawing on different skills and sensibilities from scripture copying, it attracts those attuned to the images, iconography, and aesthetics of painting. The practice applies to portrayals of sacred figures across the Japanese Buddhist pantheon. A host of Buddhas, including Sakyamuni, Amida, and the Great Sun Buddha, numerous bodhisattvas like Kannon, Monjū, and Jizō, and protector figures, like Fudō Myōō, are typically counted among the more favored figures to be copied. Predictably, Kannon, the goddess of compassion, is the most beloved figure copied. There are numerous different forms of Kannon, including Eleven-Headed Kannon and Thousand-Armed Kannon. Some images used in this aesthetic practice were originally done by recognized artists. Others are based on sculptures made famous by their singular beauty or by being associated with a famous temple. Still others are outline drawings done with careful attention to clarity, balance, and each aspect of a figure's iconography.

Unlike scripture copying where people gather and copy the same scripture, Buddhist figure copying is more individual. To begin, the practitioner chooses an image that has some meaning to her. She might choose a figure she highly respects or a figure who embodies a quality she is committed to cultivating, like compassion. A copy of the chosen image is usually printed in a faint gray, and the practitioner then follows the line with brush and ink. More advanced practitioners might paint freehand as they look at the image. As in scripture copying, there is the same process of making the ink. It not only provides a time to calm the heart-mind, but also is a time to quietly attune to the image before her.

Nagai-san is the only one among the women who has done this practice seriously. She decided to try it after she had been on a trip many years ago to seek out locations that appear in the *Manyōshū* anthology of ancient Japanese poetry. The poetry from this early period speaks to her spirit deeply. She enjoys the natural quality and lack of pretense of this poetry. Going to a place cited in one of the ancient poems generates a deep sense of being at home and belonging. While there, she was deeply moved by the Eleven-Headed Kannon statue at Dōgan-ji Kannon Hall in Shiga Prefecture. It is recognized as a national treasure and dates back to the Nara Period (710–794 C.E.), when Emperor Shōmu reigned. The exquisite sinuous lines are supple yet strong, earthy in their simplicity yet transcendent in their beauty. A powerful sense of stability and calm washed

Shabutsu Buddha figure copying of Eleven-Headed Kannon

over Nagai-san as she gazed at the statue. Later, seeing it in her mind's eye, she could regain the peace she felt then. This is the power of an image to heal. It can generate a palpable sensation that lingers beyond sight, for its image can remain whole—encoded with the fullness of the original experience, the sounds, the smells, the season. As she painted the image on paper, another was painted on her heart.

The specific image can be particularly potent if it has personal meaning and significance. Nagai-san primarily reveals her reason through the impassioned tone in her voice and excitement in her eyes as she explains, "I chose to do a Buddhist figure copying of Dōgan-ji's Eleven-Headed Kannon, because I felt her more than any other."[16] As she says this to me, it is evident that something in this image still has the power to stir her and help her experience a release from whatever strain has built up in her.[17] The kinesthetic experience was augmented by the precious medium she chose to use. "Working with the gold—to make it even—took time."[18] When Nagai-san finished renovating her house, she invited many people to come hear Aoyama Rōshi give a Dharma talk. She had her image of Eleven-Headed Kannon hanging in the background.[19] Buddhist figure copying being a much more contextualized practice than scripture copying, such events are endowed with resonant import.

Gyokko Sensei discovered for herself a notably resonant aesthetic practice that helps her heal. She did not make an explicit effort to engage in a defined practice. One day she was reflecting on how living a life in the posture of bowing—with palms pressed together in respect and gratitude—was her aim in life. For her this means being grateful, accepting, and responding with compassion. She realizes that attaining this is akin to enlightenment, but awareness that the goal is lofty does not overwhelm her. Rather, it undergirds her commitment to the importance of the goal. To amplify her determination to live ever more according to these qualities, she was inspired to create an image of Kannon, goddess of compassion, bowing with palms pressed together. Her medium of choice was colored pencils. They reflect her inclinations and level of comfort. Amazed at how healing it was to draw a rudimentary line drawing of Kannon bowing, she drew several more. It became a meditation for her and a source of buoyant joy as she exercised her creativity. Eventually she decided to add colored shading. Her eyes lit up as she explained how much fun it was to see her image come alive. Although she had become increasingly aware of the importance of enjoyment in healing, since she was a rather serious, studious, and contained woman she rarely did something just for fun. The no-pretense pencil drawing of Kannon tapped into a mode of being that she had not known before. She felt empowered as she experienced a liberating delight in engaging in a kinesthetic, visual, and aesthetic mode of religious practice. It inspired her to increase the details of the face and garment. She now draws images of Kannon and Jizō, over and over. She frequently draws on scrap paper, even on the plain side of an advertisement that came with the morning newspaper. The healing power of her homemade aesthetic practice is rooted in the meaning the image has for her.

Gyokko Sensei's experience was not an isolated experience. In an entirely unrelated context, Yamamoto-san, too, discovered how creating a simple image with her own hands gave her a deep sense of satisfaction and well-being. She had heard of a Buddhist artist, Niwa Zenkyū, who worked with the elderly to create very simple paintings with brush, ink, paper, and a handful of lines. Niwa's images of Jizō bowing with palms pressed together are so endearing that they are now mass-produced on calendars, postcards,

Colored-pencil drawing of Kannon, by
Gyokko Sensei

and little books. Moved by his work, Yamamoto-san sought him out. She
wanted to try such a painting herself, and she arranged for both of us to
visit him while he was teaching at an elder center outside of Nagoya. She
was astounded at the life-generating power she experienced when she
painted a simple Jizō herself. With brush and black ink, she formed a circle for the head, two lines running down the sides for the body, two curved
strokes fashioning an upside-down "v" for hands with palms pressed together, two gentle arcs for eyes, a tiny circle in the middle of the forehead
to mark the "wisdom eye" (*bindhi*), and a tiny "u" shape for a mouth. Vari-
ations on this can invoke quietude with no mouth, sadness with a down-
ward curving stroke, seriousness with a straight line, to say nothing of
how slight changes in the shapes of the eyes can multiply the possibilities.
Add to that the quality of the stroke, the amount of ink on the brush, the
pressure, the speed of producing the stroke, and all the emotional content
the brush reveals, and the potential is limitless.

Yamamoto-san immediately saw the benefits for her own spiritual
health. A painting that requires no expertise with a brush and fewer than

ten strokes could express her current mood or sway her to shift her mood. Until then, her engagement in aesthetic practices had been formal and required years of disciplined practice to attain a modicum of achievement, like with tea and flowers. So, this was a revelation to her. She found that doing modest creative activity is healing, and the effects are instant. Now she enjoys doing such paintings when she wants to express some joy, gratitude, or sorrow. She said it also helps when she wants to brighten her mood to paint a quick smiling Jizō. She has added this to her array of healing activities.

The hand drawings and paintings of these women have a deeper personal meaning than even Buddhist figure copying. In their healing activity of creating minimal images, the content and not the form of the image drives the practice. Such freehand, basic images are astonishingly powerful. By engaging in a creative activity, the women felt a direct and immediate emotional experience they described as seemingly disproportionately pronounced compared to the simplicity of the images they produced. The buoyancy helped them be more resilient by opening more space in their heart-minds to be accepting. It helped them open their eyes to the creative possibilities in themselves and beyond. The simplicity of the forms enabled the women to weave the healing activity of creating meaningful images into their daily lives, where the personal images have maximum impact.

The two most dramatic cases of the power of painting to heal, surprisingly, did not occur as a result of a woman creating an image herself. One incident involved Kimura-san, whom you might recall from the last chapter. She claimed a *tenugui* cloth with Aoyama Rōshi's calligraphy and images of Gasshō Dōji (two figures bowing with palms pressed together) on it was the source of her healing experience. The drama of this event is that in her case she was not only healed, she was also cured of a cancer that had been diagnosed as terminal. I was fortunate to be granted an interview with the artist who painted the images for the *tenugui* cloth, renowned Buddhist painter Sakuma Ken'ichi. It is a rare opportunity to gain access into the intention of the artist. Apparently, he had not been aware that the cloth he provided the image for had become known for miracle healing. Although visibly reluctant to claim any part of a miracle, he was, nonetheless, pleased that his images could help in some fashion.

Sakuma Sensei reflected on this new information about how his work has been experienced. He spoke slowly, generating gravity for what he was about to say. "Beauty heals by moving people's hearts. Beauty does not operate in the realm of linear words. Such words make things shallow."[20] As he continued to process the healing, he explained what he does to prepare his heart to work on his art. "I practice saying 'thank you' one hundred times."[21] Perhaps it is not surprising to hear an artist devoted to creating images of figures expressing gratitude with their hands with palms pressed together does this, but it is gratifying. The Gasshō Dōji images, he thinks, are in the person's heart. He continues his analysis of the role of beauty in healing. "Having an object of beauty is needed to draw it out and give it focus. That is the way we are wired, because we are material beings. The role of beauty is to activate the healing powers."[22] My conversation with Sakuma Sensei and his wife was lively and turned to the role of gratitude in healing. In the course of our discussion, we noted how there are various depths to gratitude. Some even experience happiness in little things, engendering profound gratitude. His wife spoke from experience: "As you get older, your gratitude deepens."[23] Sakuma Sensei nodded in agreement. I then offered my gratitude for their hospitality, not only for allowing me to spend the afternoon in their home, but also for allowing me to get a glimpse of the heart and thoughts of this artist whose work helped heal my friend.

The other case involved Nagai-san, whose fuller experience was detailed in Chapter 4. Here again we are most fortunate to learn about the artist's intentions in creating his paintings.[24] As a grandfather, Iwasaki Tsuneo wanted his grandchildren to learn the wisdom of the Buddhist teachings, because he did not want them to suffer. He saw that along with changes in Japanese society over the course of his life that there were fewer natural opportunities to learn the Buddhist teachings. Yet, he did not want to preach to them either. With his constellation of skills and concerns, he had a profound vision about what he could do. Guided by his understanding of Buddhist teachings, he applied his talents as an artist and calligrapher. He even enlisted his expertise as a scientist on many occasions. The result was nothing short of brilliant. His paintings capture the teachings of the *Heart Sutra* in a way that make them visually accessible. He illustrates emptiness (of independent existence) as a quality of every atom, every bubble, every star, every duck, every strand of DNA. The net effect of viewing several of his paintings makes it clear that everything in the universe is interrelated and integrally significant.

A testimony to the efficacy of Iwasaki's paintings to convey the teachings in a manner that communicates at the deepest level, Nagai-san called me to say that she had finally found relief from her constant pain due to paintings she had seen earlier that day. Until then, even though she had seriously studied the meaning of emptiness and its counterpart, interrelatedness, she

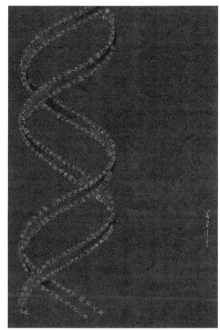

Heart Sutra "DNA," by Iwasaki Tsuneo

could not feel it. Iwasaki Tsuneo's *Heart Sutra* paintings helped Nagai-san see emptiness as a warm embrace. The particular painting that reached into her heart most deeply is of ducklings swimming in the wake of their mother. The wake was made of the characters of the *Heart Sutra*. Now she experiences how she is already compassionately embraced by the universe, and that she is not alone. Viewing Iwasaki's paintings ended her struggle to experience interrelatedness.

I had to see for myself. The day after Nagai-san's call, I went to the Nagoya City Museum. It was immediately apparent to me why Nagai-san would be healed. The art was breathtaking in its boldness and penetrating insight. It had humor and tenderness, sadness and delight. Since it was the last day of the exhibit, the artist, Iwasaki Sensei, was there. I introduced myself, because I wanted to express how profoundly the paintings moved me and hopefully to arrange to talk with him at length in the future. He was a humble man, yet he had a twinkle in his eye. He was not unaware that he had done something special. Since his motivation was to have his grandchildren and others understand the beauty of the Buddhist teachings, he was more concerned if what he had done helped anyone. On my second meeting with him, Nagai-san and I went together to his home. In the subtle exchanges of formal Japanese interactions, she conveyed how meaningful the paintings had been to her. It was not necessary to provide the wherefores and whys of her experience. It was enough that Iwasaki Sensei knew that his paintings had done their work, and that Nagai-san had been healed.

When the women turn to the dynamics of painting and drawing for healing, they have found that copying Buddhist figures, creating simple images in paint or even pencil, and viewing images that speak directly to their heart-minds have proven to be powerful healing activities. Painting or drawing an image heals by virtue of the artist being engaged with a creative activity, which inherently involves extending connections beyond the narrow confines of a heart-mind constrained by fears, pain, and weariness. When viewing images is done as a healing activity, heart-minds are open to see the potential evoked therein. Beauty directs your attention by luring you to focus in a certain direction. It is a dance between the commotion in your heart-mind and the implications evoked through the image. In either activity—creating an image or appreciating it—the healing occurs when you inhabit the present moment and feel sustained by forces your eyes cannot see.

Poetry Reading and Writing

A Dharma friend is coming	仏縁の友逢いに来し
On that morning	その朝に
The first flower blooms	初花のさく
The color of healing	いやしの色の

Umemura-san wrote this poem for me on the occasion of my return to Japan. It had been two years since our last meeting when we had shared so much—our disappointments, pains, and fears, as well as our aspirations. Our laughter was ebullient with the unabashed joy of seeing each other again, each a person who understood and cared for the other. Then she handed me a slip of paper. It was a scrap piece, like the ones she kept neatly stacked by the telephone. She cut any paper that could be used in this way to a small rectangle, so as to get maximum use of it before it was recycled. In her characteristic, beautiful hand, she had penned this poem. She said it came to her when she went out to water her plants on the veranda. At that time, she was excited about meeting me later that morning, and then she saw a flower had blossomed on a plant that had never flowered before. As soon as she saw the flower, she knew what it meant. This is how she perceives things, making connections and finding beauty in little things in daily life. Distilling it in her heart and expressing it in a poem is one of her healing activities.

All of the other women have written a verse at a meaningful or important time in their lives. In Japanese culture, this is not uncommon, given the high value placed on refined and subtle forms of expression. For some of these women, writing and even just reading poetry is an aesthetic practice they count as a healing activity. Poetry can be healing because it can evoke complex harmonies and emotions that defy linear explication, allowing the beauty inherent in wholeness to emerge. Hence, an experience that is difficult to accept as an isolated event becomes acceptable when viewed in its fuller context. Through poetry, women can embody and embrace even difficult and unwanted events, rather than resisting or denying them.

Another principle of the healing paradigm is living body-mind, which involves an effort to be fully present in the here and now. It is easy to become distracted and lose touch with your current condition by dwelling in a preferred past or desired future. Umemura-san explains how writing poetry helps her embody the present: "When someone dies or something big happens and I see something like the butterfly working so hard, I think, is there some way of putting that into words? Working hard trying to express it helps me get absorbed in the moment. This heals my heart."[25] What heals is being absorbed in something occurring at that moment, which, she says, helps her set the grievous occurrence within a web of cosmic connections.

The following are several of Umemura-san's poems written at times of emotional intensity. The first of a series of three captures when she went to see her birth mother, knowing her passing was not far. The fact that her mother had abandoned her at birth was a source of deep, lifelong pain for Umemura-san. Well into adulthood, the pain remained raw, although she tried to keep it hidden from view. It is with all those emotions that she reflected back to the tenth day before her birth mother passed.

> Gratitude flowing from her
> Ten days before going on
> My birth mother's joy
> ありがたしと言わせしめいし
> 逝く十日前の母の歓喜ぞ

Composing this poem helped Umemura-san feel her birth mother's joy upon seeing her daughter. It also helped Umemura-san recognize the gratitude in her birth mother. Crafting the poem was a potent vehicle for Umemura-san to cultivate her own gratitude, the kind of gratitude that heals old wounds.

Moistening the lips of the newly departed is a ritualized activity that expresses care for the person who is beginning a final journey. For Umemura-san, not just any water will do. She turns this ritual into a healing ritual as she makes connections with her youth, washing away the years of pain she did not have with her birth mother. The healing deepens as she finds the words to capture the significance of the moment.

> I went to fetch water from the village where I spent my youth
> Still warm
> Moisten Mother's lips

> 若く日を過ごしき村の水もらい
> まだ暖かき
> 母の唇浸す

The first night after a person breathes her last, loved ones stay together with the deceased, keeping incense lit. White clothing especially for the end marks the transition. Everyone gathers at the threshold of death, because it is a momentous occasion when impermanence is palpable. In that liminal space, emotions course through in the potent quietude of deep darkness, a chance for hearts to be cleansed.

> A fleeting night of passing vigil
> In the pure quiet
> Get the white clothing
> Unable to stop the suffering of the disease
> Purifying tears

> 仮通夜の
> 清謐の中
> 白布とり
> 病苦とどめぬ
> 清らかさに泣く

Poetry writing was a deeply healing aesthetic activity for Umemura-san at the passing of her birth mother, and it has helped her as she faced other life challenges as well. Upon her pilgrimage, itself a healing activity, she amplified the healing experience with her poems. She began with solidifying her intentions and hopes, including the phrase that distinguishes this pilgrimage as the Shikoku Island Eighty-eight Temple circuit. "Walking two together" refers to a pilgrim metaphorically walking with the Buddhist master Kūkai (774–835 C.E.), more commonly known by his title Kōbō Daishi.

> Along the way, regrets and sadness, should be purified
> So I went on a journey walking two together

> 来し方のうらみ悲しみ純化すべく
> 同行二人の旅へと出でむ

Umemura-san, however, knows in her heart that the "two" referred to in her poem can be read two ways. One is the obvious traditional meaning, telling the reader she is on the Eighty-eight Temple circuit, but the second meaning is carried in her heart as she walks through the first temple's gate.

> Passing through the gates of Ryōzan-ji Temple
> My deceased mother's
> Dream of twenty years
> Crying as I walk

> 霊山寺山門くぐる
> 亡き母の
> 二十年の夢
> 泣きつつ歩く

As her journey continues, her walking also changes. Even as she makes connections with others, she finds herself and learns how to live.

> I put a letter to a Buddhist friend
> In the post box
> I want to be alone
> Walking I become me

> 仏縁の友への便り
> ポストに入れ
> 独りになりたく
> あるく我なり

At Jizō-ji Temple, I again receive kind offerings
As I receive it, I think
This is how to live

地蔵寺で又もやさしい接対を
受けつつ思う
生きていくこと

Walking along slowly, the two of us together
I feel Dharma connections
Flowers beautiful

ゆっくりと二人とともに歩きつつ
仏縁思う
花うつくしき

Bestowing full-bloom flowers
Take evening meal
Inside joy
I become today's me

満開の花を恵でつつ
夕げとる

喜びの中の
今日の我なり

Perfectly cleared up
I take in the morning chill on my skin
On a road for one and a half *li*[26]
Gratitude flowing as I walk

澄みわたる
朝の冷気を肌に受け
一里半の道
謝しつつ歩

Writing poems helped Umemura-san go deep into the present moment and see a larger context and deeper connections. She could see herself differently. After walking alone, she saw herself rejoined, walking as two. The alone time helped her become herself. Joy and gratitude renewed her connections. Umemura-san had found what she was looking for—the buoyancy that comes from being grateful, which was a sign of her healing. Writing the poems helped her be clear to herself as she ushered in these changes in her heart. Umemura-san's poems reveal the path of her healing. Reading them later, she will be able to retrace her journey.

Gyokko Sensei also actively engages in poetry writing as part of her healing activity. She wrote the following poem at a time when she was adjusting to a completely new phase and rhythm of life. She had cared for her own home for decades, and she had just moved into a home with her oldest son's family. They built the house with this living arrangement in mind. She had her own space with a view through floor-to-ceiling windows overlooking a beautiful traditional Japanese garden, a treasure in contemporary Japan. She herself was surprised by the emotions that surfaced. She said she had never felt lonelier in her life.

> Loneliness is not in the mountains
> It is not in the city when a person is by herself
> It is when a person is among many people

> 孤独は山になく
> 街にある一人の人間にあるのでなく
> 大勢の人間の間にあるのである

She had not anticipated it, but it was the sounds that made her lonely. She could dimly hear them from the other side of the house. Her son and his family had their own established routines. As they discussed the day's activities and planned for the next, Gyokko Sensei was an outsider in her own home. Recognizing this was an opportunity to understand the human condition with deeper understanding, she brushed the poem above. Putting it into words helped her release some pain as she saw that she was not alone. Others, too, felt this kind of loneliness.

Most of her poems, however, are not "composed" by her. She "hears" the poetry coming from different Buddhas and bodhisattvas. "I can't explain why these come to me. They just pop in. This is the mysterious Dharma (*myōhō*)."[27] She elaborated that she thinks interrelatedness is a mystery. She receives the poems as teachings that illuminate an important part of the mystery in order to guide her on matters that help her respond to current situations. She takes them as cues on how to lead a lifestyle of healing.

On April 14, 1975, Gyokko Sensei "gratefully received from the universe" a poem inspired by her visit to the Inari Shrine and Sōtō Zen Myōgon-ji temple complex in Toyokawa, just outside Nagoya. In keeping with the tone and stage of her life at the time—she was in the prime of life and very busy—the poetic teaching is straightforward and practical:

> *Shugyō* (Practice)
> *Shu* is to learn, to remember.
> *Gyō* is to happen, to act.
>
> 修業
> 修とは習う、おぼえる。
> 業とは行なう、行動する。

Due to its thematic resonance, she wrote a poem from her mother on an adjacent page:

> One day, one day, one word, piling up
>
> 一日一日一口に積み重ねよ

Out loud, she adds, "this is practice, one act at a time."[28]

On another occasion, she received a more discursive message from the sacred Toyokawa environs. She keeps it with the poems she records carefully in a special notebook: "The path of life is long. The things that are revealed on the surface are none other than the tip of the iceberg. However, the depths of it I can only understand to be Dharma. What is above the sea is the present. What is below the sea is Dharma. Since we can't see everything, we best not get too anxious. Patient faith is called for, because the Dharma works."[29]

Kannon, the goddess of compassion, has also given her a number of poems over the years. Here are a few of her favorites.

> Kannon is the universe
>
> 観世音とは大宇宙の事
>
> Kannon sees with eyes
> Observes with heart
> Hears with ears
> Listens with heart

観世音目で見る
心で観る
耳で聞く
心で聴く

Hear the sound of the wind.
The sound of the wind listens.

風の音を聞く。
風の音に聴く。

Bitterness and jealousy impoverish the heart
Those with poor hearts, wait for mercy
That mercy will turn to compassion
That is the heart of Kannon!

うらみ心、ねたみ心は心を貧しくする
貧しき心の者には、あわれみを待ち
そのあわれみを慈悲にかえよ
それが観世音の心ぞよ.

Honorable Buddha has also given her numerous poems over the years. The tenor of the poems varies in nature. On the morning of August 10, 1993, she received one that portends environmental and spiritual crisis.

The planet is now becoming a desert
"Earth, too, people's hearts, too"
Wandering in search of an oasis,
People seek sacred water

地球は今砂漠化して来ている
「人地も人の心も」
オワシスを求めてさまよう
民聖なる水を求めて

The poem gave her pause to think of what she could do. Then she received another short poem, as if to answer her question.

If I think of what whetstone can polish my heart
There is no shortage

我が胸を磨く砥石と思えば
不足なし

She interpreted the poem she received from the Buddha as encouragement to examine her own heart in the face of these major concerns. She
saw she has many "whetstones" in her life. Among them, she includes
people she does not like, annoying people, and those who say irritable
things. Interaction with these people provide her with opportunities to
polish her own heart. In so doing she can better help people seeking refuge
from the desert.

Another poem Gyokko Sensei received from the Buddha also gives
her guidance in how to live more fully in the present, the only place where
action occurs.

> Long roads, short roads, winding roads
> All end up at the same place
> When not rushing and flowing, relax into the body

遠い道近い道まわり道
行きつく先は同じ
あせらず時の流れに身をまかせよう

Gyokko Sensei explains what she gained from this poem. "Once I realized that the point is to be here, there is no reason to rush or be anxious.
Ride the flow of nature. If you don't do this, you suffer a great deal. With
this, I saw how I didn't have to suffer. It's very difficult! The reasoning is
not hard to understand, but to do it is *difficult!*"[30] Being a working mother,
she was always busy and pressed for time. In her retirement with grandchildren, she still needs reminders to be present, but it is not so difficult
anymore. The various poems she "receives" and occasionally writes are
critical healing activities, keeping her focused on caring for herself and
others, polishing her heart, and embodying the present moment.

Poetry as a healing activity is not limited to those who compose or "receive" poetry. Ogawa-san finds that even reading poems is healing, because
the feelings are felt in her own heart. "I don't write poems, but I find healing
in reading poems. I resonate with the feelings in the poem. One poem I like
is the beauty that is noted in daily life. It helps me heal, because it helps me
see everyday things in a deeper way."[31] She continues, "To me the poems
express 'I am healed.' I feel it deeply."[32] One of the poems she is moved by
was also given to me by Kitō Sensei. It is by Aida Mitsuo. One of the lines is,

"Just by you being there, everyone's heart finds peace." 「あなたがそこに ただ いるだけで みんなのこころが やすらぐ。」 Ogawa-san finds affirmation and encouragement in this poem: affirmation that she belongs, and encouragement to keep polishing her heart so her presence is helpful to others.

Ogawa-san offers further reflections on the healing dimension of poetry. "Words that just leap into the heart have healing power. It does not require a lot of words."[33] Poetry operates at a level different from discursive language, and reminds us of the potent effect a few well-chosen words can have. Words in a poem can work together like sympathetic vibrations in music. For example, when the note "A" is played on the "D" string of the violin, the "A" string will vibrate as well, creating a richer sound. Other overtones are also set in motion. Thereby, by playing one well-placed note, several notes enter the harmony, creating a lush and sonorous quality. Poems can likewise evoke reverberating responses. A heart that is tuned to the frequencies that occur in a poem can tap into an exponentially larger context, providing room for healing.

Music: *Go-eika* Hymnody

Go-eika is a form of hymnody that focuses on succor for the suffering heart. It has become extremely popular in Japan in recent decades, especially among older women in the Sōtō Zen sect. Each individual singer accompanies the song with a hand-held bell and small mallet for striking a metal disc, punctuating the rhythm. Everyone plays in unison, except for the leader of the group who often starts the song to bring everyone in together. It is a relatively quiet and slow mode of musical expression, with little dynamic, tempo, rhythmic, or pitch range. Its purpose is more contemplative for the participants, rather than a form of entertainment for others. The lyrics of the songs are largely taken from Buddhist scriptures and teachings. The melodies and rhythms draw on deeply moving sounds and silences that create a poignancy that shines on the pain in the heart. Kitō Sensei explains it is easy to feel close with this singing, more than with just scriptures.[34] Her observations as a nun resonate with neuroscientist Aniruddh Patel who, through scientific research, concludes, "music appears to have much deeper power over our emotions than does ordinary speech."[35] When seeking relief, then, singing can be a powerful healing activity.[36]

Although the written word is insufficient to give you a flavor of this distinctive style of singing, here is an example of a popular hymn's lyrics.

Sanbo Gowasan (Three Treasures)
VERSE 1

Shine on the pain in my heart
The great, venerable Buddha's
Vow to save all.
Let's chant refuge to the venerable Buddha.

VERSE 2

Cross over the waves of the suffering world.
Go to the pure, charmed Dharma.
All are on a boat.
Let's chant refuge to the great Dharma.

VERSE 3

At the banks of enlightenment
It should be crossed.
Tell the Way.
We depend on the various leaders.
Let's chant refuge to the venerable community of Buddhists.

The words sung in *go-eika* hymnody are clearly articulated, but vocabulary and grammar are often scriptural, making it not as immediately accessible as contemporary speech. This enhances the experience of engaging in a deep aesthetic practice. *Go-eika* hymnody aims to help the singer feel understood, supported, and surrounded by others in the same boat. The singing draws people together as it creates a safe harbor for people to open their hearts and express their pains and aspirations. The songs transport them to a different mode of being, enabling them to find healing. Boyd and Williams describe an analogous phenomenon, although they refer to Zoroastrian manthric chant. "It is as if one enters a fluid realm of language-like sounds pregnant with potential meaning, as if one has arrived at a source of meaning deeper than any particular articulation. These sounds without sense have their own noetic function. The priest/listener moves into a perceptual state less bounded by convention and allowing for new insights and shifts in meaning."[37]

In addition to the meaning created and perspective gained from *go-eika* hymnody singing and manthric chanting, both encourage oxygen intake.

Music therapist Mitchell Gaynor observes that one tends to breathe in deeper and exhale longer with these activities. The increased oxygen is good for your health.[38] It can help slow the body-mind and help it feel safe and energized. Yamamoto-san has experienced this. She adds that another part of the healing power of singing is it helps the body find balance. "People need to use their voice loudly at times, to sing loudly, because sound vibrating through your body is needed for balance in your life."[39] Ogawa-san offers her thoughts on music and healing as well. "Sound and silence both have healing power. What matters most is the person's heart."[40] Indeed, the appeal of *go-eika* hymnody is that it is an aesthetic practice honed to reach into the worn and tired places in the heart, healing with each breath.

Flower Arranging and Viewing Nature

The women integrate the healing power of flowers into their daily life. In so doing, flowers are endowed with a meaning that animates their sense of being. The larger cultural context is that flowers are highly cherished in Japan and a formal aesthetic practice has developed around them. Many of the women have studied and attained various degrees of proficiency in this art of flower arranging, or ikebana. Their healing activities involving flowers include the formal discipline, but they also extend well beyond it.

Simple acts like watering houseplants can be an occasion to feel intimately connected to the life-giving support of nature when one experiences the Dharma in such daily tasks. Honda-san gives us a view of her inner life and sustaining activities as she tends to her eleven-year-old cyclamen plant.

> I feel that it is not just by my power that I live. I don't know anything deep, but I guess I can say that I feel the power is the Dharma in daily life. I just feel that my life is supported by the universe [*ikasareteiru*]. I don't know any theoretical things. I do feel that I am interrelated to flowers. I talk to my cyclamen. It has bloomed for eleven years. I thank it for blooming for me. In the summer when it is hot, I apologize if it is dry and ask it to be patient while I go get the water. I feel the mystery of life in things like that. When I come home from work in the summer, I apologize that I have been drinking water all day, but they haven't had any. Then I give them water. I love flowers. I enjoy talking to flowers. They bloom for me.[41]

The sublime relationship Honda-san has with her flowers is a powerful healing activity in her life. Living alone with no children is something she now accepts about the way her life unfolded. Flowers have been a daily part of her ability to release disappointments and focus on the beauty in her life as it is. Her self-assessment of not understanding "anything deep" conceals a profound wisdom in her bones.

One of the activities that Yamamoto-san consciously engaged in with her children when they were young gives us an idea of how children are enculturated to appreciate the beauty of flowers and help them cultivate their own relationships with flowers. Among all flowers, the cherry blossom (*sakura*) holds a cherished place in Japanese culture. Even in poetry, if just the word "flower" is used, it often means cherry blossom. The cherry blossom is prized for its particular kind of beauty. There are numerous varieties of cherry trees, of course, but the Japanese varieties are noted for flowering before leaves emerge. Hence, the tree in early spring is ablaze with blossoms. This is stunningly beautiful in and of itself, but it is not the primary reason the cherry blossom is revered. The cherry blossoms reveal the aesthetic and spiritual orientation of its admirers. It is the brevity of the blossoms that captures the hearts. Some blossoms peak for only a day, others three days. It is the courage to be so exquisitely beautiful in the face of impermanence that fills the heart with sublime appreciation of the nature of reality. Yamamoto-san wants her children to gain this awareness and experience its healing power.

Her approach, however, was not to give a discourse on such matters. She knew how to reach her children. Drawing on a moralistic Japanese folktale, "The Old Man Who Made Cherry Blossoms Bloom" (Hana saku jīsan), she built up excitement to play out this story with her kids.[42] They would have to wait until it was just the right time when the flowers bloom. She emphasized how they could only do it once a year, and it could only be done on just the right day. The main point of the fable is to stress it is good to be kind and generous and bad to be greedy and mean. The kind and generous person in the story is the old man who, after heartbreak, is eventually honored for his moral behavior with the task of bestowing cherry blossoms for others of like heart to enjoy. For the climax of the story, Yamamoto-san would gather petals in a basket to shower on her children. Although it was approached as just playing with her children, Yamamoto-san saw it as a critical element of what she wanted to impart to her children. She wanted them to develop a sense of affinity, and eventually a sense of intimacy, with flowers. The *sakura* is especially important to her, for it is the quintessential example of how to live well in this world: living in fear of impermanence leads to misery, living in awareness of the beauty of impermanence is liberation.

Having focused on efficiency and practicality most of her working-mother days, Gyokko Sensei is learning in retirement about the importance of "waste" and allowing cracks of space in her life to let in "water." Flowers taught her how her heart needs to be watered so it does not become a desert.

> To someone who is busy, taking time to view flowers is seen as a waste of time. If you go and look, though, you think "Oh, how beautiful!" This is what it means to be abundant and supple. If you don't have "waste" in your life, your life will not be supple. As you get older, you realize this. It's not as noticeable when you are young. Now I see "waste" and "cracks of space" are very important. It's important for the mind to work well. Children try to create abundance and suppleness. It is important to allow this. Our hearts will become a desert if we don't have suppleness. Nature teaches that we need water to survive. Nature is like reading scripture.[43]

Her views are reminiscent of the great Buddhist teacher Kūkai (774–835 C.E.), who taught the "Dharma Body expounds the Dharma" (*hosshin seppō*). In short, all things in the cosmos are teaching through embodied example, including flowers. Though Gyokko Sensei did not make a deliberate effort to follow Kūkai's teachings, her numerous practices have helped her cultivate her heart so she can listen to the teachings of flowers. She takes their teachings seriously, and incorporates them into her daily life.

Umemura-san has also found listening to flowers healing. She formulates one of her more poignant healing experiences after arranging the flowers on her home altar honoring the sixth-month anniversary of a beloved nun's passing.

> Through the form of arranging flowers,
> I interact with the spirit of flowers,
> and I can feel you.
> Although it is once a month,
> I think, How can I arrange the flowers so their spirit will shine?
> I focus my heart
> and listen to the flowers.
> In this instant my heart is healed.
> I feel this deeply.

花を生けるという形をとうして
花の命と向き合っていると
感ずる事があります。
一月に一回ですが
どう生けたらこの花の命を輝かせる事ができるかと
心をすまし
花に聞く。
この一時は私の心が癒されている。
そんな気がいたします。[44]

Poetry and flowers are often combined for twice the healing power. Umemura-san instinctively knew to do this when grieving the loss of the nun with whom she had been so close.

Umemura-san shared another experience when flowers taught her a life lesson that helped her heal. A sublime experience while riding her bike to get to work reached deeply into her sense of being. Awareness flashed through the cracks opened by profound sadness over the loss of her mother.

When I was riding my bike on a cold day in February with snow falling, I saw the bud of a plum blossom. I thought of all the energy the bud was exerting to bloom even in the winter. It is not just the energy of the bud, it is the energy of the universe working to bloom this flower. The world is working so hard to activate this flower, and it is working for me, too! At that instant, I felt embraced by that energy! [She exclaims with joy.] The *Kannon Sutra* says that there is this power that holds you. This is it: Kannon Riki [compassion power]! There is a *huge* power in the universe that aims to make flowers blossom.[45]

Plum blossoms are another extra special flower in Japan, especially in a Sōtō Zen context. The plum blossom is the symbolic flower of the sect, chosen for its quality of being strong enough to be gentle in the harshest conditions. The plum blooms as winter just begins to give way to spring. It is said the most beautiful time to see a tiny plum budding is when it is partially veiled with a light snow, for it is in such a moment the gentle flower reveals its strength and deepest beauty. As testimony to its true nature, the tiny plum bud had the strength to enter Umemura-san's heart and mind, enabling her to see the nature of the universe. She suddenly realized how she, too, is supported by the whole universe. To her delight, she found it to be a compassionate universe. The flower showed her how hard the universe works to give rise to its blooming. By implication, it is working for her, too. Her mother is gone, but she is not alone. A whole, compassionate universe, including her mother's energy, embraces her each moment of the day.

Yamamoto-san's heart is healed by flower buds, more so than with fully bloomed flowers. She always has flowers in her home and arranges them with her skilled training in ikebana. She says she does this to keep nature close and to feel part of something larger, something enticing and beautiful. "Working with flowers has brought me closer to nature, because I notice what is blooming, and I think how it would be in an arrangement. I like the quietness of flowers. In flowers, you choose buds rather than fully bloomed flowers, because they don't have as much interest. [Fully bloomed flowers] have no potential."[46] Flower buds have more power than full blooms to draw the heart in close to listen to their subtlety. This is the aesthetic quality of *yūgen*.[47] *Yūgen* is a quality that entices the observer to lose her sense of being a separate being and merge with it, for it will not reveal its beauty from a distance. It is only with an intimate connection that it does. It is making this connection that heals, because it is in that moment she feels part of something larger and something beautiful. For Yamamoto-san, keeping flowers arranged in her home is far more than the mark of a woman with refined aesthetic sensibilities: it is part of her daily healing activity.

Ogawa-san's experience of cherry blossoms is more compelling since her father passed away, for he passed away during cherry blossom season. Being a reflective and serious Buddhist, the lessons the flowers have to teach do not escape her. "My father's monthly death anniversary is tomorrow, right about when the cherry blossoms bloom. I think, oh, it is the season. Humans are like flowers, they bloom and the petals float away. Cherry blossoms repeat this cycle every year. I think humans do this, too. I think I thought this way because of the influence from Buddhist teachings of impermanence."[48]

Cherry blossoms help Ogawa-san heal by showing her the beauty of natural cycles. Impermanence is natural. Flowers demonstrate one of the most important teachings of Japanese Buddhism: the beauty of impermanence. When one can see the beauty in impermanence, delusions dissolve, anger does not have a place to grip, and suffering loosens its tenacious talons. Flowers, especially the elegant and ephemeral cherry blossom, model how to be beautiful in the present moment.

Tea Ceremony

Whether engaged in a formal tea ceremony or enjoying a cup at home, tea as an aesthetic mode of ritualized motion is about embodying tranquil beauty. In the tea ceremony, artistry and healing come together in powerful ways. The process known simply as "tea" is an elaborate observance, sometimes lasting hours, in which the hostess and guests enter a refined world that creates a space, literally and figuratively, where healing can take place. All the women are versed in the ways of tea, and some are deeply engaged in the formal practice of tea ceremony. Yamamoto-san is the most seriously involved with tea ceremony practice, so much that it imbues her movements throughout her daily life. She offers her view of the aims of tea, referring to the aesthetic qualities of *wabi* and *sabi*. These terms invoke the beauty of the natural flow of impermanence. When present, these qualities establish a reflective mood that helps people attune to the carefully executed details of simple design, listen for quiet sounds that draw the heart in, and appreciate small gestures of respect. "Subtlety is especially treasured in the tea world, where [the aesthetic qualities of] *wabi* and *sabi* are cultivated. They activate your creativity. Tea teaches the method for moving in the most beautiful way to do a task. Tea centers on beauty. The aim is that it is carried into daily life. It is true of flowers, too, but especially true of tea. The ways of flowers and tea can be woven into daily life. Tea becomes part of who you are, the way you move and see, what you notice. It takes a long time to cultivate this."[49]

Each motion is so carefully cultivated over years and years that it becomes part of who the person is. For some sense of the level of attention and care involved, a person typically takes weekly tea lessons for three years before even beginning to learn how to arrange the charcoal for heating the water. Tea ceremony is embodied learning at its highest level of refinement.

In order to provide a glimpse of this refined and subtle world the women turn to for healing, I will discuss portions of the tea ceremony, highlighting salient aspects of the process and of women's experiences of tea as a healing activity. This begins with the very first step into the garden. Generating an inviting sense of fresh life, the rock path meandering through the garden leading to the tearoom has been recently moistened. It is a subtle gesture the host makes to show guests respect. With each step, the strains and weariness of stressful demands are left behind, as each stone leads her deeper into the tranquility of the garden. On arriving at the well, she pauses to reflect on the carving in the stone basin.

"I only know satisfaction."

Reaching her right hand to lift the long, thin-handled bamboo dipper is the occasion for reflecting on how she would feel if all she knew were contentment. No desires pulling or aversions pushing, no complaints or disappointments, she pauses to imagine. She gingerly scoops water into the dipper and slowly pours it over her left hand. Switching hands, she trickles water over her right hand. Then with both hands on the handle held just so, she allows the remaining water in the dipper to run down the handle to rinse it as a courtesy to the next person. She sets it back down on the well, dipper down, handle at a slight angle, just being in the present moment, content. Now she feels purified, inside and out. She breathes in slowly to enjoy the verdant garden as she dries her hands on her handkerchief.

After removing her shoes and placing them neatly out of the way, she kneels at the tearoom door and slides it open with both hands, showing high respect. On entering, she slides the door shut, again with both hands, being careful to make little sound. Although she is alone in the small room, she bows low in the direction of the painting, calligraphy, or flowers chosen for the occasion. As she sits in silence drinking in the carefully and thoughtfully arranged items, she feels respected. Someone cared enough to tend to each detail, creating a soothing harmony of elements that draw out the tranquil beauty of the season, time of day, and qualities of the relationships of those to be gathered.

When the other two guests arrive, they bow greetings to each other. Conversation is limited and hushed, for each of them wants to maintain the purity and tranquility of the moment. The host enters and all bow out of respect for each other. This establishes them as a harmonious group. They will help each other heal as a natural byproduct of engaging fully in the aesthetic enjoyment of tea together—nothing gratuitous, nothing lacking. First, to balance the bitterness of the green tea (*matcha*) that will come later, the host offers elegantly arranged confections that reflect the spring season. It looks as if soft pink cherry blossoms have just gently fallen on the celadon ceramic plate. The guests' hearts are captivated by the refinement and delicacy of the sweets, their beauty amplified by the silence. The host then makes the tea with exquisitely flowing gestures. Each intricate detail is executed with an ease that only comes from a relaxed comfort in being fully embodied and devoted to the present moment, respecting each utensil and meticulous movement for its precise part in preparing tea for a friend. A bow of gratitude and respect accompanies each item served, passed, or returned. A heightened awareness through all the senses permeates her heart, beauty nourishing her body-mind. She experiences a finely tuned joy in just being, her heart expanding its capacity to accept and be compassionate. Tea has once again helped her inhabit her integrated place in the universe. That place is one where there is only space for satisfaction.

Yamamoto-san related to me her personal experience with the healing power of tea. She elaborates on the quality of tranquility: "Silence is treasured, because it embraces you and supports you in the deepest and weakest places. It is safe to be just as you are. You are accepted as you are. You are protected and cared for. Your deepest needs are understood and met."[50] Ogawa-san also stresses tranquility when reflecting on what occurs in tea that she finds so healing. "Tea enables me to concentrate deeply due to the tranquility. It enables me to become one with the movements, utensils, and time."[51] She goes on to more explicitly articulate how tea heals: "Tea focuses me on the present moment and encourages me to be in it with a deliberate awareness of being. You enter the world of tea where beauty is of central importance, which is a world where the heart and spirit are principal. It is also a world where all things are treated with vital significance, because everything is interrelated. The distinction between animate and inanimate is not made. It is a mix of Shinto *kami* and Buddhist interrelatedness."[52] Even when a person knows the potential for tea to heal, the depth of her experiences is remarkable. Sharing a cup of tea—when done with purity, harmony, respect, and tranquility—reveals the potential for all daily actions to be opportunities for healing.

The Role of Beauty in Healing

What emerges from an examination of these women's aesthetic practices is a particular understanding of beauty making as healing. It engages the principles of their way of healing, which holds that if you are focused on acting from your heart-mind, beauty and healing can permeate daily life. They engage the same mindfulness and aesthetic sensitivities required of the practices examined above to domestic tasks, including hanging laundry, cooking, serving food, cleaning floors, and washing dishes. When you do these activities as beauty-making activities, they become healing activities. Beauty making is a positive choice. It is a choice to perceive and approach something in its wholeness, where its deepest beauty is illuminated.

Indeed, some of the women explicitly voice that integrating beauty into daily life is the most meaningful because it instills their lives with a deep sense of wholeness. There is no dichotomy between "special" activities and "mundane" activities. It is all of a piece. Yamamoto-san reflects, "Learning all these arts [tea, flowers, calligraphy, etc.] is good, but what would give me the deepest satisfaction in life is to live according to Aoyama Rōshi's teaching: beauty in daily living."[53] Nagai-san echoes a similar view. For her it is especially the beauty of the way things are done and presented that is healing. She adds that it is not the other Buddhist teachings that help her. It is the beauty that is practiced in living that provides the deepest support.[54] Kitō Sensei is a role model of how to integrate beauty as healing activity in daily life for all the women who know her.[55] In particular, she is a master of tea, flowers, and calligraphy and seamlessly applies the insights she has gained from them to beauty making with each gesture, phrase, and facial expression. She understands the power of beauty in her bones. Many people feel healed just because she is present.

Being in the presence of beauty heals by nourishing. Whether they are creating the beauty by composing a poem or arranging flowers or are enjoying a walk to see the plum blossoms in bloom, the power of beauty to nourish depleted hearts was found by all the women. The power seems to lie in the experience of receiving the energy of the beauty. When pain fills you, receiving input from other sources does not take the pain away, but it gives you more to feed on than the pain. It takes the focus off the wound.

Otherwise, when beleaguered by tragedy and loss, the pain can be consuming. Beauty helps shift your focus of attention and provides relief from negativity in the present moment. You need to get extra nourishment when wounded, and beauty has the facility to reach in and bestow the graceful form of sustenance that brings relief to tender places. It is potent medicine, for it is loaded with ingredients that reach into the interstices of your heart, all the cracks and crevices. Beauty can heal things you did not even know were wounded until after you are healed and feel the liberating strength that replaces the wound. The act of creating is inherently positive and life affirming. Therefore, beauty-making activities can help reduce suffering, for you can gain strength from creating beauty. Experiencing beauty, whether through your own actions or appreciating that of others', can instill hope, lengthen your endurance to live with loss, and revitalize those in the midst of tragedy.

Beauty also sustains the women through its capacity to soften the rough spots in their hearts, enabling them to be more flexible in living with the present circumstances. Once you are aware of beauty in your midst, it works as an antidote to bitterness and stops calcification in the heart. It acts as a solvent that loosens debris in the heart. Your heart closes up as you seek protection from harm. A closed heart gets stuck in a time or situation, because by nature, to the extent that it is closed, it is shut off from what is going on. Since an open heart is required to be present in the "now," beauty helps you heal by encouraging you to recognize that it is safe for you to open up. Beauty can then engage you further in the fullness of the present moment in which you can recognize yourself as an integral part, as a participant. Perceiving beauty is an act of recognizing the value of something. In so doing, it awakens the beauty in yourself, to your bigger nature. In these ways, beauty helps you feel deeply connected

One of the dimensions of their practice of beauty as healing that is especially amenable to daily activities is the beauty of physical movements. Beauty in motion occurs when you act with full mindfulness on the present moment and treat everything with respect. Moreover, beauty has the power to focus your being on the life-affirming aspects of the present. Whether doing chores or a traditional art, actions done with concentrated focus and embodied awareness of meaning induce the body-mind to be in beauty-making mode. Being in this mode is healing, because it engages your entire being in a seamless experience of the present moment. Beauty and healing go hand in hand: the more beauty, the more healing; the more healing, the more beauty.

Harmonizing diverse elements into an integrated whole is beauty-making activity in its highest and strongest mode. Expansive beauty provides a safe space for healing to occur. The larger the context in which you perceive yourself to be, the stronger the support you feel. When you feel alone and perceive things narrowly, it is easy to experience suffering. Beauty draws your attention beyond this illusion and directs it to the proverbial "jewel net" of interrelationality. Beauty entices you to engage in an act with your full being, whereby the distance between things dissolves. Beauty is empowering when you experience it with all six senses, including mind-consciousness. It is not dependent on whether you are the creator of the beauty or the appreciator, for such distinctions are ultimately empty. Experiencing something as beautiful is a profoundly refined mode of acceptance. Perceiving beauty occurs when you appreciate the strengths and contributions of something, especially in the context of its larger whole. Such beauty is perceived through the heart. In other words, beauty is a lens for seeing deep interrelatedness. Healing occurs in the awareness that you, too, are an integral part of something vast and beautiful.

The healing arts help you see everything interrelated in a perpetual dance of change. Women engage the aesthetic practices because the art of healing is a creative activity. These practices facilitate a direct experience of interrelatedness that gives rise to gratitude—a place where you can feel at peace and intimately connected. You are connected to family and friends—living and dead—and connected to nature and the cosmos. The wisdom that emerges out of this awareness of your interrelated wholeness engenders ethical action, helping you respond to the needs of the present moment with compassion. For these women, nothing is more healing or beautiful than that.

CHAPTER 6

Revealing the Healing Realm of Zen

Our physical constitution is such that even the cells of our body work better if we have peace of mind, whereas an agitated mind usually brings some physical imbalance. If peace of mind is important for good health, that means the body itself is structured in a way that accords with mental peace. Therefore we can say that human nature is more inclined to gentleness and affection. Even our body structure seems designed not for fighting but for embracing. Look at our hands: if they were meant for hitting, I think they would be hard like a hoof.[1]

TENZIN GYATSO, FOURTEENTH DALAI LAMA

Healing courses through the lives of contemporary Japanese Zen women, revealing a realm of Zen that thrives in the painful dramas and quietly heroic triumphs of the domestic sphere. Mapping new territory in Zen, this study demonstrates how ritualized activities transform emotionally intense moments—charged with fear, pain, and untamed anger—into healing. Examining ritualized activities woven into daily life illuminates a side of Zen that is as at home with kitchens crowded with three different types of unmatched recycling containers as it is with the impeccably refined aesthetics of breathtakingly beautiful flower arrangements placed in the foyer. This qualitative research of Zen in the home provides a compass directing us to resourceful and resilient women who wield healing power. The women's stories and experiences inform, expand, and enrich our understanding of Buddhism, Japan, women, ritual, healing, field methodology, and Zen as they reveal to us their healing practices and wisdom. The knowledge gained from these women not only enhances our insight into the cultural and religious dimensions of healing, but it also lays the foundation for scientific exploration into the healing possibilities of ritualized activities.

The Art of Zen Healing

Engaging in ritualized activities that embody wisdom and compassion are the keys to Zen healing. It is an art to lace healing rituals into the contours and vicissitudes of daily life. It requires attunement to bodily expressions and awareness of mental conduct. Most of the healing rituals, however, are not done as healing rituals per se. For example, if I did not know how the death of Honda-san's mother affected her whole life, I would not have thought it significant when she addressed her home altar with the Japanese ritualized greetings of leaving and returning home, because this is not an uncommon practice for people of her generation. It was only in the context of her life that I could see and understand the healing power of even this apparently simple ritualized greeting. In most homes, this ritual occurs with the comings and goings of each person. If you directly asked a family member if she was healed by participating in this ritualized exchange of greetings, she is likely to have no clue why you would ask such a thing, because it is such an ubiquitous custom. This does not mean, however, no healing occurs. They might not be consciously aware, and therefore not be able to articulate how this reliable exchange helps them in any way. Furthermore, it is most likely even if they receive some benefit from the ritualized greetings, they are not doing the greeting in order to receive the benefit. These dynamics underscore the necessity of trusting relationships to discern the most potent rituals, for healing is a by-product. It occurs as a result of doing a myriad of ritualized activities. This is the beauty and power animating their ritual lives.

Understanding the women's way of healing through an analysis of its characteristic elements will enable us to more clearly see the nature of this realm of Zen. An "Integrated Model of Healing and Illness," a model developed by religion and medical anthropology scholar Linda Barnes, provides criterion for analysis to reveal the root assumptions at work in the Zen healing paradigm.[2] The model is specifically designed to foster cross-cultural understanding and communication among people working and living with diverse concepts of healing. This "Integrated Model" foregrounds the infrastructure or building blocks of a healing tradition. In other words, it asks the

medical practitioners and scholars who use the model to be critically conscious of fundamental concepts of self and worldview and to place the various dimensions of healing and illness into their larger context.

The model consists of seven foci:

1. Understandings of ultimate human possibility. In the case of the
   Japanese Buddhist women, their understanding of ultimate
   human possibility is the possibility of healing, even enlightenment in daily life. Enlightenment is guaranteed in death.
2. Understandings of affliction and suffering. The women understand these as a part of life. They are relatives. They are not en-
   emies. No matter what, they must be interacted with. *How* one
   interacts is the key.
3. Understandings of self. They see themselves as interrelated to
   everything in the universe. They do not bifurcate mind and body.
   Therefore, the realms of life and death can interact.
4. Understandings of illness and sickness. They see themselves as
   having the power to choose how to respond, positively or negatively. Positive and negative here do not refer to valuations of
   good and evil, but rather of weaving the illness into living versus
   trying to reject it. Weaving leads to healing. Rejecting leads to
   greater suffering.
5. Understandings of healers. These women consider allopathic
   doctors and acupuncturists as healers, but also stress how they
   see Zen Buddhist nuns as healers. The nuns are the ones who
   guide them in how to have better relationships with their illnesses. The most intimate healers, however, are deceased loved
   ones, their personal Buddhas who know them best and who are
   with them everywhere, all the time, no longer restricted by the
   forces of gravity or the limitations of space and time.
6. Understandings of nature of intervention. Beyond medical treatments, the nature of the care these women turn to is a transformation of perspective. Whether it is in healing from the loss of a
   loved one or dealing with the residence of cancer in your body, it
   is in being aware of how you are internally related to everything
   that helps. The nature of the intervention is to cut out the delusion that you are an isolated, independent entity.
7. Understandings of efficacy or healing. Experiencing and expressing gratitude is one of the key components of healing for these

women. After all, if you are related to everything, then the only reasonable response is gratitude for everything. The gratitude may or may not help arrest the development of cancer cells, but it makes each breath of air sweeter, every load of laundry lighter, and committee meetings feel like a slice of heaven.

Analyzing Zen healing according to the categories constituting Barnes' model gives us a basis from which comparative studies and integrative methods can be pursued. Indeed, being open to diversity and integrating various practices and approaches are vital dimensions to the women's art of healing. In this vein, all the women were open to other religious traditions. The lack of focus on sectarian and institutional matters is one of the notable things that come to light when viewing Zen from the lens of women's everyday lives in the home. Although Sōtō Zen teachings and root assumptions are the foundation for how these women interpret and experience events, the women weave in practices from a wide range of traditions. Gyokko Sensei articulates it this way. "All gods, Allah, and Buddhas and whatever are interrelated and communicate with each other. It can't be seen with the eyes or said with the mouth."[3]

> I think it is fine there are many religions among the people of the earth. I don't think it is that there is only one fundamental you must follow. I can't think any other way. I don't know if there is some god in the universe or not. But I think there is some kind of amazing power at work in humans having different ideas of how things are. I don't know what that is. Tōdai-ji has the big Buddha in a particular form, but there does not need to be a Buddha. I don't think in terms of what sect I'm in. I do things from Tōdai-ji, and do the o-sugari channeling and Heart Sutra. My mother [raised in Sōtō Zen]—who had a very refined and active spirit—mixed together things from various places. What we do is not the same thing that is done in a temple. We don't have a set way of doing things. We just learn from each other. We have not been taught these things or what to do. We hear things and read things, and we do what comes. We don't know what will come next. We don't think of whose teaching or sect something is.[4]

In fact, all the women make an art of integrating different religious teachings and practices into their lives. Umemura-san was drawn to Zen by Aoyama Rōshi. "My husband's family is Zen, but I'm not clear which sect of Zen. My birth home is the True Pure Land sect, but I personally go to the Sōtō Zen sect with Aoyama Sensei."[5] In fact, several women weave Pure Land and Zen practices together. All articulated in one fashion or another they want a balance between self-power (*jiriki;* associated with Zen) and other-power (*tariki;* associated with the Pure Land traditions). Umemura-san says Shinshū allows her to lean and rely on others and Zen helps her be strong. Another woman, Ogawa-san, has her own deliberate way of mixing Pure Land and Zen practices: "I do Pure Land chants in the morning and Sōtō Zen chants in the evening. The arrangement of items in the altar are Pure Land. My father's family is Pure Land, but he turns to Sasaki Rōshi for teachings, in Sōtō Zen."[6]

Nagai-san likes Sōtō because it brings Dharma into concrete details of daily life, like manner of cooking and eating: "It was just by chance that Aoyama Sensei and my husband's family are both Sōtō Zen. It was because of Aoyama Sensei that I thought this temple was appropriate for [the memorial for] my younger sister. I was attracted to her [Aoyama Rōshi's] seriousness. Since I had been disappointed by the monks who drank, I see her as serious. She eats with such care. And at the nunnery they use all of the radish [*daikon*], cutting it in different ways for different dishes."[7] Institutional background of a family is part of the picture, but not a determining factor. These women seek direct guidance and help because of the people to whom they want to listen.

What comes into focus when viewing Zen through this ethnographic lens is a complex picture in which constellations of practices defy sectarian boundaries. My consociates' practices are oriented in a Zen worldview, but their interest is rarely philosophical or sectarian. Indeed, for these women, the definition of Zen is not much of a concern. In the reports of these women, we see they are engaging in rituals that are not traditionally recognized as Zen. Their primary focus is on what is effective in helping them care for themselves and others in the vicissitudes of daily life. Their concern is practical. It reveals their wisdom that cognitive knowledge alone does not have the power to heal; rather, bodily experiences are the conduit for healing. Dōgen's Sōtō Zen teachings are at the root of their healing paradigm and approach to ritualized practices. For this reason, I call it Zen healing.

The women's lives illustrate how healing activity does not occur due to sectarian delineations. Rather, it thrives where beauty is perceived and gratitude is expressed. In other words, they actively seek positive potential embedded in seemingly negative conditions and respect the power inherent in complex dynamics. Honda-san sums it up in a pithy statement: "The posture of healing is to interpret things in a positive manner and to be grateful."[8]

Gratitude was a critical element during field research, too. On our last formal interview of the first year, emotions were flowing. Our voices were ebullient as we shared our joy at having met, reflections on why we met, and what the meeting had meant to us. Umemura-san had said earlier she recognized how she had actually healed in trying to explain things to me. "I have thought, why did I go up to talk with you on that day [at the nunnery]. My mother made me do it. [Her mother was deceased at the time.] It was that story of your mother, it caused me to cry, and it deeply penetrated my heart, and I thought, I must speak with her! I realize now, I had to meet you. We have a karmic link. Upon meeting you, I can see the depth of healing in my life. I can't explain it well. Please interpret it well!"[9]

Anthropologist Loring Danforth recognizes, "The practice of anthropology . . . involves a search for meaning and identity that is ultimately therapeutic in nature."[10] I have grown to increasingly respect, care about, and consider these women to be life companions. Research, in this instance, was the catalyst for deep understanding and human connection.

The Study of Zen Healing

The ethnographic material offered by the women in this research has shown us intimate specifics of their lives. Examining such concrete details inspired valuable insights and provided the impetus to develop a handful of new theories and hermeneutical categories to better understand Sōtō Zen dynamics. In kindred spirit to other scholars who have trod this kind of terrain, I have approached my material with the same understanding: "Our conviction is that the stories or testimonies gathered here have their most powerful impact as human expressions. To theorize them is not to enhance their worth, but only to locate them in fields of knowledge in order to aid readers in situating and understanding their meaning."[11]

The primary theory I created is my ten-principle paradigm of the Japanese Zen Buddhist women's way of healing. This includes an analysis of how ritualized activities function in a Sōtō Zen mode. I developed an interpretation about Zen ritualized activities that derives out of Dōgen's teachings: ritualized Zen behavior is actualization of Buddha nature. My consociates also give us a view of an aspect of Zen not found in other sources. It is what I call domestic Zen. The hermeneutical lens of domestic Zen enabled me to see characteristics of Zen distinct to life in the home versus life in the temple or monastery. Seeing how people found healing by doing rituals at their home altar showed me a novel concept of Buddhahood that emerges directly from mortuary and grieving rituals. Deceased loved ones are recognized as personal Buddhas who help the living heal. Calling the deceased "Hotoke-sama" (honorable Buddha) is a practice unique to Japanese Buddhists. These Buddhas "know" things and "assist" in things that draw on the intimate and personal relationships developed during life. The women's aesthetic practices provided a view of the healing power of beauty in a Zen frame, so I fleshed out a theory on the aesthetics of healing. Analyzing their aesthetic practices through the lens of the healing paradigm revealed how healing can occur with calligraphy, painting, poetry, music, flowers, and tea. Each of the contemplative arts has its own distinct qualities and helps the women heal in different ways. In terms of field research methodology, I advanced a "second-person" perspective. The intimacy of the subject necessitated establishing close relationships based on trust and respect. Indeed, all of the theories and hermeneutical categories I created derive directly out of the deep relationships of trust the women and I shared for more than a dozen years. We had to interact with each other with a full range of emotion, fears, pains, joys, and triumphs.

Having revealed this realm of Zen, my study offers four avenues to expand the purview of Zen studies. First, this research demonstrates the richness of an ethnographic approach and how it is essential to learn about the ritual practices employed by women in the home. Second, this ethnographic research provides points for comparison and contrast with text-based historical and philosophical views of Zen. Third, this close analysis of ritual practices in Zen Buddhism facilitates discourse with ritual studies and gender studies cross-culturally. Sōtō Zen offers a distinctive way to think about ritual. It suggests that "method of actualization" might be an appropriate way to think of "ritual." Fourth, this study illustrates how a tradition famous for strictly disciplined monasticism can simultaneously offer healing activities for everyday people navigating life's problems and opportunities.

Although Dōgen did not specify empowerment and healing rituals in his panoply of guidelines on body-mind practice, his acute insight into the kinesthetics of actualizing specific experiences suggests he would not see conflict in the women's practice of these rituals. These rituals require women to do specific motions with their bodies—bowing, chanting, letting slips of paper fly—which in turn activate the empowering and healing awareness of interrelatedness. The innovation of women's activities and rituals as exemplified in their Zen practice is a manifestation of their insight into Dōgen's teaching on the "total body." These women do not draw sectarian lines around their practice. They do not bifurcate the whole and relegate themselves into an "inferior" or "powerless" category. They are creative in their responses to daunting situations. They rarely show fear in the face of death. They have found ways to experience themselves as the "total body," where Dōgen, too, realizes, "there is no obstruction for it [total body], it is graciously smooth and tumbles freely."[12] Invoking his metaphor, these innovative and powerful not-specifically-Zen rituals are all part of that "one bright pearl" manifesting beauty as it is tossed around in the currents of human life.

Qualitative research on rituals that facilitate the physical and spiritual healing of contemporary Japanese women led me to discover a wealth of wisdom, strength, humor, and beauty. These virtuous qualities were mostly cultivated through painful, difficult, and challenging experiences. Various ritual ceremonies, gestures, and practices facilitated the healing. A picture of the features common to the women who feel that they have experienced healing and peace in their hearts is found in the thick data collected during the field research. The knowledge we gain of Zen through these women is the lived experience of householders. Their stories inform, expand, and enrich the studies of Buddhism, Japan, women, ritual, healing, field methodology, and Zen as they reveal to us their wisdom in the ways of polishing the heart.

The Science of Zen Healing

Currently the stage of scientific and religious inquiry has many players. Developments in technology are enabling research that aims to fathom the human mind and heart on an unprecedented level of detail and specificity. Through brain images, we can "see" what happens when someone prays, meditates, chants, feels happy, and is compassionate. At one level, this looks like a new development, but from cross-cultural and historical perspectives, interaction between those who seek deep understanding has long been intertwined. In Western civilization, the paths seemed to diverge, but, in a sense, it was more a matter of developing new modes of inquiry as older modes persisted. Now we are at a point where the overlap in interest and appreciation of the vast potential of multidisciplinary inquiry is emerging into the mainstream.

Cross-cultural, multidisciplinary, integrative research raises questions about the role and meaning of "objectivity" and "subjectivity." I have increasingly come to see "objectivity" as a metaphor for a perspective that ideally seeks to consider *all* influences on a matter with the hopes the conclusions are not embedded with *hidden* values, assumptions, and power. This use of "objectivity" assumes any inquiry will contain values, assumptions, and power. What makes an approach "objective" is that these elements are consciously and deliberately brought out into the open. "Subjectivity," then, becomes a metaphor for an approach that does not seek multiple perspectives, but is explicitly seeking a particular perspective. The degree of self-awareness about which elements are embedded varies. In either case, the more scholarly the mode, the more explicitly the details of the perspective are addressed. The way I have done this is to engage in a second-person mode of scholarship where I am working with particular people in particular relationships.

Qualitative studies strive for clear, rich, complicated, and nuanced de-tails that emerge out of subjective experience. Quantitative studies can then explore the dynamics of theories produced from the qualitative materials. Increasingly, research designs include both qualitative and quantitative as-pects, such as Paul Farmer's work with global health and social medicine.[13] Those engaged with matters of health are finding the need to bring humani-ties, social science, and scientific expertise and methods to bear on improv-ing the lives of people. Taking a multilevel integrative approach promises to yield helpful insights at individual and societal levels.[14]

The ethnographically driven qualitative research on healing rituals in this study has potential for further integrative exploration. Some sugges-tive areas are in deeper examination of how the body, brain, and con-sciousness are affected by different kinds of ritualized activity.[15] Rituals are a potent tool for commanding the limbic brain to respond in certain ways that reason and logic cannot compel. Although people the world round have drawn on ritual's power to heal for millennia, the possibilities for ritual to heal are only dimly being understood in scientific terms. Re-search has shown the role of ritual in healing is that it activates the limbic brain, which guides the neo-cortex, the region where reason reigns. The limbic brain activates and orchestrates a multitude of events to which the body both responds and generates sense experience.

Since the limbic brain is a channel between the external and internal, rituals have tremendous potential to draw out particular responses. Ritual-ized activities are choreographed actions that engage the senses in specific ways, like the smell of incense, the sound of drums and bells, the sight of flames and flowers, and the texture of tatami when touching your forehead to the floor. In addition, many rituals involve specific ideas the practitioner deliberately aims to follow. For example, bowing is often attended by thoughts of gratitude. The strength of such "top-down" brain activity suggests why symbols and rituals are so potent and effective. In other words, rituals function as an external regulator and can help people integrate things in a manner that can calm. More research on different types of rituals will help us learn what types of responses are evoked and what is activated in the brain and body. The research in this study has given us a glimpse of what is activated in the heart and mind when people engage in certain rituals. It suggests rituals that heal use the limbic system to help people resonate with something deemed helpful, regulate the environment in hopes of eliciting certain responses, and revise the sense of things, with the aim of healing.

Ritualized activities are like cultural nodes, or concentrated spots of meaning and symbols in society. They have "real" power to effect change and shape ethos. Among cultures, Japanese culture has made an art of ritualization. Regardless of the culture, though, aesthetics, worldview, environment, traditions, economic conditions, social structure and relations, history, and personal sensibilities all are embedded in ritualized activities. The Buddhist rituals cherished and vital to the women who offered their experiences up for scholarly scrutiny are specific to their inclinations and needs. These women demonstrate it is often the homemade rituals that are most meaningful, and therefore most effective. There is no right or wrong way to do a ritual that heals. If it helps, it helps. If not, then do something else. Some types of elements, however, have shown notable consistency and reliability, so testing them in your own context might prove fruitful. For example, bowing might be a "staple" to weave into a ritual if the aim is to activate respect, gratitude, and awareness that you are supported by a myriad of things. This could be tested by individuals, communities, and scientists.

Dr. Sascha du Lac, a neuroscientist and Howard Hughes Medical Investigator at the Salk Institute, and I have begun exploring the potential in focusing on ritualized gestures, especially bowing.[16] We see it as a complement to the burgeoning studies on the meditating brain, led by Richard Davidson. As I was reading about all the findings generated by research on meditators and trying to see how this research might resonate with my on-the-ground Zen findings, the differences in the cultures we were addressing became increasingly apparent. Many of the women I work with are recognized among their community as notably "good" Buddhists. But most of them do not do seated meditation. Moreover, although common for monastics, the majority of Buddhists throughout history have not focused on meditating. Most if not all Buddhists engage in ritual practices. However, in the

modern West, a culture has developed in this most recent transformation of
Buddhist teachings and practices that associates being a good Buddhist to
being a good meditator. It is true that meditation is easier to import than
rituals. Rituals tend only to have power in their particular cultural and aesthetic contexts. Yet the primary reason a central focus on meditating has
emerged, I think, is training the mind does bring about the kind of results
that have become associated with Buddhist ideals: equanimity, increased attention stamina, mindfulness, and awareness. Meditation practice also ap-
peals to the largely more intellectual and reason-driven orientation of many
Western converts to Buddhism. Given the rich ritual resources for healing
in Buddhism, I think it is unfortunate, however, that in this subculture if
you do not meditate, then you are either considered not a "real" Buddhist or
else a lazy, and, oftentimes, guilt-ridden Buddhist.

My elderly Japanese women consociates do not think in these terms.
These Zen Buddhist women are concerned with responding to the immediate needs of their families, including themselves. They do what is
needed. That is their "practice," but they do not even use that term. They
do not bifurcate life activities (like cooking, making offerings at the home
altar, cleaning, laundry, caring for sick family members, chanting, and
taking out the trash) and "religious" activities. Moreover, Sōtō Zen is especially concerned with nondualistic modes that center on the details of
each activity in the present moment. A root assumption is that the body-
mind moves as one and can only move in the present. The women who
contributed to this study rarely if ever meditate, yet they have a paradigm
of healing in a Zen mode that is embedded in everyday details and fully
embodied in the traumas, sicknesses, and challenges of their lives.

Due to the overarching orientations, concerns, and assumptions about
how things work, it is no wonder neuroscientists and Buddhists have come
together to explore what goes on in the meditating brain. Given, however,
that most Buddhists do not meditate on a regular basis but do perform rituals, I am interested in seeing what we can learn about the effects of ritual,
especially Sōtō Zen–based rituals. My research offers that such rituals are
an actualization of a person's Buddha-nature.

Zen viewed through my qualitative research encompassing the domestic sphere opens up avenues of conversation and potential collaborative research in the realms of Zen studies, ritual studies, cross-cultural healing
studies, and neuropsychobiology. My consociates, however, do not need
research or scientific studies to experience healing. They already know deep
in their bones how ritualized activities are a potent means to experiencing

interrelatedness and opening the heart to accept reality as it is. The Japanese Buddhist women elders in my study reveal how healing can be done in the home on a daily basis or in the throes of a traumatic crisis. These women discovered how healing can emerge at the convergence of deepest despair and highest ideals and put this principle into practice in the Zen rituals they adopted, adapted, and developed to evoke the powers of healing by accepting interdependence, embracing emptiness, creating beauty, cultivating gratitude, and embodying compassion.

Notes

Prologue

1. Personal interview with Suzuki Kakuzen Rōshi on February 22, 1999, in Nagoya, Japan.

Chapter 1: Mapping the Terrain

1. Roland Scholz and Olaf Tietje outline a process for working with in-depth qualitative materials. See Scholz and Tietje, *Embedded Case Study Methods*, pp. 30–31. The three-part process explained in terms of how my approach resonates with their process is (1) *understanding* the people as a whole, including empathetic and intuitive levels; (2) *conceptualizing* the materials for organizing the knowledge gained through understanding; and (3) *explaining* the material, which requires analyzing the original field materials in a manner that takes into account the body of knowledge in relevant fields. Based on the findings, specific and well-designed quantitative studies can then be designed.

2. Bell, "Yes, Virginia, There Is a Feminist Ethnography," p. 29. Bell discusses three practices she identifies as necessary for critical feminist scholarship in order to overcome criticisms of hegemonic discourse: (1) building on connections between investigator and subjects, (2) decentering the researcher's perspective, and (3) drawing on the power of strategic collaborations.

3. For a fuller discussion of the ethics of power in research relationships, see Christians, "Ethics and Politics in Quantitative Research," p. 233.

4. Faure, *The Rhetoric of Immediacy,* addresses this issue. See especially pp. 284–303.

5. Catherine Bell's books have helped in the formulation of ritual analysis. See *Ritual Theory, Ritual Practice* and *Ritual Perspectives and Dimensions.* The editors d'Aquili, Laughlin, McManus (*The Spectrum of Ritual*) have also informed this study.

6. For more on longitudinal "intraindividual" and "interindividual" research designs, see Lazarus, "Relational Meaning and Discrete Emotions," pp. 47–48.

7. This generation is known for having had a difficult youth due to the war. See Plath, "The Last Confucian Sandwich Becoming Middle Aged," pp. 51–63.

8. In a separate study, Lebra also has found that Japanese elder women are the healers in the household. See Lebra, *Japanese Women,* p. 289.

9. Most names of these consociates are pseudonyms and details about their lives are changed to conceal their identities. In order to further ensure their privacy, I have employed fourteen different names to refer to the twelve people. The names of public figures I consulted, such as monastic and academic teachers, and those who preferred the use of their own name, however, are real. For contextual and comparative purposes on mature Japanese of this generation, you might find the study by David Plath helpful. See Plath, *Long Engagements.*

10. Umemura interview, September 3, 1998.

11. Northup cites Elizabeth Ozorak on this point of memory. See Northup, *Ritualizing Women,* p. 79.

12. Spickard discusses the issue of understanding versus explaining in the context of humanities and postcolonial ethnographies. See Spickard, "On the Epistemology of Post-Colonial Ethnography," p. 243.

13. Ornish, *Love and Survival,* p. 125, citing Francis and Pennebaker, "Putting Stress into Words," pp. 280–287.

14. My approach resonates with the concerns expressed by McGuire, especially "attention to the epistemological grounds of all method" and putting "a special emphasis on human language, bodies, and subjectivity, as both objects of our search for understanding and vehicles for accomplishing understanding." See McGuire, "New-Old Directions in the Social Scientific Study of Religion," p. 198.

15. Depraz and Cosmelli, "Empathy and Openness," pp. 168–170.

16. Gilbert, "The Science of Happiness."

17. In-depth interviews are regarded as the most positive for self-report methods. See Schorr, "Subjective Measurement in Appraisal Research," pp. 331–349; and Wallbott and Schere, "Assessing Emotion by Questionnaire," pp. 44–82.

18. Arisaka, "The Ontological Co-Emergence of 'Self and Other' in Japanese Philosophy," p. 199.

19. Thompson, "Empathy and Consciousness," p. 9.

20. The research on mirror neurons is beginning to generate interesting possibilities for understanding how people learn, understand, and affect each other. Exactly how mirror neurons work and what impact they have is still being investigated. For more on this topic, see Decety and Ickes, eds., *The Social Neuroscience of Empathy;* Dobbs, "A Revealing Reflection"; Gallese, Fadiga, Fogassi, and Rizzolatti, "Action Recognition in the Premotor Cortex"; and Iocaboni, *Mirroring People.*

21. Bell, "Introduction: The Context," p. 8.

22. Therefore, "what appears to be a retreat from science is actually a sign of increased commitment to it" (Spickard, "On the Epistemology of Post-Colonial Ethnography," p. 248).

23. Ibid., p. 248.

24. Yamamoto interview, August 4, 1998.

25. Accommodation refers to the thought process of modifying existing schema to adapt to the environment. Assimilation refers to modifying your perception of the environment according to preexisting schema. For further discussion of these concepts, see works by Piaget: *The Equilibration of Cognitive Structures* and *The Mechanisms of Perception.*

26. "Subjects who do not personally know the researcher are likely to hide or distort information because they do not trust the researcher or the ultimate purpose of the research, and there is no reason to believe that field workers who are not trusted will ever discover that they have been given inaccurate information." (Johnson and Johnson, "Quality Into Quantity," pp. 162–163.)

27. My research experience corresponds with Meredith McGuire who found, "To comprehend others' illnesses, suffering, transformation, and healing, I had to be open to the experiential grounds of understanding." See McGuire, "New-Old Directions in the Social Scientific Study of Religion," p. 205.

28. Natural developments in the field furthered the research in important ways. "It is an axiom of qualitative research that if we are to develop authentic descriptions of individual behavior and beliefs, we must accompany the subject into several significant settings that evoke the many facets of the whole person. We must know our subjects well, and be known to them, if we are to obtain the most valid information about them" (Johnson and Johnson, "Quality Into Quantity," p. 163).

29. An extensive study of this topic can be found in Ames, Dissanayake, and Kasulis, eds., *Self as Person in Asian Theory and Practice.* Especially relevant to this study is Part II, "Person in Japanese Theory and Practice." For an excellent examination of various dimensions and considerations in conducting fieldwork in Japan, see Bestor, Steinhoff, and Bestor, eds., *Doing Fieldwork in Japan.*

30. Based on extensive anthropological field research in *Crafting Selves,* Dorinne Kondo gives a detailed analysis of Japanese construction of identity.

31. Takeo Doi has done an extensive explication and analysis of this aspect of the Japanese concept of self in his book *The Anatomy of Self.*

32. Throughout the field research, book research, and writing phases of this study, I was constantly met with questions and concerns that emerged out of different concepts of knowledge. The Japanese Buddhist–based concept of knowledge is primarily focused on particular and concrete matters. The Greek-based concept of knowledge that is implied in much of Western scholarly paradigms focuses more on abstract theories and ideas. For more discussion on this topic, see Ames and Hall, *Anticipating China.* See also Smith, *Decolonizing Methodologies,* pp. 47–48.

33. As is true with Karen McCarthy Brown's work, I found that "telling the truth required me to perform an intellectual balancing act, in which the order and clarity of abstraction were placed in tension with the dense tangle of lived experience" (Brown, "Writing About 'The Other,' Revisited," p. 130). Yet, it is the "dense tangle" that breathes life and significance into the study. Anthropologist Spickard explains that ethnography "remains a particularizing science—one that seeks truth in the particulars in life and presumes human equality as the way to reach it" (Spickard, "On the Epistemology of Post-Colonial Ethnography," p. 251).

34. The criteria for evaluating the strength of qualitative research is discussed in Flick, "Triangulation Revisited," especially p. 194. The criterion of "validation" does not suit the nature of qualitative research. It is a category that comes out of quantitative research, which is suited to matters than can be counted and reproduced. The nature of intimate human experience is such that it cannot be quantified or controlled without distorting the very matters that are being researched. See also Flick, *An Introduction to Qualitative Research.*

35. According to Thomas and Eisenhandler, to learn about religiosity of mature adults, especially its potential health benefits, it is important to understand the content of the religiosity and not just the frequency of activities. Thomas and Eisenhandler, eds., *Religion, Belief, and Spirituality in Late Life,* p. xvii.

36. Smith, *Decolonizing Methodologies,* p. 48.

37. I developed this graphic rubric to help students understand how religious traditions have varying root assumptions. It is especially helpful when learning and comparing several traditions, and is now a staple pedagogical tool in my classroom. It helps students learn that there *are* different root assumptions, which is a major and required step in understanding multiple worldviews. Without this tool, inadvertent projection of your own worldview onto another's is hard to avoid. Applying the worldview compass raises awareness as it trains one in critical, analytical, and comparative thinking. It helps diminish unfounded fears of the "foreign" and encourages the cultivation of respect for the unfamiliar. This tool facilitates seeing yourself more clearly in the context of a diverse world.

38. This explanation and insight is from my late mentor, Masatoshi Nagatomi Sensei, of Harvard University. Buddha nature is a concept that refers to the capacity to manifest wisdom and compassion.

39. Birnbaum, *The Healing Buddha,* p. 3.

40. The conjugation of this verb is passive (shown in past form), but the meaning of it as used by my consociates includes an expression of gratitude. The gratitude implied is that you are not alone, but that there is support from beyond. You are considered an integrated part of a vast whole, which is the implied agent to whom you owe a debt of gratitude. In a healing context, then, the agent is the universe.

41. See Tanabe and Reader, *Practically Religious,* p. 31; and Traphagan, *The Practice of Concern,* pp. 20–22.

42. Danforth, *Firewalking and Religious Healing,* p. 52.

43. Ibid., p. 53.

44. Meredith McGuire also found that empowerment is a core element of religious experience in healing groups. See McGuire, "Discovering Religious Power."

45. Ronald Grimes explains, "Ritual is not a 'what,' not a 'thing.' It is a 'how,' a quality, and there are 'degrees' of it. Every action can be ritualized" (Grimes, *Ritual Criticism,* p. 13).

46. Ritual studies is a growing field that includes those with concerns about the functions of ritual in society, including Durkheim and Radcliffe-Brown. Tom Driver, also, is taking a structuralist approach in delineating three major functions of ritual: making and preserving order, fostering community, and effecting transformation (Driver, *Liberating Rites,* p. 71.) He also asserts that through such patterned and repetitive activity ritualization can be used to store and transmit information across time and across generations (ibid., p. 26). Van Gennep contributed insightful analysis of the logic of ritual movements in space in his effort to find universal patterns. Zen ritual departs from Arnold Van Gennep and Victor Turner's works that highlight rituals that involve a process. Other scholars are concerned with cultural meaning, notably Malinowski, Geertz, and Jan van Bremen, who draws on Catherine Bell's nuanced work on ritual in his assessment of ritual in Japan. "Ritual is not an entity but a practice that exists only in the specific cultural schemes and strategies for ritualization embodied and accepted by persons of specific cultural communities" (van Bremen, "Introduction," in *Ceremony and Ritual in Japan,* p. 9). Bell herself explains that ritual "is a cultural and historical construction that has been heavily used to help differentiate various styles and degrees of religiosity, rationality, and cultural determinism" (Bell, *Ritual Perspectives and Dimensions,* p. ix). For more discussion of different frames for contextualizing ritual, see Clothey, "Toward a Contemporary Interpretation of Ritual."

47. Bloch, *How We Think They Think,* p. 23.

48. Krondorfer, "Bodily Knowing, Ritual Embodiment, and Experimental Drama."

49. Lopez, Jr., ed., *Curators of the Buddha.* This important work discusses how European Orientalists constructed a false philosophical/ritual split in Buddhist representations.

50. Lesley Northup discusses some of these elements in *Ritualizing Women,* p. 29.

51. For an insightful discussion of the concept of *li* (ritual propriety), see Fingarette, *Confucius.* Japanese scholar Ikemi explains this with reference to the central Chinese concept of *li:*

> Although the Japanese appreciated the basic notion of *li* as a method of civilizing and improving human nature through the proper observation of ceremonies and rituals, they did not import the Chinese patrilineal kinship system along with the writings of Confucius and consequently found it impossible to transfer the observance of the ceremonial injunction of Chinese *li.* The absence of these ceremonies did not mean that the ancient Chinese system of *li* had no influence on Japanese culture. The Confucian classics,

including those works devoted to *li*, were read and absorbed by the Japanese people. From models of letter writing to *li* as a system of moral reflection, Confucianism influenced Japanese cultural practices in many ways. (Ikegami, *Bonds of Civility*, p. 346)

52. Ritual studies specialist Ronald Grimes explains "ritual usefulness" in the context of Zen practice. "Magic is ritual usefulness. If Zen practice is viewed as beneficial to everyday life, if it contains therapeutic possibilities, and if we can live a more fruitful or centered life because of practice, we are engaged in magic, because it puts meditative rites in service of work. Magic is mindful of empirical consequences and would produce them by transcendent means" (Grimes, *Beginnings in Ritual Studies*, p. 115).

53. Hasebe Kōichi, "Zenmon no Girei (I) [The ritual of the Zen school]." Cited in Faure, *The Rhetoric of Immediacy*, p. 298.

54. Kuromaru Kanji, "Eihei shingi no seikaku [The life of Eihei regulations: Special emphasis on the relationship with bodhisattva vows]." Cited in Bodiford, *Sōtō Zen in Medieval Japan*, p. 386.

55. Hori, "Teaching and Learning in the Rinzai Zen Monastery," p. 29.

56. Faure, *The Rhetoric of Immediacy*, p. 68.

57. Sharf, "The Rhetoric of Experience and the Study of Religion," p. 273.

58. Faure, *Ch'an Insights and Oversights*, p. 98.

59. See the following works by Faure: *The Rhetoric of Immediacy, Ch'an Insights and Oversights*, and *Visions of Power*. See the following works by Bodiford: "The Enlightenment of Kami and Ghosts," *Sōtō Zen in Medieval Japan*, and "Zen in the Art of Funerals." See the following work by Ishikawa Rikizan: "Chūsei Bukkyō ni okeru bosatsu shi Sōtō-shū ni okeru Jizō Bosatsu Shinkō wo chūshin toshite [Bodhisattvas in medieval Buddhism: Centered on the Faith in Jizō Bodhisattva]."

60. See the following works by Fujii Masao: *Sosen saishi no girei kōzō to minzoku* [The ritual structure and people of ancestor ceremonies], *Bukkyō girei jiten* [Dictionary of Buddhist rituals], and edited volume *Sōgi o kangaeru* [Thoughts on funeral rites].

61. Faure, *Chan Buddhism in Ritual Context;* and Heine and Wright, eds., *Zen Ritual*.

62. See the following works by Ohnuki-Tierney: *Illness and Culture in Contemporary Japan;* and *The Monkey as Mirror*.

63. See LaFleur, *Liquid Life*. See Hardacre, *Marketing the Menacing Fetus in Japan*

64. I agree with Michel Strickmann, who notes that the best understanding of ritual comes from a combination of textual and ethnographic approaches. See Strickmann, "A Survey of Tibetan Buddhist Studies, Review Essay," especially p. 141.

65. Northup, *Ritualizing Women*, p. 33.

66. Sered, *Priestess, Mother, Sacred Sister*, p. 258.

67. Ibid.

68. Bell, *Ritual Perspectives and Dimensions*, p. 265.

69. Ibid.

70. Ibid., p. 267.

71. Dōgen, "Bendōwa," p. 28.

72. Dōgen, "Genjo Kōan."

73. See Dōgen's *Eihei shingi* for more examples of this type of concern and activity.

74. For a resonant understanding of ritual in Buddhist context, see Sharf, "Ritual." He stresses ritual as "enactment," which is somewhat different from actualization. The difference stems from the distinctive and thoroughgoing nondualistic orientation of Dōgen's teachings.

75. The women under consideration in this work include nuns at Aichi Senmon nunnery (*nisōdō*) in Nagoya, Japan, and laywomen who are affiliated with this Sōtō Zen nunnery. I did not strive to find a sample that represents the spectrum of women in terms of demographics or types of practices because there are no data available to ascertain what the spectrum includes. For more detailed information on Dōgen's teachings about women and his female disciples, see Arai, *Women Living Zen*, Chap. 2.

76. Grimes, *Ritual Criticism*, p. 120.

77. Northup, "Emerging Patterns of Women's Ritualizing in the West."

78. Martinez, "Women and Ritual," especially p. 196.

79. Heine explains some relevant developments of the Sōtō tradition: "Although Dōgen himself seems to have been clear, consistent, and conscientious in internalizing and spiritualizing the meaning of rituals and symbols, later developments in the Sōtō sect beginning with Keizan were more eager to incorporate and syncretize elements of local, mythico-ritualistic religiosity into the selection of successors and the transmission process" (Heine, *Dōgen and the Kōan Tradition*, p. 77). Heine draws on Kim, *Dogen Kigen*, pp. 137–143.

80. Along with many others, including Maurice Bloch, I am in complete agreement that ample descriptions are a fundamental part of understanding and conveying ritual materials. "Perhaps we should make much more use of description of the way things look, sound, feel, smell, taste, and so on—drawing on the realm of bodily experience—simply for heuristic purposes, to remind readers that most of our material is taken from the world of non-explicit, expert practice and does not come from linear, linguistic thought" (Bloch, *How We Think They Think*, p. 15).

81. Nara, "May the Deceased Get Enlightenment."

82. Bodiford, "Zen in the Art of Funerals."

83. Shinto influence is part of the explanation of how this developed in Japanese Buddhism. See Sasaki Kōkan, *Kami to Hotoke no Jinruigaku* [The anthropology of Kami and Buddha]. See also Kizaemon Ariga, *Hito to no nihon bunka-ron* [People and the discourse on Japanese culture], Chap. 1.

84. Anthropologist Michael Jackson has found traditions that elevate the qualities of the deceased also help the living. "At funerals . . . the living succeed in

simultaneously metamorphosing the dead into an ideal type . . . and experiencing for themselves an ability to go on with life" (Jackson, *Minima Ethnographica,* p. 24).

85. Kawasaki interview, December 12, 1998.

86. This is the history I wrote about in Arai, *Women Living Zen.*

87. Noguchi interview, February 26, 1999.

88. Lewis, Amini, and Lannon, *A General Theory of Love,* p. 189.

89. For a discussion of rituals and the various ways and things that can misfire, see Grimes, *Ritual Criticism,* pp. 204–205.

90. Snyder and Lopez, eds., *The Handbook of Positive Psychology.*

91. Bloch, *How We Think They Think,* p. 24.

Chapter 2: The Way of Healing

1. Tatz, trans., *Buddhism and Healing,* p. 2.

2. See, for example, Birnbaum, *The Healing Buddha;* and Zopa, *Ultimate Healing.*

3. I substitute "Awakened" for the more common usage "Right" because it facilitates a clearer understanding of the Buddhist worldview, which does not turn upon designations of "right" and "wrong." The concern is to be awakened to the ultimate nature of reality, which is interrelated and impermanent.

4. Gyokko interview, February 9, 1999.

5. Tanaka interview, December 14, 1999.

6. Kawasaki interview, August 14, 2003.

7. Gyokko interview, May 17, 2003.

8. Gyokko interview, April 6, 1999.

9. Umemura interview, February 22, 1999.

10. Plath, *Adult Episodes in Japan,* 49.

11. Teachings of Aoyama Rōshi given on August 22, 2003, at Aichi Senmon nunnery.

12. Ibid.

13. Gyokko interview, August 13, 2003.

14. Articulated during several consultations with Honda-san during winter and spring of 1999.

15. Umemura interview, March 8, 1999.

16. Umemura interview, February 8, 1999.

17. Driver, *The Magic of Ritual,* p. 174.

18. Ibid.

19. Boyd and Williams, "Ritual Spaces."

20. Hori, "Teaching and Learning in a Rinzai Zen Monastery," p. 28.

21. Yamamoto interview, August 12, 2003.

22. d'Aquili and Laughlin, "The Neurobiology of Myth and Ritual," p. 159. For other studies that indicate the limbic system plays a major role in religious and

spiritual experiences, see Joseph, *The Transmitter to God;* and Saver and Rabin, "The Neural Substrates of Religious Experience."

23. Personal correspondence with Dr. Sascha duLac, Howard Hughes Medical Investigator at the Salk Institute for Biological Studies.

24. Consultation on, June 1, 1998, with Dr. Fujii Masao of Taisho University.

25. Honda interview, April 20, 1999.

26. Noguchi interview, February 16, 1999.

27. Taniguchi interview, December 21, 1998.

28. Nagai interview, January 27, 1999.

29. Gyokko interview, June 22, 2001.

30. Tenzin Gyatso and Dalai Lama IV, *Healing Anger,* p. 35.

31. Gyokko interview, April 6, 1999.

32. Umemura interview, February 2, 1999.

33. Umemura interview, February 22, 1999.

34. Cousins, *Anatomy of an Illness as Perceived by the Patient.*

35. Davidson and Harrington, eds., *Visions of Compassion,* p. 94.

36. Noguchi interview, March 25, 1999.

37. Kawasaki interview, August 14, 2003.

38. Umemura interview, March 30, 1999.

39. Ornish, *Love and Survival,* p. 132.

40. Gyokko interview, January 4, 2007.

41. Emmons and McCullough, "Counting Blessings Versus Burdens."

42. Yamamoto interview, July 28, 1998.

43. Yamamoto interview, September 30, 1998.

44. Gyokko interview, January 14, 1999.

45. Noguchi interview, March 8, 1999.

46. Quotation from dialogue with Dean Ornish, author of *Love and Survival,* p. 182.

47. Gyokko interview, January 6, 1999.

48. Gyokko interview, August 13, 2003.

49. Gyokko interview, July 10, 2006.

50. Gyokko interview, January 4, 2007.

51. Gyokko interview, July 10, 2006.

52. Ibid.

53. Ibid.

54. Ibid.

55. Gyokko interview, April 2, 1999.

56. Honda interview, April 20, 1999.

57. Ibid.

58. Kitō Sensei interview, March 2, 1999.

59. Ibid.

60. Dharma talk by Aoyama Rōshi on, June 14, 2004, at Aichi Senmon nunnery.
61. Gyokko interview, April 6, 1999.
62. Umemura interview, February 8, 1999.
63. Noguchi interview, March 25, 1999.
64. Honda interview, March 14, 1999.
65. In accordance with their general practice, the Japanese did not translate the *Heart Sutra* into Japanese, but retained the Chinese version.
66. Tanabe and Reader's volume, *Practically Religious,* offers numerous examples of this phenomenon.
67. Ornish, *Love and Survival,* p. 145.
68. Bell, *Ritual Perspectives and Dimensions,* p. xi.
69. Taniguchi interview, August 11, 2003.
70. Dharma talk by Suzuki Kakuzen Rōshi delivered during a Sesshin at Aichi Senmon nunnery on July 26, 1998.
71. Taniguchi interview, August 11, 2003.
72. Gyokko interview, August 13, 2003.
73. Ekman, *Emotions Revealed,* p. 180.
74. Dalai Lama, "Understanding Our Fundamental Nature," p. 68.
75. Honda interview, April 20, 1999.
76. Ogawa interview, March 26, 1999.
77. Honda interview, April 3, 1999.
78. Yamamoto interview, August 4, 1998.
79. Kitō Shunkō interview, August 15, 2003.
80. Ornish, *Love and Survival,* p. 127.
81. Ibid., p. 2.
82. Ibid., p. 131.
83. Ibid., p. 122.
84. Kitō Shunkō interview, August 15, 2003.
85. Taniguchi interview, August 11, 2003.
86. Taniguchi interview, August 21, 2003.
87. Umemura interview, February 22, 1999.
88. This healing theory contributes to the advances in biomedical and socio-behavioral sciences. For more on studies that cover similar areas of concern, see Fredrickson, "What Good Are Positive Emotions?"; Ickovics and Park, eds., "Thriving"; Kessel, Rosenfield, and Anderson, eds., *Expanding Boundaries of Health and Social Science;* Thoits, "Stressors and Problem-Solving"; and Wong and Fry, *The Human Quest for Meaning.*
89. Kitō Sensei interview, March 2, 1999.
90. Dharma talk by Aoyama Shundō on May 2, 1999.
91. Tanaka interview, April 9, 1999.
92. Gyokko interview, February 9, 2009.

93. Honda interview, April 3, 1999.

94. Addiss, trans., "*Hekiganroku*," p. 117.

Chapter 3: Personal Buddhas

1. Suzuki Kakuzen Rōshi interview, February 22, 1999.

2. Komazawa University Professor, specializing in Dōgen's *Shōbōgenzō*.

3. Yamaguchi interview, July 28, 1998.

4. Cited in Bodiford, "Zen in the Art of Funerals," p. 164.

5. Aoyama Shundō, Dharma talk at Aichi Senmon nunnery in Nagoya, Japan, March 15, 1999.

6. In Japanese society, death is not considered a pathological state. The concept of reincarnation is woven into the Japanese worldview that directs notions of death, even though reincarnation is not actively believed by all Japanese. See Ohnuki-Tierney, *Illness and Culture in Contemporary Japan*, p. 71. For a broader historical examination of death rituals and concepts, see Hur, *Death and Social Order in Tokugawa Japan;* Stone and Walter, eds., *Death and the Afterlife in Japanese Buddhism;* and Suzuki, "Japanese Death Rituals in Transit."

7. Nara Yasuaki explains how the Japanese Buddhist funeral service helps both the living and the dead; see esp. "May the Deceased Get Enlightenment," p. 34.

8. Traditionally, a person becomes an ancestor thirty-three or fifty years after passing away. By this time, few, if any, of the people continuing to perform the rituals would have actually known the deceased. At the final memorial ritual, the deceased is formally recognized as an ancestor. From thereon, a person is not ritually referred to by *kaimyō* (their Buddhist name), but is an ancestor (*go-senzo-sama*). For further discussion on Zen funeral rituals, see Faure's *The Rhetoric of Immediacy*, pp. 191–208.

9. Obon is an annual ritual that usually takes place in August or July. It is a three-day period when ancestors return for a visit. The living also often return to their hometowns at this time.

10. See Glassman, "Chinese Buddhist Death Ritual and the Transformation of Japanese Kinship"; Hardacre, *Lay Buddhism in Contemporary Japan;* Smith, *Ancestor Worship in Contemporary Japan;* Yanagida Kunio, *About Our Ancestors.*

11. Lindemann, "The Symptomatology and Management of Acute Grief," p. 143.

12. Hardacre observes that in Reiyukai, "ancestors are simply a category of deities on a par roughly with Buddhas and kami" (*Lay Buddhism in Contemporary Japan*, p. 66).

13. For more information, see Fujii Masao's *Sosen saishi no girei kōzō to minzoku* [The ritual structure and people of ancestor ceremonies].

14. The notable monthly death anniversaries include the eighteenth for Kannon, the twenty-first for Kōbo Daishi (Kūkai), the twenty-fourth for Jizō Bosatsu, and the twenty-eighth for Fudō Myōō. A death anniversary that coincides with the memorial dates for one of these Buddhist figures is considered auspicious.

15. Upon arriving at the grave, the gravestone is washed with water. Then offerings are made, most commonly fresh flowers, incense, and three ladles full of water poured over the top of the gravestone. Oftentimes the women will also mark the monthly death anniversary by preparing a favored dish or treat to offer at the home altar. For a discussion on contemporary practices in dealing with remains, see Rowe, "Grave Changes."

16. The schedule of rituals after death are given metaphoric reason in the T'ang Dynasty, reflecting Chinese bureaucratic process. There are Ten Kings of Hell that one must visit after death. The first seven kings are seen, in turn, once a week. On the forty-ninth day, the seventh king is met. The eighth king is met on the one hundredth day after death. After one year, the ninth king is met. The tenth king is met on the "third" year after death. There is also a way of organizing time around thirteen Buddhas: Fudō Bosatsu, Shaka Nyorai, Monju Bosatsu, Fugen Bosatsu, Jizō Bosatsu, Miroku Bosatsu, Yakushi Nyorai, Kannon Bosatsu, Seishi Bosatsu, Amida Nyorai, Ashuku Nyorai, Dainichi Nyorai, and Kokuzō Bosatsu. The first Buddha oversees *shonanoka* (the seventh day after death). The thirteenth oversees *sanjūsankaiki* (the last memorial rite thirty-three years after death).

17. Honda interview, March 7, 1999.

18. Ibid.

19. Driver explains how "it is precisely when we do not know in our conscious minds what we ought to do that the ritualizing impulse, laid down for us in structures older than consciousness, is brought into play" (Driver, *Liberating Rites*, p. 50).

20. Kawasaki interview, January 8, 1999. Zen Buddhists are the ones who popularized Buddhist funerals for the average people. See Tamamuro Taijō, *Sōshiki Bukkyō* [Funeral Buddhism].

21. Kawasaki interview, January 8, 1999.

22. For more on the funeral business, see Suzuki, *The Price of Death*.

23. Tanaka interview, March 10, 1999.

24. Ibid.

25. Ibid.

26. This is the only time two people can simultaneously hold the same object with chopsticks, hence the taboo of passing food directly from chopstick to chopstick at the dinner table.

27. Noguchi interview, March 25, 1999.

28. A *nodobotoke* directly translates into "throat Buddha." It is actually the second cervical vertebra. The shape is likened to a figure sitting in meditation or with palms pressed together, bowing. The person closest to the deceased is recognized by being the one to pick that bone up. It is often seen as an indication of the deceased's level of attainment when they have a nice clear one, and therefore it is treasured in a separate container and not put in the urn with the other bones that remain after cremation. Honda interview, April 24, 1999.

29. Honda interview, March 20, 1999.

30. Interview with Aoyama Shundō on March 15, 1999, at Aichi Senmon nunnery.

31. Nagai interview, January 20, 1999.

32. Noguchi interview, February 26, 1999.

33. Taniguchi interview, August 10, 2000.

34. Honda interview, April 3, 1999.

35. Hardacre, *Lay Buddhism in Contemporary Japan*, p. 229.

36. For further elaboration of the concept of *amae,* see Takeo Doi, *The Anatomy of Dependence.*

37. Noguchi interview, March 25, 1999; Honda interview, March 14, 1999.

38. Nagai interview, January 20, 1999.

39. For further explication of the clan or structure in Japanese society, see Hendry, *Understanding Japanese Society,* p. 22.

40. Chen Gang, "The Old Tradition in a New Setting."

41. Honda interview, March 14, 1999.

42. Traphagan, *The Practice of Concern,* p. 81.

43. Ogawa interview, March 26, 1999.

44. Honda interview, April 3, 1999.

45. Gyokko interview, April 14, 1999.

46. Nagai interview, January 27, 1999.

47. Kawasaki interview, December 22, 1998.

48. Ibid.

49. These three types of ritual spaces—physical space, meaning space, and virtual space—are developed in Williams and Boyd's book *Ritual Art and Knowledge,* pp. 33–45.

50. Selye, *Stress Without Distress.*

51. Gyokko interview, April 8, 1999.

52. Nagai interview, January 20, 1999.

53. Yamaguchi interview, June 29, 1998.

54. Kawasaki interview, January 27, 1999.

55. Interestingly, Japanese distinguishes the heart organ *shinzō* and *kokoro,* the heart as a locus of love and concern (or more fully translated as "heart-mind"). The *shinzō,* of course, is in the chest area, and the *kokoro* is understood to be in the abdomen.

56. Perhaps the ritualized gift exchange helps people maintain open hearts by generating explicit circumstances for bowing. Although I am aware that much bowing in general society are not occasions for notable heart-felt exchanges, the sincerity proscribed in a genuine bow would lubricate the heart. It is perhaps not insignificant that Japanese culture is famous for its profuse expressions of gratitude and the ubiquitous nature of bowing when communicating in that cultural context. When speaking English, there is no specific bodily motion that accompanies saying "thank you" like there is in Japanese. It is nearly impossible, however, to say *"arigatou"* (thank you) without

bowing. Perhaps pairing the words and the motion has an effect on how deeply or frequently one experiences gratitude, because the body and mind are both engaged.

57. Kawasaki interview, December 22, 1998.

58. Gyokko interview, April 2, 1999.

59. Although examining a different group of people, evidently "immersion in one's own sonic vibrations *does* have healing effects. UCLA researchers found that if hospitalized schizophrenics hummed an *mmm* sound, they experienced around 60 percent reduction in auditory hallucinations" (Dossey, *The Extraordinary Healing Power of Ordinary Things*, p. 100). For more on this topic, see Green and Kinsbourne, "Auditory Hallucinations in Schizophrenia."

60. Kawasaki interview, February 19, 1999.

61. Yamamoto interview, July 21, 1998.

62. Gyokko interview, February 9, 1999.

63. Gyokko interview, March 17, 1999.

64. Gyokko interview, February 9, 1999.

65. Gyokko interview, March 17, 1999.

66. Gyokko interview, February 9, 1999.

67. Kawasaki interview, January 27, 1999.

68. Kawasaki interview, January 8, 1999.

69. Ibid.

70. Ibid.

71. Ibid.

72. Gyokko interview, February 9, 1999.

73. There are four "Bodhisattva Vows." (1) Vowing to liberate all beings, (2) Vowing to extinguish inexhaustible defilements, (3) Vowing to master immeasurable Dharma gates, and (4) Vowing to actualize the supreme way of the Buddhist Path (of wisdom and compassion). They are often chanted quietly at the end when chanting at the home altar. My translation does not include "I vow" as is often included in English versions. Not only does the Japanese version not include the subject "I," but when "I" is added, grammatically required in English at the beginning, the focus stresses your personal experience. The stress in Japanese is on the commitment to continuously act in a certain way.

74. Honda interview, April 3, 1999, in Nagoya, Japan.

75. Aoyama Shundō, "Foreword" in Arai, *Women Living Zen*, p. viii.

76. Barnes, "From Ritual to Meditative Piety," p. 1.

77. Honda interview, April 3, 1999.

78. Gyokko interview, February 9, 1999.

79. Ibid.

80. Ibid.

81. Tanaka interview, March 31, 1999.

82. Tanaka interview, April 15, 1999.

83. Gyokko interview, February 29, 1999.

84. Gyokko interview, April 2, 1999.

85. Nagai interview, January 20, 1999.

86. Honda interview, April 3, 1999.

87. For more information on this ritual, see Shibasaki Terukazu, *Obon to Urabongyō*.

88. Kawasaki interview, August 14, 2003.

89. Kawasaki interview, February 19, 1999.

90. Ibid.

91. Ibid.

92. Kawasaki interview, August 14, 2003.

93. Kawasaki interview, February 19, 1999.

94. Kawasaki interview, January 8, 1999.

95. Honda interview, April 3, 1999.

96. Garrick, "The Work of the Witness in Psychotherapeutic Rituals of Grief," p. 110. For discussions on how physicists note the effect of observation on events, see Davies, *Other Worlds;* Overbye, *Lonely Hearts of the Cosmos*.

97. Aoyama Shundō interview, June 14, 2004.

98. Strickmann notes that I-Ching, a Chinese monk who took a pilgrimage to India in 673–685, wrote in 692 about a practice among monastic and lay Buddhists to "impress the Buddha's image on silk or paper" (Strickmann, *Chinese Magical Medicine,* p. 124). This does not tell us the origins of the practice of imprinting images of Jizō on paper, but it indicates that a kindred practice was done in India more than 1,300 years ago.

99. Honda interview, March 14, 1999.

100. Gyokko interview, August 2, 2000.

Chapter 4: Domestic Zen

1. Dharma talk by Aoyama Shundō, July 24, 1998, at Aichi Senmon nunnery.

2. Pure and impure are indigenous Japanese categories that demarcate important distinctions, but they are not absolute. Though purity is preferred, impurity can be transformed into purity, and vice versa. Mircea Eliade developed the distinction of "sacred" and "profane" in *The Sacred and the Profane.* The conceptual category of sacred and profane, however, does not illuminate the dynamics of Japanese religious experience and practice to the degree found in other contexts.

3. Noddings and Witherell, eds., *Stories Lives Tell,* p. 280.

4. Seligman, *Authentic Happiness.*

5. Singer and Ryff, eds., *New Horizons in Health,* p. 57.

6. Williams and Boyd, *Ritual Art and Knowledge,* p. 53.

7. Ibid. Williams and Boyd used Wittgenstein's phrase "form of life."

8. Kawasaki interview, December 22, 1998.

9. Ibid.

10. Gyokko interview, February 9, 1999.

11. Singer and Ryff, eds., *New Horizons in Health,* p. 46.

12. Japanese medical anthropologist Margaret Lock notes that in interpersonal conflict, especially among Japanese women, "non confrontational tactics are considered more appropriate than an outward, abrupt shattering of the peace." Being nonconfrontational is seen as morally higher. The aim is peace, so ritualized activities embedded with harmonizing dynamics are a more direct route to their goal. Lock and Norbeck, eds., *Health, Illness, and Medical Care in Japan,* pp. 130–157.

13. Kawasaki interview, December 22, 1998.

14. Kawasaki interview, January 8, 1999.

15. Ingesting script is not unique to this practice. Among others, not only is Ezekiel in the *Hebrew Bible* noted for having ingested scripture, but a practice in Chinese medicine includes "written prescriptions [are] frequently rolled up and eaten by . . . Chinese patients" (Strickmann, *Chinese Magical Medicine,* p. 9). Strickmann also draws on the *Book of Incantations and Dhāraṇī of the Jāṅgalī* (*Ch'ang-chü-li tu-niu t'o-lo-ni chou ching,* Taishō 1265, vol. 21: 295a) and points out the practice of writing a spell "in vermillion on paper and then swallowed" (Strickmann, p. 154).

16. Gyokko interview, March 17, 1999.

17. Ibid.

18. Kawasaki interview, January 8, 1999.

19. Kawasaki interview, January 22, 1998.

20. Gyokko interview, March 17, 1999.

21. Kawasaki interview, December 22, 1998.

22. Ibid.

23. Ibid.

24. Ibid.

25. Dhonden Yeshi describes how, in Tibetan medicine, "if the disease has progressed to the point that the patient is mentally imbalanced, the physician or an accomplished vajrayana practitioner writes down certain *mantras* on a piece of paper, rolls it up, and recites *mantras* over a volume of water. The water is then empowered with *mantras*. Then the *mantra*-inscribed paper is given to the rabid person to swallow and then wash down with the water that has been empowered with the *mantra*." Dhonden Yeshi, *Healing from the Source,* p. 143.

26. Kawasaki interview, December 22, 1998.

27. Benson and Spark, *Timeless Healing.*

28. Duncan Williams discusses Sōtō temples that engage in the distribution of medicines in *The Other Side of Zen.*

29. Kawasaki interview, January 8, 1999.

30. Umemura interview, March 30, 1999.

31. Taniguchi interview, August 10, 2000.

32. Dharma talk at Sunday event for laity and nuns on May 2, 1999, at Aichi Senmon nunnery, Nagoya, Japan.

33. Honda interview, March 20, 1999.
34. Gyokko interview, February 9, 1999.
35. Ibid.
36. Kawasaki interview, January 8, 1999.
37. Long, *Family Change and the Life Course in Japan,* p. 61.
38. Interview with Aoyama Shundō on June 14, 2004, at Aichi Senmon nunnery.
39. Ibid.
40. Ibid.
41. Driver, *Liberating Rites,* p. 190.
42. Gyokko interview, March 17, 1999.
43. Yamaguchi interview, July 28, 1999.
44. Yamaguchi interview, July 21, 1998.
45. Yamaguchi interview, August 4, 1998.
46. Gyokko interview, April 6, 1999.
47. Ibid.
48. A Buddhist text, *Amoghapāśahṛdayadhāraṇī,* describes an incantation recommended by Kuan-yin (Kannon in Japanese) for healing the sick. Reciting it 108 times is potent enough to cure demonically provoked illnesses. Just one recitation done forcefully relieves seasonal illnesses. The practice of chanting "Nenpi Kannon Riki" in times of distress and illness must come out of this larger context where such chants are also invoked with the aid of Kannon. See Meisezahl, "The *Amoghapāśahṛdayadhāraṇī.*" Also see Kōya-san Daigaku, ed., "The *Amoghapāśahṛdayadhāraṇī* Manuscript Formerly Kept in the Reiunji Temple and Its Collateral Texts in Tibetan Transliteration."
49. Among others, Wade Wheelock makes a case for words spoken in ritual being efficacious, not just representational. See his 1982 article, "The Problem of Ritual Language."
50. Kawasaki interview, January 9, 1999.
51. Kawasaki interview, February 19, 1999.
52. Gyokko interview, February 9, 1999.
53. Gyokko interview, April 14, 1999.
54. Umemura interview, December 9, 1998.
55. Kawasaki interview, October 11, 2005.
56. Yamaguchi interview, June 29, 1998.
57. Ogawa interview, March 26, 1999.
58. Yamaguchi interview, August 4, 1998.
59. Umemura interview, September 3, 1998.
60. Gyokko interview, February 23, 1999.
61. Ibid.
62. It was only in recent years that they started adding chairs in the large entryway area open to the worship hall. Increasingly, people have included chairs in their homes, so temples have started adding chairs as a gesture of kindness for those with sore knees who had discovered the comforts of them. Choosing a chair was becoming

less a novel and awkward blending of tradition and modernity than it had been. It was even losing the moral overtone that those who sit in traditional style are more respectful and more disciplined people.

63. Michel Strickmann's research on the *Mahāprajñaparamitā* explains when the text is placed on the shoulder, "through this direct ritual contact, the sufferer is sealed with the wisdom of all the Buddhas" (*Chinese Magical Medicine*, p. 187).

64. Referring to the *Lotus Sutra*, Michel Strickmann concludes "the book itself is both physician and medicine; it provides both diagnosis and cure" (*Chinese Magical Medicine*, p. 97). Both sūtras circulated in the same realms, so it is not surprising to see both understood to have healing dimensions. In a tangentially related discussion of a Taoist text (*The Book of the Devil-Destroyers of Wisdom/Hsiao-mo chi-hui-ching*, HY 1333)—also available in the same circles as the *Lotus Sutra* and *Wisdom Sutra*—Strickmann explains that "for demonically induced diseases, Chih-i, the patriarch of T'ien-t'ai, recommended insight meditation and the use of incantations but also warned that meditation, wrongly practiced, could cause illness rather than cure it. Other Buddhists who saw all ailments as caused by demonic agencies (and this, often, as a corollary of the demonic nature of the apocalyptic times) saw powerful ritual means as the primary mode of response" (ibid., p. 50, fn 157, Chap. 1).

65. For more information about similar Buddhist rituals see Bodiford, "Sōtō Zen in a Japanese Town"; Gellner, "'The Perfection of Wisdom'"; Schopen, "The Phrase '*saprthivipradesas des'as' caityabhutobhavet*' in the *Vajracchedika*."

66. Williams and Boyd further explain, "ritual as artistic masterworks are indissoluble wholes comprising physical, formal, and symbolic elements" (*Ritual Art and Knowledge*, p. 80).

67. Schechner, "The Future of Ritual," p. 13.

68. Dharma talk on Dōgen's "Mountains and Water Sutra" by Aoyama Shundō at Aichi Senmon nunnery on May 2, 1999.

69. Kawasaki interview, January 8, 1999.

70. Ibid.

71. Gyokko interview, March 17, 1999.

72. Gyokko interview, February 9, 1999.

73. Numerous books and articles have been written about this pilgrimage. For a more detailed understanding of it, Statler's *Japanese Pilgrimage* is an inviting place to start. See also Reader, *Making Pilgrimages*.

74. Umemura interview, October 24, 2005.

75. For historically contextualized information about pilgrimage to Kuan-yin (Kannon) in China, see Chün-Fang Yü, *Kuan-yin*.

76. The Saigoku and Bandō pilgrimage temples are largely Shingon and Tendai sect temples.

77. Kitō Sensei interview, April 28, 2009.

78. Yamaguchi interview, September 30, 1998.

79. Yamaguchi interview, July 21, 1998.

80. Traphagan, *The Practice of Concern*, p. 60.

81. Remen, *Kitchen Table Wisdom,* p. 225.

82. Gyatso and Dalai Lama XIV, *Healing Anger,* p. 11.

83. Dharma talk by Aoyama Shundō on June 14, 1998, at Aichi Senmon nunnery.

84. When Aoyama Rōshi drew diagrams to illustrate her point, the fact that time functions as a convention was underscored by her line running from past to future ran from right to left.

85. Dharma Talk by Aoyama Shundō on June 14, 1998, at Aichi Senmon nunnery.

86. Ibid.

87. Ibid.

88. More detailed discussion of scripture copying practice is in Chapter 5, this volume.

89. See Selye, *Stress Without Distress.* For a multidisciplinary volume on eustress, see Perrewé and Ganster, eds., *Emotional and Physiological Processes and Positive Intervention Strategies.*

90. Tedeschi, Park, and Calhoun, eds., *Posttraumatic Growth.*

91. Yamaguchi interview, October 15, 2005.

92. Ibid.

93. Ibid.

94. Ibid.

95. Conversation with Nagai on January 8, 1999.

96. Nagai interview, January 20, 1999.

97. Noddings and Witherell, eds., *Stories Lives Tell,* p. 10. They cite Toni Morrison's "The Site of Memoir," p. 112.

98. Nagai interview, January 20, 1999.

99. Nagai interview, January 27, 1999.

100. Nagai interview, January 20, 1999.

101. Nagai interview, February 24, 1999.

102. "Self power" and "other power" is a rubric invoked to contrast practices that one must do on one's own in order to experience enlightenment, like Zen, versus Pure Land Buddhist practices that rely on the compassion of Amida Buddha to be re-born in the "Pure Land." Although within Pure Land Buddhist traditions and teachings there are various understandings of the specifics of the vow, they all stress that one is not alone. Amida has power to help.

103. Nagai interview, February 24, 1999.

104. Ibid.

105. Interestingly, out of twelve consociates, two women in addition to Nagai also pursued Christianity. Despite the appealing aspects, it was not suitable for them either, mostly for cultural reasons.

106. Adding "chan" at the end of the name indicates a warm intimacy between these adult women, because "chan" is a diminutive primarily reserved for beloved children and pets.

107. Nagai interview, January 20, 1999.

108. Ibid.

109. Ibid.

110. Ibid.

111. Ibid.

112. Ibid.

113. Others have done elaborate pagodas and outlines of Kannon using the characters of the *Heart Sutra* to make the lines of the images, but no one has made the qualitatively powerful step to create images that are designed to convey the meaning of the sutra. My next book, currently entitled *Painting Emptiness: Buddhist Scripture for the Modern World,* will be on Iwasaki Tsuneo's work.

114. Research on cancer patients who engage in mindfulness-based interventions have shown noteworthy increase in immunological and physiological function. See Carlson, Speca, Patel, and Goodey, "Mindfulness-Based Stress Reduction."

115. Kimura interview, July 7, 1998.

116. Noddings and Witherell, eds., *Stories Lives Tell,* p. 9.

117. Yamaguchi interview, July 28, 1998.

118. Sakuma interview, April 23, 1999, in Kyoto, Japan.

119. Yamaguchi interview, July 28, 1998.

120. Ibid.

121. Dossey, *The Extraordinary Healing Power of Ordinary Things,* p. 259.

122. See Bloom, Richardson, and Harris, "Natural History of Untreated Breast Cancer 1805–1933." Dossey cites this article because it is an example of how survival statistics are often calculated omitting anomalies like two women surviving forty years without treatment. Without them, the median survival time is 3.3 years for untreated breast cancer (Dossey, *The Extraordinary Healing Power of Ordinary Things,* p. 246).

123. Dossey, *The Extraordinary Healing Power of Ordinary Things,* p. 253. He goes on to write, "in 2000, a *Newsweek* poll did just that, and found that 63 percent of Americans say they know someone who experienced a miracle, and 48 percent say they have experienced or witnessed one." See also Challis and Stam, "The Spontaneous Regression of Cancer"; and O'Regan and Hirschberg, *Spontaneous Remission.*

124. Honda interview, April 20, 1999.

125. Ornish, *Love and Survival,* p. 16.

126. Lebra, *Japanese Patterns of Behavior,* p. 112.

127. McVeigh, "Ritualized Practices of Everyday Life," p. 53.

Chapter 5: The Healing Power of Beauty

1. Tenzin Gyatso and Dalai Lama XIV, "Understanding Our Fundamental Nature," in Davidson and Harrington, eds., *Visions of Compassion,* p. 69.

2. Kawasaki interview, December 22, 1998.

3. Kawasaki interview, January 8, 1999.

4. Kitō Sensei interview, December 8, 1998.

5. Ibid.

6. Published by the Sōtō-shū Shūmuchō (Sōtō Zen Sect Administration).

7. Honda interview, April 20, 1999.

8. Nagai interview, October 10, 2005.

9. Nagai interview, February 10, 1999.

10. Honda interview, March 7, 1999.

11. Honda interview, April 3, 1999.

12. Honda interview, March 7, 1999.

13. Noguchi interview, March 25, 1999.

14. Honda interview, April 3, 1999.

15. Ibid.

16. Nagai interview, October 10, 1999.

17. Strickmann, *Chinese Magical Medicine,* p. 152. There is historical precedence for healing powers of images in the Buddhist tradition. Strickmann found a text, *Ch'ang-chü-li tu-niu t'o-lo-ni chou ching* [Book of the Incantations and Dhāraṇī of the Jāṅgalī Woman], that describes a ritual of painting an image of a Buddhist goddess as part of healing.

18. Nagai interview, October 10, 1999.

19. Nagai interview, August 15, 2003.

20. Mr. Sakuma interview, April 23, 1999, at his home in Kyoto, Japan.

21. Ibid.

22. Ibid.

23. Mrs. Sakuma interview, April 23, 1999, at her home in Kyoto, Japan.

24. Several interviews with Iwasaki Tsuneo in the period between spring 1999 through his death in the spring of 2002. The working title of the book I am writing on his work is *Painting Emptiness: Buddhist Scripture for the Modern World.*

25. Umemura interview, September 28, 1998.

26. One *li* is about four kilometers.

27. Gyokko interview, April 14, 1999.

28. Ibid.

29. Ibid.

30. Gyokko interview, April 6, 1999.

31. Ogawa interview, March 26, 1999.

32. Ibid.

33. Ibid.

34. Kitō Sensei interview, August 23, 2003.

35. Patel, *Music, Language, and the Brain,* p. 4.

36. Music therapy research has shown that music helps enhance "melatonin release via pineal gland stimulation and for unlocking and restoring the expression of emotional connections with our deeper self, whether in a state of health or disease." See Kumar et al., "Music Therapy Increases Serum Melatonin Levels in Patients with

Alzheimer's Disease," p. 56. For other scientific studies and activities on music and health, see Harvard Medical Schools' Institute for Music and Brain Science, Mark Jude Tramo, Director and Neurology Professor; Gaynor, *Sounds of Healing*.

37. Boyd and Williams, "Ritual Spaces," p. 24.

38. Gaynor, *Sounds of Healing*, pp. 62–63.

39. Yamamoto interview, March 18, 1999, in Nagoya, Japan.

40. Ogawa interview, March 26, 1999, in Nagoya, Japan.

41. Honda interview, April 3, 1999.

42. Yamamoto interview, December 4, 1998.

43. Gyokko interview, April 2, 1999.

44. Umemura interview, March 30, 1999.

45. Umemura interview, September 3, 1998.

46. Yamamoto interview, March 18, 1999.

47. *Yūgen* is a Japanese aesthetic concept referring to the mysterious and sublime. No English rendering can directly capture its meaning. Yet, it is a quality that artists of all types seek to embody in their painting, poetry, musical and dramatic performances, and movements during tea. For further discussion, see Kamo no Chōmei's *Mumyōshō* [Treatise without a name] cited in Addiss, Groemer, and Rimer, *Traditional Japanese Arts and Culture*, pp. 93–94.

48. Ogawa interview, March 26, 1999.

49. Yamamoto interview, March 18, 1999.

50. Yamamoto interview, July 28, 1998.

51. Ogawa interview, October 19, 2005.

52. Ibid.

53. Yamamoto interview, March 18, 1999.

54. Nagai interview, August 15, 2003.

55. Honda interview, April 3, 1999.

Chapter 6: Revealing the Healing Realm of Zen

1. Gyatso, *Transforming the Mind*, pp. 150–151.

2. Linda Barnes, associate professor of Pediatrics at Boston University Medical School, developed this model, which takes into account concerns of medical anthropology, comparative religions, and medical practice.

3. Gyokko interview, February 9, 1999.

4. Ibid.

5. Umemura interview, September 3, 1998.

6. Ogawa interview, March 26, 1999.

7. Nagai interview, January 27, 1999.

8. Honda interview, March 20, 1999.

9. Umemura interview, March 3, 1999.

10. Danforth, *The Death Rituals of Rural Greece*, p. 298.

11. Gold and Gugar, *In the Time of Trees and Sorrows,* p. 5.

12. Dōgen, "Ikka myōju" [One bright pearl], p. 105.

13. Paul Farmer, anthropologist, medical doctor, and chair of Harvard Medical School's Department of Global Health and Social Medicine, is committed to global health equity. See his *Pathologies of Power.*

14. Singer and Ryff, eds., *New Horizons in Health,* p. 12.

15. In brief, the parts of the brain involve the vestibular system (for balance), limbic system (emotional balance), reticular activating system (the brain's wake-up call), cerebellum (automatic movement), basal ganglia (intentional movement), and frontal lobes (reasoning).

16. Arai, "Healing Zen: Exploring the Brain on Bowing," with Sascha duLac (forthcoming).

Kanji Glossary

Aida Mitsuo　相田みつを
aigo　愛護
akamatsu　赤松
amae　甘え
Amida Buddha　阿弥陀仏
Bandō Kannon *meguri*　坂東観音巡り
Batō Kannon　馬頭観音
bōkō　母港
bonji　梵字
Bukkyō　仏教
buppō　仏法
butsudan　仏壇
Butsudō　仏道
butsuma　仏間
Daihannya　大般若
Daihannya-e　大般若會
daijobu　大丈夫
Dainichi Nyorai　大日如来
　　(Mahavairocana Buddha)
Dōgan-ji Kannon-dō　渡岸寺観音堂
Dōgen　道元
eitai kuyō　永代供養
ema　絵馬
ensō-jikan　円相時間
fujin-byō　婦人病
Fuku wa uchi. Oni wa soto.　福は内。鬼
　　は外。
gadō　画道
gasshō　合掌

Gasshō Dōji　合掌童子
girei　儀礼
gishiki　儀式
go-eika　御詠歌
go-senzo-sama　ご先祖様
Gozan Bunka　五山文化
Hana Matsuri　花祭
Hana saku jīsan　花咲く爺さん
Hannya Shingyō　般若心経
hara-obi　腹帯
haru wa hana　春は花
Hatsubon　初盆
hihō　秘法
hondō　本堂
honne　本音
hosshin seppō　法身説法
Hotoke-sama　仏様
Hotoke-sama no go-en　仏様のご縁
hōyō　法要
Hyaku Kannon *meguri*　百観音巡り
Hyakumanben　百万遍
ie　家
ikasareteiru　生かされている
ikasu　生かす
ikiteiru　生きている
inochi　命
iyasaremashita　癒されました
iyasareteiru　癒されている
iyasareteiru keiken　癒されている経験

iyashi no deai　癒しの出会い

iyashita　癒した

jihi　慈悲

Jikku Kannon-gyō　十句観音経

Jizō Bosatsu　地蔵菩薩

Jizō Nagashi　地蔵流し

Jōdoshinshū　浄土真宗

Joya no Kane　除夜の鐘

Jūichimen Kannon　十一面観音

juzu　数珠

kadō　華道 (flower)

kadō　歌道 (poetry)

kaerubasho　帰る場所

kaimyō　戒名

kamidana　神棚

kanashimi　悲しみ

kanbun　漢文

Kanjizai bosatsu　観自在菩薩

Kannon　観音

Kannon-gyō　観音経

Kannon *meguri*　観音巡り

Kannon-sama, *tasuketekudasai*　観音
　様、助けてください

Kannon-yū　観音湯

kata　型

katakarahairu　型から入る

Kegonshū　華厳宗

keiken　経験

kekkonshiki　結婚式

kenkōcha　健康茶

Kinshō-ji　金昌寺

ki o tsukau　気を使う

kokoro　心

kokoro no furusato　心の古里

Kōrin-ji　香林時

Kosodate Kannon　子育観音

kotobuki　寿

Kūkai　空海

kyōbon　経本

li　禮

mamemaki　豆巻

meinichi　命日

michi　道

Mizu Tori　水取

mochū　喪中

mono o daiji ni suru　ものを大事にする

mu　無

muda　無駄

Mu-enbotoke-sama　無縁仏様

mugen　無限

mukaebi　迎え火

muri o shinai　無理をしない

mushin　無心

Myōgon-ji　妙厳寺

myōhō　妙法

Nagoya-shi Hakubutsukan　名古屋市
　博物館

nande　何で

nanoka nanoka　七日七日

nanten　南天

Nara Kōmyō Yasuaki　奈良康明

Nembutsu　念仏

Nenpi Kannon Riki　念彼観音力

Nihon-ji　日本寺

Niwa Zenkyū　丹羽善久

nodobotoke　喉仏

Obon　お盆

o-fuda　お札

o-haka　お墓

o-haka-mairi　お墓参り

Ohigan　お彼岸

o-ihai　お位牌

okaerinasai　お帰りなさい

Oku-no-In　奥の院

omairi　お参り

omamori　お守り

omiai　お見合い

onkakakabisanmanesowaka　オンカカ
　カビサンマンエソワカ

o-segaki kuyō　お施餓鬼供養

otsuge　お告げ

rei　礼 (etiquette)

rei　怜 (spirit)

reigi　礼儀

Rishu-kyō 理趣経

Sadō 茶道

sahō 作法

saidan 祭壇

Saigoku Kannon *meguri* 西国観音巡り

Sakuma Ken'ichi 佐久間顕一

Sangemon 懺悔文

Sansui-kyō 山水経

Sanzu no Kawa 三途の川

Seigan-ji 誓願寺

seijinshiki 成人式

Seikan-ji 清閑寺

seishinkyōiku 精神教育

Senju Kannon 千手観音

sennin 仙人

Setsubun 節分

Setsubun Mamemaki 節分豆まき

shabutsu 写仏

shakyō 写経

shamisen 三味線

shiki 式

Shikoku hachijūhakkasho 四国八十八カ所

shingon 真言

shinjin 身心 (body-mind)

shinjin 心身 (mind-body)

shinzō 心臓

Shitarachō of Kitashitaragun 北設楽郡設楽町

Shōbōgenzō 正法眼蔵

shodō 書道

shōjusen 松寿仙

Shōmu Tennō 聖武天皇

shūkyō 宗教

shūkyū wa seikatsu de aru 宗教は生活である

shushō ittō 修證一等

Sonshōdarani 尊勝陀羅尼

Sōrintō 相輪塔

sōshiki 葬式

soto 外

Sōtōzenshū 曹洞禅宗

sotsugyōshiki 卒業式

sugaru 縋る

sugata 姿

sunao 素直

Suzuki Kakuzen Rōshi 鈴木格禅老師

taiken 体験

Tanagyō 棚経

tenchi 天地

tenugui 手ぬぐい

Tōgan-ji 桃巌寺

toshikoshi soba 年越しそば

tsukaregadeta 疲れが出た

tsukiau 付き合う

uchi 内

Uji 有時

utsukushimi 慈しみ

wagen 和顔

wagen aigo 和顔愛護

Yawase Kannon 矢合観音

yozakura 夜桜

Yudō 癒道

yūgen 幽玄

yurusu 許す

zazen 座禅

Bibliography of Sources Cited

Addiss, Stephen, Gerald Groemer, and J. Thomas Rimer. *Traditional Japanese Arts and Culture: An Illustrated Sourcebook.* Honolulu: University of Hawaiʻi Press, 1996.

Addiss, Stephen, Stanley Lombardi, and Judith Roitman, eds. *Zen Sourcebook: Traditional Documents from China, Korea, and Japan.* Introduction by Paula Arai. Indianapolis, IN: Hackett Publishing, 2008.

Ames, Roger, and David Hall. *Anticipating China: Thinking Through the Narratives of Chinese and Western Culture.* Albany: University of New York Press, 1995.

Ames, Roger, Wimal Dissanayake, and Thomas Kasulis, eds. *Self as Person in Asian Theory and Practice.* Albany: State University of New York Press, 1994.

Aoyama Shundō. "Foreword." In Paula Arai, *Women Living Zen.* New York: Oxford University Press, 1999.

Arai, Paula. *Women Living Zen: Japanese Sōtō Buddhist Nuns.* New York: Oxford University Press, 1999.

Arai, Paula, with Sascha duLac. "Healing Zen: Exploring the Brain on Bowing." *Studies in Medicine, Science and Society.* Special Edition on "Convergence and Collisions: Disease, Religion and Healing in Asia." Hong Kong: Hong Kong University, forthcoming.

Arisaka, Yoko. "The Ontological Co-Emergence of 'Self and Other' in Japanese Philosophy." In "Between Ourselves: Second-Person Issues in the Study of Consciousness," edited by Evan Thompson. *Journal of Consciousness Studies* 8, no. 5–7 (March–July 2001): 197–208.

Barnes, Andrew E. "From Ritual to Meditative Piety: Devotional Change in French Penitential Confraternities from the 16th to the 18th Century." *Journal of Ritual Studies* 1, no. 2 (1987): 1–26.

Bell, Catherine. *Ritual Theory, Ritual Practice.* New York: Oxford University Press, 1992.

———. *Ritual Perspectives and Dimensions.* New York: Oxford University Press, 1997.

Bell, Diane. "Yes, Virginia, There Is a Feminist Ethnography: Reflections from Three Australian Fields." In *Gendered Fields: Women, Men, and Ethnography,* edited by Diane Bell, Pat Caplan, and Wazir Jahan Karim. London; New York: Routledge, 1993.

———. "Introduction: The Context." In *Gendered Fields: Women, Men, and Ethnography*, edited by Diane Bell, Pat Caplan, and Wazir Jahan Karim. London; New York: Routledge, 1993.

Benson, Herbert, and Marg Stark. *Timeless Healing: The Power and Biology of Belief.* New York: Scribner, 1997.

Bestor, Theodore, Patricia Steinhoff, and Victoria Bestor, eds. *Doing Fieldwork in Japan.* Honolulu: University of Hawai'i Press, 2003.

Birnbaum, Raoul. *The Healing Buddha*, rev. ed. Boston: Shambhala, 1989.

Bloch, Maurice. *How We Think They Think: Anthropological Approaches to Cognition, Memory, and Literacy.* Boulder, CO: Westview Press, 1998.

Bloom, H. D. G., W. W. Richardson, and E. J. Harris. "Natural History of Untreated Breast Cancer 1805–1933." *British Medical Journal* 2 (1962): 213–221.

Bodiford, William M. "The Enlightenment of Kami and Ghosts: Spirit Ordinations in Japanese Sōtō Zen." In *Chan Buddhism in Ritual Context,* edited by Bernard Faure, 250–265. New York: Routledge Curzon, 2003.

———. "Sōtō Zen in a Japanese Town: Field Notes on a Once-Every-Thirty-Three-Years Kannon Festival." *Japanese Journal of Religious Studies* 21, no. 1 (1994): 4–36.

———. "Zen in the Art of Funerals: Ritual Salvation in Japanese Buddhism." *History of Religions* 32, no. 2 (1992): 146–164.

———. *Sōtō Zen in Medieval Japan.* Honolulu: University of Hawai'i Press, 1993.

Boyd, James W., and Ron G. Williams. "Ritual Spaces: An Application of Aesthetic Theory to Zoroastrian Ritual." *Journal of Ritual Studies* 3, no. 1 (1989): 1–43.

Brown, Karen McCarthy. "Writing about 'The Other,' Revisited." In *Personal Knowledge and Beyond: Reshaping the Ethnography of Religion*, edited by James Spickard, J. Shawn Andres, and Meredith McGuire, 127–133. New York: New York University Press, 2002.

Carlson, L. E., M. Speca, K. D. Patel, and E. Goodey. "Mindfulness-Based Stress Reduction in Relation to Quality of Life, Mood, Symptoms of Stress and Levels of Cortisol, Dehydroepiandrosterone sulfate (DHEAS) and Melatonin in Breast and Prostate Cancer Out-Patients." *Psychoneuroendocrinology* 29 (2004): 448–474.

Challis, G. B., and H. J. Stam. "The Spontaneous Regression of Cancer: A Review of Cases from 1900 to 1987." *Acta Oncologica* 29, no. 5 (1990): 545–550.

Chen Gang. "The Old Tradition in a New Setting: A Preliminary Study of Mortuary Ritual in a Chinese Village." *Journal of Ritual Studies* 10, no. 2 (Summer 1995): 41–57.

Christians, Clifford. "Ethics and Politics in Quantitative Research." In *The Landscape of Qualitative Research: Theories and Issues*, 2nd ed., edited by Norman Denzin and Yvonna Lincoln, 208–243. Thousand Oaks, CA: Sage Publications, 2003.

Clothey, Fred W. "Toward a Contemporary Interpretation of Ritual." *Journal of Ritual Studies* 2, no. 2 (Summer 1988): 147–161.

Cousins, Norman. *Anatomy of an Illness as Perceived by the Patient: Reflections on Healing and Regeneration.* New York: Norton, 1979.

Dalai Lama. "Understanding Our Fundamental Nature." In *Visions of Compassion: Western Scientists and Tibetan Buddhists Examine Human Nature,* edited by Richard Davidson and Anne Harrington, 66–80. New York: Oxford University Press, 2002.

Danforth, Loring M. *The Death Rituals of Rural Greece.* Princeton, NJ: Princeton University Press, 1982.

———. *Firewalking and Religious Healing: The Anastenaria of Greece and the American Firewalking Movement.* Princeton, NJ: Princeton University Press, 1989.

d'Aquili, Eugene, and C. Laughlin. "The Neurobiology of Myth and Ritual." In *The Spectrum of Ritual: A Biogenetic Structural Analysis,* edited by Eugene d'Aquili, Charles Laughlin, and John McManus, 152–183. New York: Columbia University Press, 1979.

d'Aquili, Eugene, Charles Laughlin, and John McManus, eds. *The Spectrum of Ritual: A Biogenetic Structural Analysis.* New York: Columbia University Press, 1979.

Davidson, Richard, and Anne Harrington, eds. *Visions of Compassion: Western Scientists and Tibetan Buddhists Examine Human Nature.* New York: Oxford University Press, 2002.

Davies, Paul. *Other Worlds: A Portrait of Nature in Rebellion, Space, Superspace, and the Quantum Universe.* New York: Simon & Schuster, 1980.

Decety, Jean, and William Ickes, eds. *The Social Neuroscience of Empathy.* Cambridge, MA: MIT Press, 2009.

Depraz, Natalie, and Diego Cosmelli. "Empathy and Openness: Practices of Intersubjectivity at the Core of the Science of Consciousness." In *The Problem of Consciousness: New Essays in Phenomenological Philosophical of Mind,* edited by Evan Thompson, 163–203. Calgary, Alberta: University of Calgary Press, 2003.

Dhonden Yeshi. *Healing from the Source: The Science and Love of Tibetan Medicine.* Translated by Alan Wallace. Ithaca, NY: Snow Lion Publications, 2000.

Dobbs, David. "A Revealing Reflection." *Scientific American Mind* (April/May 2006): 22–27.

Dōgen. "Bendōwa." In *Shōbōgenzō,* Vol. 1, translated by Mizuno Yaoko. Tokyo: Iwanami Shōten, 1993.

———. "Genjo Kōan." In *Shōbōgenzō,* Vol. 1, translated by Mizuno Yaoko. Tokyo: Iwanami Shōten, 1993.

———. "Ikka myōju" [One bright pearl]. In *Dōgen,* Vol. 1, edited by Terada Toru. Tokyo: Iwanami Shōten, 1980.

———. *Pure Standards for the Zen Community: A Translation of the Eihei Shingi.* Translated by Taigen Daniel Leighton and Shohaku Okumura. Albany: State University of New York, 1996.

———. *Shōbōgenzō* [Treasury of the true dharma eye]. Four volumes. Mizuno Yaoko, commentator. Tokyo: Iwanami Shoten, 1993.

Doi Takeo. *The Anatomy of Self.* Tokyo: Kodansha International, 1986.

———. *The Anatomy of Dependence.* Translated by John Bester. Tokyo; New York: Kodansha International, 1973.

Dossey, Larry. *The Extraordinary Healing Power of Ordinary Things.* New York: Three Rivers Press, 2007.

Driver, Tom F. *Liberating Rites: Understanding the Transformative Power of Ritual.* Boulder, CO: Westview Press, 1998.

———. *The Magic of Ritual: Our Need for Liberating Rites That Transform Our Lives and Our Community,* 2nd ed. San Francisco: Harper, 1992.

Ekman, Paul. *Emotions Revealed: Recognizing Faces and Feelings to Improve Communication and Emotional Life.* New York: Henry Holt, 2003.

Eliade, Mircea. *The Sacred and the Profane: The Nature of Religion.* Translated by Willard Trask. New York: Houghton Mifflin Harcourt, 1968.

Emmons, R. A., and M. E. McCullough. "Counting Blessings Versus Burdens: Experimental Studies of Gratitude and Subjective Well-Being in Daily Life." *Journal of Personality and Social Psychology* 84, no. 2 (2003): 377–389.

Farmer, Paul. *Pathologies of Power: Health, Human Rights, and the New War on the Poor.* With a foreword by Amartya Sen. Berkeley: University of California Press, 2003.

Faure, Bernard. *Ch'an Insights and Oversights: An Epistemological Critique of the Chan Tradition.* Princeton, NJ: Princeton University Press, 1993.

———. *The Rhetoric of Immediacy: A Cultural Critique of Ch'an/Zen Buddhism.* Princeton, NJ: Princeton University Press, 1991.

———. *Visions of Power: Imagining Medieval Japanese Buddhism.* Translated by Phyllis Brooks. Princeton, NJ: Princeton University Press, 1996.

———, ed. *Chan Buddhism in Ritual Context.* New York: Routledge Curzon, 2003.

Fingarette, Herbert. *Confucius: The Secular as Sacred.* New York: Harper & Row, 1972.

Flick, Uwe. *An Introduction to Qualitative Research: Theory, Method, and Applications.* London: Sage Publications, 1998.

———. "Triangulation Revisited: Strategy of Validation or Alternative?" In *Journal for the Theory of Social Behavior* 22 (1992): 175–198.

Francis, M. E., and J. W. Pennebaker. "Putting Stress into Words." *American Journal of Health Promotion* 6 (1992): 280–287.

Fredrickson, Barbara. "What Good Are Positive Emotions?" *Review of General Psychology* 2/3 (September 1998): 300–319.

Fujii Masao. *Sosen saishi no girei kōzō to minzoku* [The ritual structure and people of ancestor ceremonies]. Tokyo: Kobundo, 1993.

———. *Bukkyō girei jiten* [Dictionary of Buddhist rituals]. Tokyo: Tokyo Do Shuppan, 1977.

———, ed. *Sōgi o kangaeru* [Thoughts on funeral rites]. Tokyo: Chikuma Shobo, 1990.

Gallese, Vittorio, Luciano Fadiga, Leonardo Fogassi, and Giacomo Rizzolatti. "Action Recognition in the Premotor Cortex." *Brain: A Journal of Neurology* 119, no. 2 (1996): 593–609.

Garrick, David. "The Work of the Witness in Psychotherapeutic Rituals of Grief." *Journal of Ritual Studies* 8, no. 2 (1994): 85–113.

Gaynor, Mitchell. *Sounds of Healing: A Physician Reveals the Therapeutic Power of Sound, Voice, and Music.* New York: Broadway Books, 1999.

Gellner, David N. "'The Perfection of Wisdom'—A Text and Its Uses in Kwā Bahā Lalitpur." In *Change and Continuity: Studies in the Nepalese Culture of the Kathmandu Valley,* edited by Siegfried Lienhard, 223–240. Torino, Italy: CESMEO, 1996.

Gilbert, Daniel. "The Science of Happiness." *Edge: The Third Culture* (May 22, 2006 at www.edge.org/documents/archive/edge182.html#gilbert).

Glassman, Hank. "Chinese Buddhist Death Ritual and the Transformation of Japanese Kinship." In *The Buddhist Dead,* edited by Jacqueline Stone and Bryan Cuevas, 378–404. Honolulu: University of Hawai'i Press, 2007.

Gold, Ann Grodzins, and Bhoju Ram Gugar. *In the Time of Trees and Sorrows: Nature, Power, and Memory in Rajasthan.* Durham, NC: Duke University Press, 2002.

Green, M. F., and M. Kinsbourne. "Auditory Hallucinations in Schizophrenia: Does Humming Help?" *Biological Psychiatry* 27, no. 8 (1990): 934–935.

Grimes, Ronald L. *Beginnings in Ritual Studies.* Washington, DC: University Press of America, 1982.

———. *Ritual Criticism: Case Studies in its Practice, Essays on its Theory.* Columbia: University of South Carolina Press, 1990.

Gyatso, Tenzin, and Dalai Lama XIV. *Healing Anger: The Power of Patience from a Buddhist Perspective.* Translated by Geshe Thupten Jinpa. Ithaca, NY: Snow Lion Publications, 1997.

———. "Understanding Our Fundamental Nature." In *Visions of Compassion: Western Scientists and Tibetan Buddhists Examine Human Nature,* edited by Richard Davidson and Anne Harrington. New York: Oxford University Press, 2002.

Hardacre, Helen. *Lay Buddhism in Contemporary Japan: Reiyukai Kyodan.* Princeton, NJ: Princeton University Press, 1984.

———. *Marketing the Menacing Fetus in Japan.* Berkeley: University of California Press, 1997.

Hasebe Kōichi 長谷部好一. "Zenmon no girei (I)" [The ritual of the Zen school] 禅門の儀礼. *Aichi Gakuin Zen Kenkyu sho kiyō* 2 (1972): 40–52.

Heine, Steven. *Dōgen and the Kōan Tradition: A Tale of Two* Shōbōgenzō *Texts.* Albany: State University of New York Press, 1994.

Heine, Steven, and Dale S. Wright, eds. *Zen Ritual: Studies of Zen Buddhist Theory in Practice.* New York: Oxford University Press, 2008.

Hendry, Joy. *Understanding Japanese Society.* New York: Routledge, 1995.

Hori, G. Victor Sogen. "Teaching and Learning in the Rinzai Zen Monastery." *Journal of Japanese Studies* 29, no. 1 (1994): 5–35.

Hur, Nam-lin. *Death and Social Order in Tokugawa Japan: Buddhism, Anti-Christianity, and the Danka System.* Cambridge, MA: Harvard University Press, 2007.

Ickovics, J. R., and C. L. Park, eds. "Thriving: Broadening the Paradigm Beyond Illness to Health." *Journal of Social Issues* 54, no. 2 (1998): 237–244.

Ikegami, Eiko. *Bonds of Civility: Aesthetic Networks and the Political Origins of Japanese Culture.* New York: Cambridge University Press, 2005.

Iocaboni, Marco. *Mirroring People: The New Science of How We Connect to Others.* New York: Farrar, Straus, & Giroux, 2008.

Ishikawa Rikizan. "Chūsei Bukkyō ni okeru bosatsu shi Sōtō-shū ni okeru Jizō Bosatsu Shinkō wo chūshin toshite" [Bodhisattvas in medieval Buddhism: Centered on the Faith in Jizō Bodhisattva]. *Nihon Bukkyō Gakkai Nenpō* 51 (1986): 473–488.

Jackson, Michael. *Minima Ethnographica: Intersubjectivity and the Anthropological Project.* Chicago: University of Chicago Press, 1998.

Johnson, Allen, and Orna Johnson. "Quality Into Quantity: On the Measurement Potential of Ethnographic Fieldnotes." In *Fieldnotes: The Makings of Anthropology*, edited by Roger Sanjek, 161–186. Ithaca, NY: Cornell University Press, 1990.

Joseph, Rhawn. *The Transmitter to God: The Limbic System, the Soul, and Spirituality.* San Jose: University of California Press, 2000.

Kessel, Frank, Patricia Rosenfield, and Norman B. Anderson, eds. *Expanding Boundaries of Health and Social Science: Case Studies in Interdisciplinary Innovation.* New York: Oxford University Press, 2003.

Kim, Hee-Jin. *Dogen Kigen: Mystical Realist.* Tucson: University of Arizona Press, 1975.

Kizaemon Ariga. *Hito to no nihon bunka-ron* [People and the discourse on Japanese culture]. Tokyo: Mirai-sha, 1976.

Kondo, Dorinne. *Crafting Selves: Power, Gender, and Discourses of Identity in a Japanese Workplace.* Chicago: University of Chicago Press, 1990.

Kōya-san Daigaku, ed. "The *Amoghapāśahṛdayadhāraṇī.* Manuscript Formerly Kept in the Reiunji Temple and Its Collateral Texts in Tibetan Transliteration." In *Mikkyōgaku Mikkyōshi Ronbunshū*, 179–216. Kyoto: Nagai Press.

Krondorfer, Bjorn. "Bodily Knowing, Ritual Embodiment, and Experimental Drama: From Regression to Transgression." *Journal of Ritual Studies* 6, no. 2 (Summer 1992): 27–38.

Kumar, A. M., F. Tims, D. G. Cruess, M. J. Mintzer, G. Ironson, D. Loewenstein, et al. "Music Therapy Increases Serum Melatonin Levels in Patients with Alzheimer's Disease." *Alternative Therapies in Health and Medicine* 5, no. 6 (1999): 49–57.

Kuromaru Kanji. "Eihei shingi no seikaku: Toku ni bosatsu daikai to no kankei ni oite" [The traits of Eihei regulations: Special emphasis on the relationship with Bodhisattva vows]. *Indogaku Bukkyōgaku Kenkyū* 9, no. 2 (March 1961): 233–235.

LaFleur, William R. *Liquid Life: Abortion and Buddhism in Japan.* Princeton, NJ: Princeton University Press, 1992.

Lazarus, Richard. "Relational Meaning and Discrete Emotions." In *Appraisal Processes in Emotion: Theory, Methods, Research*, edited by Klaus Schere, Angela Schorr, and Tom Johnstone. New York: Oxford University Press, 2001.

Lebra, Takei Sugiyama. *Japanese Patterns of Behavior.* Honolulu: University of Hawaiʻi Press, 1976.

———. *Japanese Women: Constraint and Fulfillment.* Honolulu: University of Hawaiʻi Press, 1984.

Lewis, Thomas, Fari Amini, and Richard Lannon. *A General Theory of Love.* New York: Vintage Books, 2000.

Lindemann, Erich. "The Symptomatology and Management of Acute Grief." *American Journal of Psychiatry* 101 (1944): 141–148.

Lock, Margaret, and Edward Norbeck, eds. *Health, Illness, and Medical Care in Japan: Cultural and Social Dimensions.* Honolulu: University of Hawaiʻi Press, 1987.

Long, Susan. *Family Change and the Life Course in Japan.* Ithaca, NY: Cornell University Press, 1987.

Lopez, Donald S., Jr., ed. *Curators of the Buddha: The Study of Buddhism Under Colonialism.* Chicago: University of Chicago Press, 1995.

Martinez, D. P. "Women and Ritual." In *Ceremony and Ritual in Japan: Religious Practices in an Industrialized Society,* edited by Jan van Bremen and D. P. Martinez, 183–200. New York: Routledge, 1995.

McGuire, Meredith. "Discovering Religious Power." *Sociological Analysis* 44 (1983): 1–10.

———. "New-Old Directions in the Social Scientific Study of Religion: Ethnography, Phenomenology, and the Human Body." In *Personal Knowledge and Beyond: Reshaping the Ethnography of Religion,* edited by James Spickard, J. Shawn Andres, and Meredith McGuire, 195–211. New York: New York University Press, 2002.

McVeigh, Brian. "Ritualized Practices of Everyday Life: Constructing Self, Status, and Social Structure in Japan." *Journal of Ritual Studies* 8, no. 1 (1994): 53–71.

Meisezahl, R. O. "The *Amoghapāśahṛdayadhāraṇī.*" *Monumenta Nipponica* 17 (1962): 267–328.

Morrison, Toni. "The Site of Memoir." In *Inventing the Truth: The Art and Craft of Memoir,* edited by William Zinsser, 101–124. Boston: Houghton Mifflin, 1987.

Nara, Yasuaki. "May the Deceased Get Enlightenment: An Aspect of the Enculturation of Buddhism in Japan." *Buddhist-Christian Studies* 15 (1995): 19–42.

Noddings, Nel, and Carol Witherell, eds. *Stories Lives Tell: Narrative and Dialogue in Education.* New York: Teachers College Press, 1991.

Northup, Lesley. *Ritualizing Women.* Cleveland, OH: Pilgrim Press, 1997.

———. "Emerging Patterns of Women's Ritualizing in the West." *Journal of Ritual Studies* 9, no. 2 (Summer 1995): 109–136.

Ohnuki-Tierney, Emiko. *Illness and Culture in Contemporary Japan: An Anthropological View.* Cambridge, UK: Cambridge University Press, 1984.

———. *The Monkey as Mirror: Symbolic Transformations in Japanese History and Ritual.* Princeton, NJ: Princeton University Press, 1989.

O'Regan, Brendan, and Caryle Hirschberg. *Spontaneous Remission: An Annotated Bibliography.* Petaluma, CA: Institute of Noetic Sciences, 1993.

Ornish, Dean. *Love and Survival: The Scientific Basis for the Healing Power of Intimacy.* New York: Harper Collins Publishers, 1998.

Overbye, Dennis. *Lonely Hearts of the Cosmos: The Scientific Quest for the Secret of the Universe.* New York: Harper Collins, 1991.

Patel, Aniruddh. *Music, Language, and the Brain.* New York: Oxford University Press, 2007.

Perrewé, Pamela, and Daniel Ganster, eds. *Emotional and Physiological Processes and Positive Intervention Strategies.* Bingley, UK: Emerald Group Publishing, 2004.

Piaget, Jean. *The Equilibration of Cognitive Structures: The Central Problem of Intellectual Development.* Translated by Terrance Brown and Kishore Julian Thampy. Chicago: University of Chicago Press, 1985.

———. *The Mechanisms of Perception.* Translated by G. N. Seagrim. New York: Basic Books, 1969.

Plath, David. "The Last Confucian Sandwich Becoming Middle Aged." In *Adult Episodes in Japan,* edited by David Plath, 51–63. Leidan: E. J. Brill, 1975.

———. *Long Engagements: Maturity in Modern Japan.* Stanford, CA: Stanford University Press, 1980.

———, ed. *Adult Episodes in Japan.* Leidan, Netherlands: E. J. Brill, 1975.

Reader, Ian. *Making Pilgrimages: Meaning and Practice in Shikoku.* Honolulu: University of Hawai'i Press, 2005.

Remen, Rachel Naomi. *Kitchen Table Wisdom: Stories That Heal.* New York: Riverhead Trade, 1997.

Rowe, Mark. "Grave Changes: Scattering Ashes in Contemporary Japan." In *The Buddhist Dead,* edited by J. Stone and B. Cuevas, 405–437. Honolulu: University of Hawai'i Press, 2007.

Sasaki Kōkan. *Kami to Hotoke no Jinruigaku: Bukkyō bunka no shinsō kōzō* [The anthropology of Kami and Buddha: The deep structure of Buddhist culture]. Tokyo: Shunjūsha, 1993.

Saver, Jeffery, and J. Rabin. "The Neural Substrates of Religious Experience." *Journal of Neuropsychiatry and Clinical Neurosciences* 9, no. 3 (August 1997): 498–510.

Schechner, Richard. "The Future of Ritual." *Journal of Ritual Studies* 1, no. 1 (1987): 5–33.

Scholz, Roland, and Olaf Tietje. *Embedded Case Study Methods: Integrating Quantitative and Qualitative Knowledge.* Thousand Oaks, CA: Sage Publications, 2002.

Schopen, Gregory. "The Phrase 'saprthivipradesas des'as' caityabhutobhavet' in the *Vajracchedika:* Notes on the Cult of the Book in Mahayana." *Indo-Iranian Journal* 17 (1975): 147–181.

Schorr, Angela. "Subjective Measurement in Appraisal Research: Present State and Future Perspectives." In *Appraisal Processes in Emotion: Theory, Methods, Research,* edited by Klaus Schere, Angela Schorr, and Tom Johnstone, 331–349. New York: Oxford University Press, 2001.

Seligman, Martin E. P. *Authentic Happiness: Using the New Positive Psychology to Realize Your Potential for Lasting Fulfillment*. New York: Free Press/Simon and Schuster, 2002.

Selye, Hans. *Stress without Distress*. Philadelphia: J. B. Lippincott, 1974.

Sered, Susan Starr. *Priestess, Mother, Sacred Sister: Religions Dominated by Women*. New York: Oxford University Press, 1994.

Sharf, Robert H. "Ritual." In *Critical Terms for the Study of Buddhism*, edited by Donald Lopez, 245–270. Chicago: University of Chicago Press, 2005.

———. "The Rhetoric of Experience and the Study of Religion." *Journal of Consciousness Studies* 7, nos. 11–12 (2000): 267–287.

Shibasaki Terukazu. *Obon to Urabongyō*. Tokyo: Daitō Shuppansha, 2006.

Singer, Burton, and Carol Ryff, eds. *New Horizons in Health: An Integrative Approach*. Washington, DC: National Academy Press, 2001.

Smith, Linda Tuhiwai. *Decolonizing Methodologies: Research and Indigenous Peoples*. New York: Zed Books, 1999.

Smith, Robert. *Ancestor Worship in Contemporary Japan*. Stanford, CA: Stanford University Press, 1974.

Snyder, C. R., and Shane J. Lopez, eds. *The Handbook of Positive Psychology*. New York: Oxford University Press, 2002.

Spickard, James K. "On the Epistemology of Post-Colonial Ethnography." In *Personal Knowledge and Beyond: Reshaping the Ethnography of Religion*, edited by James Spickard, Shawn Andres, and Meredith McGuire. New York: New York University Press, 2002.

Statler, Oliver. *Japanese Pilgrimage*. New York: William Morrow, 1983.

Stone, Jacqueline, and Mariko Namba Walter, eds. *Death and the Afterlife in Japanese Buddhism*. Honolulu: University of Hawaiʻi Press, 2008.

Strickmann, Michel. *Chinese Magical Medicine*. Edited by Barnard Faure. Palo Alto, CA: Stanford University Press, 2002.

———. "A Survey of Tibetan Buddhist Studies: Review Essay." *Eastern Buddhist* 10, no. 1 (May 1977): 128–149.

Suzuki, Hikaru. *The Price of Death: The Funeral Industry in Contemporary Japan*. Palo Alto, CA: Stanford University Press, 2000.

———. "Japanese Death Rituals in Transit: From Household Ancestors to Beloved Antecedents." *Journal of Contemporary Religion* 13, no. 2 (1998): 171–188.

Tamamuro Taijo. *Sōshiki Bukkyō* [Funeral Buddhism]. Tokyō: Daihōrinkaku, 1963.

Tanabe, George, and Ian Reader. *Practically Religious: Worldly Benefits and the Common Religion of Japan*. Honolulu: University of Hawaiʻi Press, 1998.

Tatz, Mark, trans. *Buddhism and Healing: Demieville's Article "Byo" from Hobogirin*. Lanham, MD: University Press of America, 1985.

Tedeschi, Richard, Crystal Park, and Lawrence Calhoun, eds. *Posttraumatic Growth: Positive Changes in the Aftermath of Crisis*. Philadelphia: Lawrence Erlbaum Associates, 1998.

Thoits, Peggy A. "Stressors and Problem-Solving: Individual as a Psychological Activist." *Journal of Health and Social Behavior* 35 (June 1994): 143–159.

Thomas, L. Eugene, and Susan A. Eisenhandler, eds. *Religion, Belief, and Spirituality in Late Life.* New York: Springer Publishing, 1999.

Thompson, Evan, ed. *Between Ourselves: Second-Person Issues in the Study of Consciousness.* Charlottesville, VA: Imprint Academic, 2001.

———. "Empathy and Consciousness." *Journal of Consciousness Studies* 8, nos. 5–7, (March–July 2001): 1–32.

Traphagan, John. *The Practice of Concern: Ritual, Well-Being, and Aging in Rural Japan.* Durham, NC: Carolina Academic Press, 2004.

van Bremen, Jan, and D. P. Martinez, eds. *Ceremony and Ritual in Japan: Religious Practices in an Industrialized Society.* New York: Routledge, 1995.

Wallbott, H. G., and K. R. Schere. "Assessing Emotion by Questionnaire." In *Emotion, Theory, Research, and Experience: The Measurement of Emotions,* edited by R. Plutchik and H. Kellerman, Vol. 4 (1989): 44–82.

Wheelock, Wade. "The Problem of Ritual Language: From Information to Situation." *Journal of the American Academy of Religion* 50, no. 1 (1982): 49–71.

Williams, Duncan. *The Other Side of Zen: A Social History of Soto Zen in Tokugawa Japan.* Princeton, NJ: Princeton University Press, 2004.

Williams, Ron, and James Boyd. *Ritual Art and Knowledge: Aesthetic Theory and Zoroastrian Ritual.* Columbia, SC: University of South Carolina Press, 1993.

Wong, Paul, and Prem Fry. *The Human Quest for Meaning: A Handbook of Psychological Research and Clinical Applications.* Mahwah, NJ: Erlbaum Associates, 1998.

Yanagida Kunio. *About Our Ancestors.* Translated by Fanny Mayer and Ishiwara Yasuyo. Kyoto: UNESCO, 1970.

Yü, Chün-Fang. *Kuan-yin: Chinese Transformation of Avalokiteshvara.* New York: Columbia University Press, 2001.

Zopa, Thubten. *Ultimate Healing: The Power of Compassion.* Boston: Wisdom Publications, 2001.

Index

About the Author

Paula Arai received her Ph.D. in Buddhist Studies from Harvard University under the mentorship of Masatoshi Nagatomi. She is the author of *Women Living Zen: Japanese Buddhist Nuns* (Oxford University Press, 1999), as well as numerous articles and chapters in edited volumes. Arai has received funding for her work from the Fulbright Association, American Council of Learned Societies, Reischauer Institute, Mellon Foundation, Hong Kong University of Science and Technology, Vanderbilt University, Carleton College, and the Louisiana State University Board of Regents. She is currently associate professor of religion at Louisiana State University.